CULTURE SHOCK!

Iran

Maria O'Shea

Graphic Arts Center Publishing Company
Portland, Oregon

In the same series

Australia	*France*	*Malaysia*	*Sweden*
Bolivia	*Germany*	*Mauritius*	*Switzerland*
Borneo	*Greece*	*Mexico*	*Syria*
Britain	*Hong Kong*	*Morocco*	*Taiwan*
Burma	*India*	*Nepal*	*Thailand*
California	*Indonesia*	*Netherlands*	*Turkey*
Canada	*Iran*	*Norway*	*UAE*
Chile	*Ireland*	*Pakistan*	*Ukraine*
China	*Israel*	*Philippines*	*USA*
Cuba	*Italy*	*Singapore*	*USA—The South*
Czech Republic	*Japan*	*South Africa*	*Venezuela*
Denmark	*Korea*	*Spain*	*Vietnam*
Egypt	*Laos*	*Sri Lanka*	

Chicago At Your Door	*A Globe-Trotter's Guide*
Jakarta At Your Door	*A Parent's Guide*
London At Your Door	*A Student's Guide*
New York At Your Door	*A Traveller's Medical Guide*
Paris At Your Door	*A Wife's Guide*
Rome At Your Door	*Living and Working Abroad*
	Working Holidays Abroad

Illustrations by TRIGG
Cover photographs by Riboud/A.N.A. Press Agency
Photographs from Maria O'Shea

© 1999 Times Editions Pte Ltd
Reprinted 1999

This book is published by special
arrangement with Times Editions Pte Ltd
Times Centre, 1 New Industrial Road, Singapore 536196
International Standard Book Number 1-55868-403-4
Library of Congress Catalog Number 98-87494
Graphic Arts Center Publishing Company
P.O. Box 10306 • Portland, Oregon 97296-0306 • (503) 226-2402

Printed in Singapore

To my sons, Sheerwan and Nirwan, with love.

CONTENTS

CONTENTS

ACKNOWLEDGEMENTS

This book represents the personal experiences and opinions of the author and many of her acquaintances. It was written with no assistance from any particular organisation, and without recourse to the assistance of the Iranian government or its representatives. It is not intended to cause offence to Iranians, foreigners in Iran or to the Iranian government, and I hope that any initial reservations about unfair bias or unreasonable stereotyping will be allayed by reading the entire book. Clearly, my perceptions of Iran and Iranians will have been influenced by my own background, as well as my experiences inside Iran, so a fair degree of Eurocentricism is unavoidable, and I have tried to bear this in mind.

I would like to thank everyone in Iran who has helped with the factual information in the book, especially Azita and Hessam, and all my friends and relatives in Iran and Europe who helped with, advised on, read and commented on sections of the manuscript, particularly Professor Philip Kreyenbroek and Dr. Yadi Jayran-Nejad. Many of the photographs were provided by Ardeshir Khajepour-Khouei.

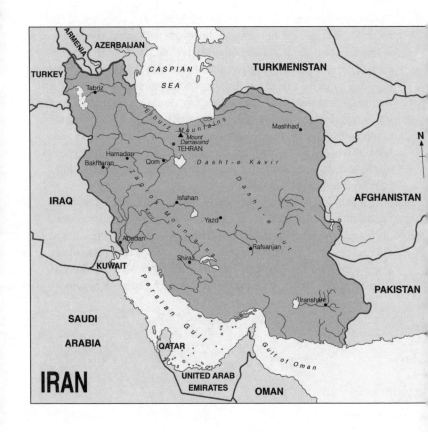

INTRODUCTION

SHIFTING IMAGES

Not too long ago, Iran conjured up a certain image in the West's popular imagination. It was Persia, the land of flying carpets, long-haired cats, oriental splendour and incalculable oil wealth. Iranians were perhaps best known as visiting students with apparently unlimited funds and a taste for luxury, white suits and discotheques. Westerners working in Iran enjoyed a life that was both luxurious and exotic. The Iranian government offered generous stipends and facilities to foreign academics and researchers, who found Iran a pleasantly relaxed and open society compared to other Middle Eastern states. For tourists, Iran was an enjoyable interlude on the overland 'hippie trail' from Turkey to India. All foreigners seemed welcome, and life was good there for them.

However, something rotten lay underfoot in Iran. The widespread human rights abuses, the consolidation of absolute power by the Shah, uncontrolled (and uneven) economic expansion, corruption and preferential treatment for foreigners all fuelled widespread discontent. Most foreigners, as well as entire sections of Iranian society, were too busy having a good time to notice the undercurrents, and certain events came as a complete shock both inside and outside Iran.

In 1979, everything suddenly changed. Iran became associated with another, completely different set of images, captured vividly on Western newsreels: fanaticism, hatred for the West and international terrorism. These images were as distorted and as opaque as those they had supplanted. In this book, I have tried to take the reader beyond the fragmented images of Iran and Iranians to expose the subtleties of a complex and often contradictory society. Anyone who travels in or lives in Iran, or who establishes relationships with Iranians, will soon realise that there is no real substitute for experience as the best guide to feeling comfortable in Iranian society. However, this book offers a head start. By giving the benefit of many individual experiences (not just my own) in Iran and with Iranians, I hope to explain much that might initially seem inexplicable. Most books on Iran are aimed at academics, rather than those who simply wish to live, work or travel in Iran. There are even fewer books daring to gently poke fun at Iran's idiosyncrasies and to describe life with Iranians in a lighthearted manner without attempting to denigrate them and their country. I hope that this book will fill that gap, and encourage people to take a new look at a remarkable country and an equally fascinating people, who are, if anything, better endowed with a healthy ability to laugh at themselves then most of us.

CONTRAST UPON CONTRAST
Iran is like no other place on earth—it is rife with contradictions and internal contrasts. Iran is part of the Middle East, although not an Arab country. It is firmly within the Islamic world, but its people

practise a distinctly different form of Islam compared to other Muslim countries. It is a developing country, yet it has substantial oil wealth. Politically, Iran is a revolutionary state, but one with conservative values.

Iran has seen two revolutions in this century, and four forms of government: absolute monarchy, military dictatorship, constitutional monarchy and Islamic government. The country has undergone stupendous economic, political, social and demographic changes, and dramatic shifts in foreign policy, as well as in the ways in which the world perceives it.

Iran is also a geographical contradiction, exhibiting a continental diversity of climate and landscape within its borders and having few unifying topographical features. This geographical diversity results in diversity of culture and human lifestyles. Iran shows an astonishing variety of architectural styles, clothing, culinary traditions and material culture. Iranians speak several languages and many dialects, and follow several religions, despite their state's title as an 'Islamic Republic'.

Within Iran, the contrast between the rural and urban areas, as well as between the capital Tehran and the rest of the country, is perhaps greater than usual in a developing country. Iran has oil wealth and yet is larger and more populous than most oil-rich countries. These factors, along with its political and social upheavals, mean that Iran has remarkably uneven development and this exaggerates the existing diversity. Iran is riven with divisions—cultural, ethnic, religious, political, economic and class-based.

THE PROBLEM OF GENERALISATION

It is difficult to generalise about any country and its people, but in Iran, this is a particularly complex challenge. The Persian-speakers of central Iran actually form a slight minority of the population, but they are the dominant cultural group, particularly in most of the major central cities of Iran, including Tehran. Even in the remotest and least developed provinces of Iran, where one may hardly hear the national language, there is to some extent an overarching Persian cultural tradition that binds Iranians together. This book inevitably concentrates on that dominant culture, but does not deliberately exclude the many strands of culture that exist alongside, or even in opposition to it.

The majority of visitors to Iran confine their travels and certainly their residence to certain regions, and this book therefore is obliged to concentrate on Iranian life as it is lived in those areas. As so much of life in Iran is concentrated in Tehran, some degree of concentration on that city and its lifestyle is unavoidable. This is a true reflection of the Iranian preoccupation with its capital, to whence all roads, or at least all railroads, really do lead.

The problem of generalisation applies not only to geography but to social groups in Iran. Space does not permit me to make the necessary distinctions in cultural expectations between even the stereotypical norms for all social groups in Iran, if indeed such groups could be clearly defined. In general, it is assumed that travellers to Iran will mix with mainly middle-class urbanites, although I have erred on the side of caution in the degree of 'traditional' attitudes that one might encounter. It is always safer to assume that new Iranian acquaintances are both 'traditional' and religious. Your behaviour can be adjusted afterwards to suit your circumstances if you find yourself in less conservative company, and caution will rarely be regretted (whereas indiscreet behaviour may leave a hangover—the only sort you can safely experience in Iran). I do hope that Iranian readers will forgive the necessary extent of generalisation inherent in this book. It is a short introduction to Iranian customs and etiquette, not an attempt to be a definitive guide, if indeed such a work were possible.

Although I have concentrated on the dominant Persian culture, I have tried to give some sense of the richness of diversity within Iran, geographically and socially, and I hope that the reader will grasp any opportunity to experience this diversity. Fortunately for the foreign visitor, Iranians are generally warm and friendly towards foreigners and eager to adjust to your standards of behaviour, especially when they are hosting you in their country. Iranians have been noted for their chameleon-like ability to adjust to other cultures. Do not let this lull you into avoiding cultural immersion in Iran—the more effort you make, the closer you will get to both Iranians and Iran, and the richer your experience will be.

Remember, although in Iran some generalisation is necessary, one should always expect the unexpected, as Iranians do themselves. In fact, this expectation informs most of Iranian social as well as political life, both its standards and its aberrations.

CULTURE SHOCK?

Some degree of culture shock is inevitable for foreigners in Iran. Iranians themselves usually suffer from some degree of culture shock when they travel within their country. Such travels need not be spatial, but can be metaphorical. The social divisions within Iran ensure that many Iranians really have no idea how 'the other half lives', and may experience a serious shock when they encounter one of the very different social types at close quarters. Do not fear your alienation— you are in good company. One of Iran's most perceptive writers, Jalal Al-e Ahmad, wrote that Iranians themselves are almost completely alienated from their own culture and prone to adopting negative aspects of Western culture. As was fashionable with other writers of the 1960s and 70s, he attempted to explore Iran's indigenous cultures, both regionally and socially generated. The events of 1979 clearly demonstrated the degree of social alienation prevalent in Iran and events since then have left many Iranians alienated to the extent that they have joined the large Iranian diaspora, where they have created a new identity and self-image.

THE IMAGE SHIFTS AGAIN?

Iran's image abroad is slowly undergoing some changes, as it seems increasingly likely that the Islamic Republic has matured and mellowed, at least in the eyes of the rest of the world. For the first time in almost twenty years, foreigners are being encouraged to visit Iran, and many restrictions are being lifted to facilitate this. Iran many not seem the most obvious tourist destination, nor an ideal place to work or study, but I hope that this book will in a small way overcome some of your reservations.

Chapter One

INSIDE THE
ISLAMIC REPUBLIC

CULTURE SHOCK
WARD

Iran is an overwhelmingly Muslim country, yet it is markedly different in atmosphere and political style from all other Muslim countries. You may have travelled in or lived in Muslim countries, or may feel that you are familiar with Islam, but if you are expecting the same religious practices or philosophy as in, for example, the Arab states or Pakistan, think again. In order to comprehend the unique form of Iranian Islam, it is necessary to examine Iran's religious history. Almost 99% of the population of Iran are Muslims—90% of whom are Shi'ite Muslims.

WHAT IS A MUSLIM?

A Muslim is anyone who accepts two basic premises which form the *shahada*, or the first pillar of Islam: firstly, that there is no God but Allah, and secondly, that Mohammed was his last and final prophet. It follows on from these beliefs that a Muslim will try to obey the other four pillars of Islam: *salat* (offering prayers five times a day), *sawm*, (fasting during Ramadan), *zakat* (giving alms to the needy), and the *haj*, (the pilgrimage to Mecca, which should be undertaken at least once in a Muslim's lifetime).

SHI'ITE MUSLIMS

The Prophet Mohammed died in the year A.D. 632, or A.H. 11. (The Islamic Era begins with the Prophet's emigration, or Hejira, to Medina on July 16, 622—this date marks the first 'year of the Hejira,' or *Anno Hejirae*.) Unfortunately, immediately Mohammed's death, the Muslim community underwent a serious upheaval caused by a dispute over leadership. The majority of Muslims (the Sunnis) accepted that a new leader, or caliph, should be chosen without giving priority to the family of the Prophet. This meant that Ali, the Prophet's cousin and son-in-law (Mohammed had no surviving sons at the time of his death), was passed over for the title of caliph in favour of Abu Bakr, the Prophet's friend and father-in-law. Throughout the caliphates of Abu Bakr, Umar, and then Uthman, the minority Shi'ah, or Shi'ite, Muslims, insisted on the right of Ali to succeed the Prophet. In 656, Ali finally became caliph, but by this time the Muslims were hopelessly divided. Five years later, after Ali's murder by a rival Shi'ite faction, Ali's son Husayn abdicated his succession rather than pursue the conflict.

In 680, the Sunni-Shi'ite rivalry reached a dreadful climax in Kerbela, Iraq, making the schism irreconcilable. At the behest of the Shi'ites, Husayn led an expedition to overthrow the unlawful and unjust Yazid, who had been installed as caliph in Baghdad. Husayn's expedition party, which included his family, was intercepted by

Yazid's army on the desert plain of Kerbela. The Shi'ites were all cruelly tortured, dying of thirst or by the sword. Husayn himself—the grandson of the Prophet Mohammed—was slain by the army's commander, Shemr, a character most despised by Shi'ite Muslims.

The Shi'ites became concentrated in Iran and Iraq, although Iran is the only officially Shi'ite state. We can see that the genesis of Shi'ism was a reaction to the question of leadership, and that the vexed question of political and religious leadership has troubled Iranian society ever since.

The Twelfth Imam

According to Shi'ites, the rightful spiritual leadership of Islam passed from Ali into the hands of successive Imams, or descendants of the Prophet Mohammed who were not recognised by the Sunni majority. Iranian Shi'ites are often known as 'Twelvers', as they believe that there were twelve Imams, the last of whom went into some sort of hidden spiritual state, to return at a later date and guide the world to a righteous state of being. The Shi'ite clergy have a major role in leading the population and explaining religious matters until the return of the Twelfth Imam. Many Iranians gave Ayatollah Khomeini the honorific title of *Imam*, clearly hoping that his leadership signalled the long-awaited arrival of the Twelfth Imam.

Iranians frequently swear by the Twelfth Imam, and one of the reasons that there are so many holidays in Iran is the preponderance of Imams' anniversaries to celebrate or mourn. The other branches of Shi'ism prevalent in other regions often recognise a different number of Imams—for example, the Ismailis in South Asia recognise only seven. For many Sunni Muslims, the term 'Imam' simply means a mullah, or clergyman; this is never the case in Iran.

Shi'ites are considered a secretive bunch by many Sunni Muslims. This is partly because Shi'ites were, and are, persecuted by the Sunni majority, and so developed a doctrine of concealment, whereby, it was acceptable to hide one's religious practices in order not to be known as a Shi'ite. This explains why in many parts of the Middle East, Shi'ism has fused with pre-existing religious practices, creating new religions, such as Alevism in Turkey and Syria. Generally however, you will find modern Iranian Shi'ites quite willing to discuss their religion with you if you express a sincere interest. Be aware that many Iranians are as ignorant of religious dogma as are the masses in any country, and much religiosity is a matter of habit rather than belief.

Visible Shi'ism

One sees few Iranians praying in public in the way that Muslims do in other Islamic states, possibly because Shi'ites pray only four times a day, rather than the prescribed five times. Islam is visible in manifestations unique to Iran, particularly in the omnipresence of pictures of religious figures, both living and deceased. Ali is every-

Portraits of Ali, the son-in-law of Mohammed, can be found all over Iran.

where. Shi'ites pray with their foreheads touching a piece of clay from Kerbela, and decorate their homes, cars and offices with holy pictures (one can see such items for sale everywhere). The Shi'ite festivals, as described later on in this book, offer the most visible demonstration of Iranian Islam.

THE 1979 REVOLUTION

Since 1979, Iran has been an Islamic Republic. This came about as a result of a revolution which overthrew the monarchy of Mohammad Reza Shah Pahlavi. This was the second revolution in this century—the previous 1906 Constitutional Revolution forced the monarch to accept constitutional government, at least in principle. The 1979 revolution was much more than a return to religious values; it was a rejection of many of the economic, political and cultural policies of the old regime. Like all revolutions, this one devoured many of its own children, and the broad spectrum of right-wing and left-wing supporters was narrowed down to those who shared the same vision as the revolution's figurehead, the Ayatollah Ruhollah Khomeini—the vision of Iran as a Shi'ite Muslim state.

HIS HOLINESS AYATOLLAH KHOMEINI

Despite his death in 1989, Ayatollah Khomeini's presence is still strongly felt, both as a result of his political legacy, and through the omnipresent portraits of him throughout the country. Iran's postrevolution constitution, ratified by a plebiscite in 1979, declares Iran an Islamic Republic, and that until the Twelfth Imam returns to rule the earth, the *faqih*, or supreme leader, will rule in his place. The *faqih* is the person accepted as the most just, pious, and able person to be found. Khomeini clearly fulfilled this role, and since his death, the succeeding Ayatollah Ali Khamenei has not been completely accepted as having quite the same credentials. It is this uniquely Shi'ite principle of *vali-e faqih*—investing final and absolute author-

19

ity in a spiritual leader—which distinguishes Iran from any other possible Islamic state.

In order to appreciate the role of Khomeini and of other clerics, it is useful to understand the complexities of the Shi'ite clerical system.

Shi'ite Clerics

Mullahs (a generic term for cleric) are literally everywhere in Iran, and are highly visible, due to the special robes that they usually wear, although a few mullahs wear normal street clothes. A black turban denotes a *sayyed* (descendant of the Prophet Mohammed). 'Mullah' can be used as rather mocking title, and Iranian people have long had a curious love-hate relationship with their clerics. Mullahs are credited with many misdeeds and negative character traits, and are maligned as uneducated parasites, yet now they form an elite who effectively rule the country.

Shi'ite Muslims, unlike Sunni Muslims, have an organised clergy, its hierarchy dating back to the establishment of Shi'ism as the state religion by the Safavids in the sixteenth century. The underpinning of this hierarchy consists of the many theological colleges in Iran and Iraq. The most important centre of religious learning is the city of Qom, home of many prominent Shi'ite clerics. Najaf in Iraq was historically the second centre of Shi'ite study, but the friction between Iran and Iraq makes contact difficult. Mashhad in Iran is now the second most important city for theological studies. The colleges are generally built on land endowed by wealthy people, and supported by similar endowments. The colleges are usually under the guidance of one senior cleric, who influences the overall style of teaching.

All mullahs enter one of the theological colleges, probably as a residential student, where they study the introductory course of Arabic grammar, syntax, rhetoric, literature, logic, the Koran (Qur'an), Islamic texts and the lives of religious figures, including the recorded sayings of the prophet (the Hadith). After seven years of this curriculum, they spend another eight years at intermediate level, studying philosophy, natural sciences, literature, and the works of the great theologians. Further research and study will lead ultimately to qualification as a *mujtahid*, or one qualified to interpret Islam for the public.

This style of traditional education has barely changed since medieval times. Neither the period nor the manner of graduation is pre-planned or compulsory. Classes are open to interested parties, and students choose the classes and teachers that they most admire. Teaching is mostly by means of studying set texts and their accompanying commentaries, and debating their merits and points out loud, much like Talmudic studies in the classical European world. Many students will study at more than one seminary to widen their knowledge. In modern Iran, the primary stage is considered equivalent to secondary school, the intermediate stage is comparable to university level, and a *mujtahid* has reached doctorate level. There are about 21,500 theological students in Iran, five times the pre-1979 number. Most mullahs leave after a few years, and seek (or are assigned) positions all over the country. Many graduates take on more divergent occupations, particularly in commercial industries, and regard the seminary as a source of a traditional education. Relatively few continue to the highest levels, after which time they can be honoured with the title Hojat-ul-Islam. After further study, including the publication of a text on some aspect of Islamic learning, a Hojat-ul-Islam can graduate to an ayatollah.

A Model for Imitation

Not only do clerics advise the people on complex religious matters, but they demonstrate appropriate standards of behaviour. All devout Shi'ite Muslims choose a living model for emulation in piety and knowledge (Majar-eh-Taqlid). Each follower will pay up to one fifth of his income to him as alms to be redistributed. The Majar-eh-Taqlid must be an ayatollah with a particularly deep and wide knowledge, and whose personal character is beyond reproach. He will have written a treatise laying down his views on personal practices, so that his followers can refer to this in copying his behaviour. Once he has attracted many imitators, he will be styled a Grand Ayatollah. Very few Grand Ayatollahs exist at any one time in the world—usually no more than six, usually all in Iran, but possibly in Iraq. The credibility of each Grand Ayatollah depends on the number of his followers, the amount of religious alms paid to him, and his publications. Generally the Grand Ayatollahs practise very different styles of life. Ayatollah Khomeini's main rival was Ayatollah Khoyee of Najaf (now also deceased), who espoused non-involvement in politics.

The Role of the Mullahs in the Revolution

Like most mullahs, Khomeini was the son of a cleric, and his sons were all mullahs. The mullahs form a distinct social group in Iran, with marital and commercial links with certain conservative land-owning families and the bazaar merchants. In addition to their links to traditionally powerful groups, the clergy owns vast estates of endowed land, investments and possessions, all of which are untaxed. As Shi'ites generally give their alms to mullahs to redistribute, the financial liquidity of the clerical order has always been awesome.

The autonomous structures of the theological colleges allowed the mullahs to be the main source of dissent against the Shah's govern-ment. It was from his position as a teacher in Qom in the 1960s that Khomeini encouraged his students and imitators to protest against government attempts to reduce clerical property rights and to eman-cipate women. In exile in Iraq, Khomeini remained steadfast in his opposition to the Shah, despite considerable personal danger and the possible murder of his son, using the theological colleges and mosques as conduits to play his tape-recorded speeches.

Unlike other opposition organisations in Iran, the clergy had money, property, a visible and established hierarchy, its own education and distribution networks, popular legitimacy and a highly revered and untainted charismatic leader. Although for

Westerners, Khomeini's charisma was hard to appreciate, his asceticism was genuine and his piety and personal sacrifices for his beliefs were beyond doubt. He also had a coterie of more worldly and capable characters.

A WHO'S WHO OF IRANIAN POLITICS

The Supreme Leader

Iran's supreme leader, currently Ayatollah Khamenei, successor to Ayatollah Khomeini, is Iran's paramount political and religious authority. He is chosen for life by the Experts Assembly, a panel of eminent theologians. It is with him that the final decision rests in all matters of state.

Revolutionary art on the side of a luxury hotel in Isfahan depicts two supreme leaders of Iran: Ayatollah Khomeini (left) and Ayatollah Khamenei (right).

The Council of Guardians

Chosen by the supreme leader, the Council of Guardians is a panel of twelve theologians and Islamic jurists who are the second tier of power in the state. They safeguard the constitution, uphold Islamic ideals, and check any corruption in the parliament. They also review bills in the way that a senate does.

The President

The President of Iran is chosen by direct election every four years, and can serve no more than two terms. Candidates must be approved by the Council of Guardians. (In the 1997 election, only four candidates were considered acceptable.) The President appoints twenty-four cabinet ministers, who then must be approved by the Parliament (Majlis). The Presidency was almost symbolic in reality until Hashemi Rafsanjani made the position much more dynamic over his eight-year tenure in office. The current President is Mohammed Khatami, a liberal who was elected in a landslide victory in 1997. The office of Prime Minister has been abandoned.

The Majlis

Iran's parliament, or Majlis, has 270 elected members who serve for four years, and although no political parties are allowed, they fall into groupings of conservatives, liberals, left-wingers and so on. There are a few women members, including Faizeh Rafsanjani, the daughter of ex-president Rafsanjani. The parliament is very lively, and members can be very outspoken—in fact the liveliness of debate often far exceeds that of the British Parliament. Tehran elects more members than the twenty-six provinces, and it could be said that the capital's interests are over-represented in the Majlis. The speaker of the parliament is a potentially powerful position, currently held by the conservative Ali Akbar Nateq Nouri. There is also the Expediency Council, a twenty-five-member body, which has the power to overturn the decisions of the Council of Guardians on legislation. Ex-President Rafsanjani is head of this council and has succeeded in revamping its powers from largely honorary to something more substantial.

What's a Liberal?

The words liberal and conservative are used relatively in Iran. All political actors within the system are essentially supporters of the Islamic Republic and its theocratic foundations. Dissenters operate outside the system, largely from abroad, and there exists no real opposition base in Iran anymore, following years of persecution.

Liberals generally support more freedom of expression and 'middle-class' values, including economic reform and artistic freedom. Foreign policy is open to review, with a pragmatic approach taking precedent. It must be remembered that freedom of expression can be tolerated only with certain boundaries—not all subjects are up for open discussion. Conservatives generally support a harder line on any perceived dissent from 'revolutionary' values, and favour a combination of government subsidies to the poor and free market policies of benefit to the bazaar economy.

Support for the liberals comes mostly from middle-class urbanites, technocrats, artists, and the irreligious. The original revolutionary power base of the proletariats and the *bazaaris* (merchants) supports the conservatives, who can mobilise mobs of people from poorer areas in their support. There are often street battles between conservatives and liberals. The Western definition of a liberal has no real place in Iranian politics, and the conservatives are really revolutionaries!

Who Runs the Show?

Iranian politics has become essentially a battle between liberal and conservative forces. The holders of executive positions have tended to be pragmatic, due to a gradual recognition that the demands of running the country force one to sacrifice ideals for practicalities. Those who have the luxury of abstaining from the dirty business of foreign relations and the daily political grind, as well as those not directly elected by the populace, are able to retain their pure revolutionary stance.

For every liberal in office, there is always a conservative who checks his or her power. Currently, however, liberals appear to have the upper hand, although they must be careful that the painful effects of economic reform do not create a conservative backlash.

NON-MUSLIMS IN THE ISLAMIC REPUBLIC

Certain religious minorities are formally represented (and guaranteed representation by means of reserved seats) in the Majlis. Freedom of worship is guaranteed by the constitution, which sees religious minorities as protected but unequal. They are generally concentrated in Tehran and in certain professions or trades. Official minorities are Christians, Jews, and Zoroastrians, who are all exempt from military service. Religious conversion is only tolerated when it is to Islam; it is punishable by death for a Muslim to renounce his or her religion. To encourage or suggest such conversion is also highly illegal, and one should take great care not to be thought of as a religious proselyte. The open practice of the Baha'i religion is outlawed. Many Iranians are very sensitive to perceived past interference by non-Muslims, although you are unlikely to be besieged by demands that you convert to Islam. Most Europeans are expected to be Christians, and concepts such as atheism or agnosticism are poorly understood. Conversion to another religion (for example, Buddhism) is best concealed, as this is likely to meet with disapproval or blank incomprehension. For the duration of your stay in Iran, it is best to describe oneself as a Christian, unless you were born into another faith, in which case, apply that label. Foreign Jews might prefer to conceal their religious faith except amongst trusted friends.

Christians

There are about 200,000 Christians (0.3% of the population), and they are exempted from certain Muslim restrictions on lifestyle. Christians are allowed to consume alcohol in private, hold non-sex-segregated parties with dancing in private places, and they have a nonsegregated sports centre in Tehran.

The majority of Christians are Armenians, who were originally settled in Isfahan, where Shah Abbas I put their skills as artisans to spectacular use. There are also Protestants, Roman Catholics, Chaldeans, and Assyrians. Christians live primarily in Tehran, Isfahan, Shiraz and Tabriz. Armenians have cathedrals in Tehran and Isfahan, and most large towns in Iran have Christian churches. Like all religious minorities, Christians live quietly, and their places of worship are usually discreetly hidden behind high walls. The Anglican Episcopal Church of Iran has churches in Tehran, Isfahan, and Shiraz; this church is probably the safest bet for Christian foreigners who want spiritual succour. Most of the churches in Tehran are concentrated in one area near the Sarkas Armenian Cathedral. Embassies can give details of regular Protestant and Catholic services in English, German and possibly French.

Jews

Only 20,000 to 25,000 Jews remain in Iran, and Jewish Iranians or foreigners are likely to be suspected of pro-Zionist sympathies. There are around thirty synagogues remaining in Iran, but it is often difficult to find them, and your presence may not be welcomed by the dwindling congregation, who generally favour emigration as their future option. When sightseeing, it is probably best to avoid Jewish buildings, as your interest in them is easily misinterpreted.

Zoroastrians

The 100,000 or so remaining Zoroastrians live mostly in Yazd and other central parts of Iran. Zoroastrianism is the ancient religion of Iran, probably the world's first monotheistic religion, founded by the Prophet Zoroastar (Zarathrustra). This religion exerted a lasting influence on Judaism, Christianity and Islam, and Zoroastrian ideas remain prevalent in Iranian society. Zoroastrian religious symbology is evident in Iranian arts, architecture and many other aspects of culture. Following a period after the 1979 revolution when it was associated with monarchism and antirevolutionary ideas, Zoroastrianism has retained a strong fascination, even among Iranian Muslims, who admire the religion for its Iranian peculiarity.

Baha'is

The world's 6 million Baha'is see their religion as a logical development of Shi'ite Islam which supersedes all previous religions as the ideal. Baha'ism began in Iran in the mid–nineteenth century, but the religion's spiritual centre is in Accra, Israel, the resting place of Baha' Ullah, the founder of the Baha'i faith. The Baha'is are thus associated with Zionism, although they refuse to be involved in politics. They espouse peace and harmony, seeking converts from all religions, and have built temples all over the world, including the United States.

Only around 300,000 Baha'is remain in Iran, as they are forbidden to openly practice their religion. Baha'is have been executed for apostasy, although espionage is the most usual charge. Few Iranians are sympathetic to the Baha'i claim that Shi'ism can be purified or perfected, and opinions on their plight should be voiced only in company which is known to be sympathetic. Generally Baha'is and Jews are not thought of kindly by Muslim Iranians.

TABOOS IN THE ISLAMIC REPUBLIC

Since Iran is an Islamic country, and in particular a Shi'ite one, it is wise to be aware at all times of Islamic sensibilities, even when people don't seem particularly religious. Obviously, one should observe taboos on touching religious people as well as comments which can be perceived as anti-Islamic or anti-Shi'ite. There are some other aspects of daily life that should be carefully noted, in order to avoid offence.

Conversational Taboos

Several topics of conversation should be either avoided or tactfully skirted around in Iran. It is a criminal offence to insult the religious figures of Islam or the religious leaders. Even though Iranians may offer endless unflattering diatribes about their own leaders and their actions, you should really be noncommittal in response. Apparently even secular Iranians can be quite sensitive to implied criticism of Islam, so always tread warily in discussions about Islam. Unless you know your friends and their opinions very well, avoid criticising the Islamic revolution or Iran's part in the Iran-Iraq War.

Again, unless you are sure of your friends' opinions, avoid discussion of the superiority of the West, women's rights in Iran, homosexuality or sexual freedom. Iranians feel free to ask many questions that Europeans might consider impertinent, such as how much you earn, why you don't have children or what family problems you have. However, it is generally safer to allow the Iranian party to lead conversational gambits until you get a feel for what topics are acceptable.

Do not try to defend banned or controversial works, such as Salman Rushdie's *Satanic Verses*, and, in fact, it is generally safer to deny having read such works. Betty Mahmoudy's *Not Without My Daughter*, the supposed story of her incarceration by a brutal Iranian husband and her subsequent escape from Iran, is deeply offensive to Iranians, and certainly portrays Iran and Iranians in an exaggeratedly unflattering way, whatever the truth of her adventures. The fact that the book is so well-known abroad, and that the film version was made in Israel is considered further evidence that this was another plot to discredit Iran.

Espionage Everywhere

As well as the authorities, many ordinary Iranians are inordinately sensitive about espionage (discussed later in Chapter Four). Expect to have many of your actions and activities misconstrued, and when dealing with the authorities, take espionage anxieties very seriously. Photography is banned in certain sensitive areas—near military installations, airports and public buildings. Signs will be clearly displayed. Do not photograph people without their permission.

Iranians are great conspiracy theorists and rarely take coincidences at face value—sometimes conversations may seem quite surreal as the latest plot against Iran is expounded. Do not be tempted to mock, as most Iranians are unshakeable in their beliefs that America and Britain created the 1979 revolution, and that the British Secret Service masterminded Salman Rushdie's *Satanic Verses*.

These conversations will imbue you with a new respect for American and European intelligence agencies, as you were doubtlessly unaware that they were really so omnipresent and capable.

ISLAMIC PUNISHMENTS

Much media attention is focused on Iran's use of 'Islamic punishments', such as stoning for adultery, limb amputation for theft, and lashing for minor offences. In fact the first two are very rare. Lashing (usually between twenty-five and eighty lashes) is a common punishment for drinking or possessing alcohol, and is carried out on the court premises, after sentencing. The lashes are applied to the back (through the clothing) with a whip and are very painful, although unlikely to inflict any lasting damage. Iranian prisons are clearly not compatible with Western models of penal reform. Deterrence and punishment, rather than reform, are the aims of the Iranian penal code.

Executions are much less frequent now than in the years immediately following the 1979 revolution, but death remains a mandatory punishment for murder and drug trafficking. Major drug traffickers or mass murderers are sometimes executed by hanging from a crane in public. There is widespread public approval of the death penalty for such offences, and Iranians often do not comprehend Western (or liberal) dismay at the their penal code—especially when they perceive that Western countries have high crime rates and are unsafe due to lax law enforcement and weak deterrents. The question of political executions and punishments is a different one, and again, it is a subject best left for discussion with really intimate friends.

Any revulsion for the Iranian penal code should be wisely translated into a rigorously law-abiding stance. Being foreign will not necessarily protect you against such punishments.

The Pasdaran

The Revolutionary Guards, or Pasdaran, are voluntary militia in charge of enforcing Islamic law. They have all the powers of the police, but are ideologically committed to supporting the Islamic revolution. Each town has its own *komiteh*, or headquarters run by these characters, who wear army fatigues and drive landcruisers with blacked-out windows. The *komiteh* is the first port of call in town for foreigners who need any sort of official permits. Foreigners are often asked to report to the *komiteh* for vetting. The Pasdaran often stop people in the street to check their clothing or to make sure couples walking together are married, and they used to regularly enter people's houses to ensure the observation of Islamic standards. They are often very rude or even brutal, but you should always be very polite with them. There are female volunteers who are more likely to accost female travellers. The Pasdaran refer to each other as *baradar* (brother) or *khohar* (sister)— thus, these simple terms may actually refer to the Pasdaran rather than family members in many conversations with Iranians. In recent years, the government has tried, with some success, to limit the Pasdaran's enormous power to interfere with people's private lives.

ISLAMIC CLOTHING

The most visible symbol of Iran as an Islamic Republic is the compulsory, public application of a particular interpretation of Islamic dress to *all* women—even those who are non-Muslim citizens or non-Muslim tourists. In no other country, over such a long period of time, has such a blanket restriction been in operation. Although Islamic dress regulations also apply to men, it is the clothing of the women that initially is so startling.

The Background of Islamic Dress

As befits a multinational state, Iran possesses an enormous number of traditional and regional costumes for both men and women, and in certain villages and peripheral regions of the country (such as Kurdistan and Baluchistan) these are still in daily use. Throughout much of the country, and in all cities, European clothes have thoroughly infiltrated and sometimes even taken over as normal attire. This is the case in Tehran, where only provincial visitors wear traditional costumes. Before the Islamic revolution, the only items of Iranian traditional attire that were worn across the entire country were the mullah's robes, and the woman's *chador*, an expansive semicircle of cloth that covers the wearer from head to toe. It must be held closed with the hands, as it has no fastenings, and can cover most of the face, being held between the teeth. Although its use had once been universal in cities, it had been banned under Reza Shah's modernising drive in the 1930s, and its use had gradually declined, even when those dress restrictions were lifted in the 1940s.

During the 1970s, women were not allowed to wear head scarves or *chadors* when employed by the government, and the population was divided into urban European dressers, who wore all the latest fashions, however immodest, and rural dressers, who wore traditional clothing. Many intellectuals felt that women had become like manne-quins—offered employment on the basis of their looks. As the revolution took shape, it took on board all forms of disgust with the materialistic, West–obsessed, shallow values of the regime. Islam offered a weapon of revolt, even for the leftist and liberal protesters. The main supporters of the Islamic revolution were students and intellectuals who had previously worn only European clothes, and, following the lead of the religious students, they developed a sartorial style out of their existing wardrobes. Many women initially wore jeans with raincoats and headscarves as a sign of rebellion against the Shah's anti–Islamic values. Iranian antipathy to everything Arab ensured that they did not adopt the Arab clothes that would fulfill the same function. The *chador* was a symbol of Iranian values, as well as Islamic dress. For men, wearing only long–sleeved shirts and aban-doning both ties and shaving served the same purposes.

As the Islamic revolution advanced, women found themselves under pressure to adopt Islamic clothes. Shortly after the consolidation of the revolution, it was decreed that Islamic clothes would be compulsory—first for all government employees, and then for all women in public. Although many women protested, the revolutionary government had a general mandate from the people, and thus was able to impose their will. Initially women had to wear one of two types of scarves covering the forehead, chin and neck; a below-the-knee, long–sleeved shapeless coat (*manteau* or *roopush*); trousers; socks; and proper low-heeled shoes. Clothes could be black, grey, navy or brown, with no pattern, and, ideally, a black opaque *chador* should finish off the outfit. Make-up and jewellery were forbidden. Of course, for men, the regulations were less demanding, disallowing only ties, short sleeves, extremely tight trousers, and bright colours.

The Present Situation

The clothing restrictions in Iran have gradually softened, but only to a point. Initially, even clearly religious older women who showed a small amount of hair, or who wore skirts, were terrorised, as were villagers who wore traditional clothing in bright colours. The revolutionary clothing laws were aimed at conformity and were a general reaction against the cult of beauty, much like Mao Zedong's Cultural Revolution in China. The horror stories of punishments for wearing lipstick—involving razor blades and slashed bare arms—are fading. However, the dress code, despite all its subversions, seems set to stay. Government employees are still have a very restricted dress code, as do schoolgirls and students. Otherwise, women are resigned to the rules (as they try to develop fashion solutions), and are always attuned to changes in the level of official tolerance. Currently, *manteaus* are tolerated in most pastel and even some primary colours, apart from red. Women wear skirts, but these should be below the knee, and flesh should not be visible through the socks. Scarves can be almost any colour, and a portion of hair is usually exposed at the front—often a vertical couple of inches of bouffant. Mid-thigh length jackets are seen, and some women wear trousers with no socks, or even sandals and socks.

The degree to which *hejab* (literally 'veil'), or Islamic dress, is enforced varies with political climate, time of year and location. The rules are enforced by civil servants in government buildings, at airports, and, only occasionally now, in the street. When in doubt, I find it is best to dress conservatively. Although certain Iranians may mock, it is safer than a scene with the Pasdaran, who always leave one feeling soiled. Foreign women are not expected to wear the *chador*. After some time, one becomes attuned to the nuances of scarf wearing, and where it is safe to wear thin nylons or no socks. Initially it is wise to seek advice from friends.

General Iranian Attitudes to Clothing

Middle-class and wealthy Iranians take clothing very seriously. Scruffy, comfortable, casual clothing is an alien concept for many Tehranis. In a society where so much is dictated by law, clothing is an important tool to show status and opinions. The *hejab* varies in its application, and every loophole is exploited. Fashions in *manteaus* and headscarves are subtle but definite. Labels are important to certain people, and gifts of foreign fashion-wear are very popular. Pirate copies of designer clothes and accessories are widely available, although at the cheaper end of the market, these are quite laughable. Iranian fashions are generally quite fussy, relying on a lot of detail and trimmings. Sunglasses, a bouffant hairstyle and impossibly padded shoulders are the hallmarks of most stylish Tehrani women. The newest *manteau* or winter coat probably conceals chic and carefully accessorised clothing, probably made to order by a tailor, who can copy any design at a reasonable price. It is also possible in high summer that it conceals nothing more than a petticoat.

Many Iranians find Westerners' attire embarrassingly casual and tatty. Jeans are worn, but always pressed and tidy, except for the teenager, perhaps. Although many Iranians wear nightwear at home, they would not do so when there are guests. Wearing smart clothes for visiting guests is a must.

It is common, when you are visiting someone's house, to hold onto the scarf (having surrendered the *manteau) in* case it is needed to cover the knees when sitting down in the presence of older people or men. Conservative women generally leave their blouses untucked outside their skirt, and an artificial silk blouse, worn loose over a straight, black, below the knee skirt, is the standard form of dress for most mature women. Jewellery is very popular and a subject of common discussion and comment. Iranian women usually wear as much make-up as they possibly can without risking arrest outside. Make-up and hair are formal and elaborate, relying largely on black eyeliner and red lipstick for effect.

One of the lasting visual impressions of Iran is the women's knee-high nylons, which are more common than other form of hosiery and come in an astounding range of designs, always black. When women take off their *manteaus*, the slits at the back of their straight skirts often shows the top of these socks. Another Iranian sight is that of scarfed heads sprouting curious growths—caused by the large butterfly clips that the women generally use to put up their hair. Anyone with a fringe or bangs might well be advised to grow it out, so that hair can be restrained under a scarf.

Men favour smart clothes also, although ties less so, unless mature in years. It is quite acceptable for foreign men to wear ties and suits, although ties are officially unacceptable as symbols of Western values! Sports jackets or smart casual are common. Iranian officials tend to wear double-breasted suits with collarless shirts, known as *mulla'ee*, as clerics also wear such shirts. Of course male clothing is less restrictive, but shorts are never allowed and short sleeves are potentially troublesome, although rolled-up is fine for all but formal situations and in certain areas. Short, very tidy haircuts are the only acceptable ones in almost all circles; moustaches are popular and varied. Beards are generally a social statement, unless in mourning, as most religious Muslim men wear beards. Fashionable clothes for men in Iran tend to be fairly flamboyant in cut, colour and style. Jewellery is popular, despite its dubious status for men in Islam.

The Exceptions That Prove the Rule

Although there is an Iranian 'look', Iranian society is complex, and there are of course many groups of Iranians who have their own style codes. Iranian intellectuals who have lived abroad may well not like the Iran-Chanel look, and they will dress in understated clothes, much as they would in the West. Indeed, there are certain designers in Iran who create expensive fashions, which would be coveted in Paris. Once you establish a group of friends, you will undoubtedly be influenced by their style and solutions to the clothing dilemmas, or even find your own. Individuality of style is not usually highly admired in Iranian society, and foreigners' creative attempts to circumvent the clothing regulations, such as wearing Arab clothing or regional costumes will often be accepted by the authorities, but met with hostility by other Iranians.

Chapter Two

A TOUR OF IRAN

The idea of achieving economic independence in today's Iran—a country that has attracted the attention of the entire world like a diamond in a ring, a country whose strategic position and political and economic status makes it coveted by the world's greedy vultures who have always thought of dominating it, a country in which every colonialist has always sought a foothold for himself; to achieve economic independence in a country like Iran which for hundreds of years has been crushed under the boot of the world's dastardly enemies—is no doubt difficult.

> —Iranian President Ali Akbar Hashemi Rafsanjani,
> inaugural address, August 1989.

GEOGRAPHY

Iran is 1,650,000 square kilometres in area—about the size of France, the United Kingdom, Spain, Italy, and Switzerland combined (or, slightly bigger than the size of Alaska). Iran is also one of the highest countries in the world; most of the country, except for narrow strips along the coast, lies on a high plateau, about 1200 to 1500 metres above sea level. Three main mountain ranges—the Zagros to the west, the Makran to the south and the Elburz to the north—surround the plateau, the centre of which consists largely of salt flats, deserts, and wastelands. The Dasht-e Kavir (Great Salt Desert) to the north and the Dasht-e Lut (Great Sand Desert) to the south cover about one third of the country and appear as an empty white space on most maps. The Zagros mountains reach heights of over 4,500 metres, and, at their northern end, join the Elburz Mountains, at the centre of which, to the north of Tehran, lies Mount Damavand, soaring to 5,604 metres.

Iran has only one partially navigable river, the Karun, which runs through the southwest, and very few lakes. There are two coastlines, one along the Caspian Sea, the other along the Persian Gulf. The overwhelming impression of Iran is that of fawn rocks and mountains, interspersed by villages or cities on the sites of green oases. Contrary to popular imagination, Iran has few palm trees, except in the balmy south. The national tree of Iran is in fact the tall, slim poplar, whose frail silhouette is part of the national landscape. Almost all villages are shaded by these trees, which also line the banks of streams.

Distances between cities are enormous, and although the main roads are good, journeys between many of the central cities and towns are long and tedious. Journeys to the peripheral highlands can be extremely picturesque, but the roads tend to be less maintained, and often the routes are quite hazardous.

The Weather

Iran has very diverse weather patterns. It is possible to ski in the mountains and swim in the sea at the same time of the year. The

Tehran's tower blocks do not diminish the majestic Elburz Mountains to the north.

uplands have hot summers and very cold winters, with snow in the winter and rain in the spring and autumn. The central plateau has scorching summers and bitterly cold winters, with almost no rainfall. The Caspian littoral has its own microclimate, with high rainfall (200 centimetres per year) and high humidity due to clouds that cannot escape over the high Elburz Mountains. The Caspian region is generally warm all year. Along the south, the Persian Gulf Coast is always warm, with blisteringly hot summers up to 51°C (124°F) and low rainfall.

Qanats and Joobs

Iran's varied climate means that almost any agricultural produce can be grown somewhere in Iran, although great human effort is needed—especially in the arid central plateau. In these areas, water is found only in oases or under the mountains. This latter source prompted the invention of the *qanat*, a system of underground wells and tunnels used to channel water for irrigation. *Qanats* are not unique to Iran, but they are more common here than anywhere else in the world. Skilled workers dig wells in the lower slopes of mountains, which collect the seepage from melting winter snow during the spring thaw. Underground tunnels lead from these wells downhill to villages and cities, and the water flows along them to where it is needed.

Some of these tunnels, which are very dangerous to dig out, are up to 100 kilometres long and 30 metres deep. Many *qanats* are very old indeed; they often determined both the birth and the death of ancient cities in arid regions. The digging and maintenance of *qanats* was traditionally an expensive affair, requiring much cooperation amongst farmers, landowners, and townspeople. This is why many cities, including Tehran, lie directly on the lower slopes of mountains—the closer to the source of the *qanat*, the more reliable the water supply.

Unfortunately, new technology (which is less harmonious with the environment) has replaced many *qanats*, and the workmanship skills needed to create and maintain them are vanishing. A journey by plane over central Iran allows the paths of the *qanats* to be clearly seen, as they have circular air openings to the surface at regular intervals. Rich people often had their own private *qanats*, and the British Embassy compound in Tehran is built over its own personal *qanat*, which was vitally important during past outbreaks of waterborne epidemics.

Throughout Iranian cities and towns you will see channels of water, or *joobs*, running alongside streets. Before tap water was supplied, these were the main water supplies for the population. They may originate in *qanats* or springs, and the supply could be diverted into individual houses, to fill their courtyard pools. The water was used for drinking, washing and waste disposal, so the nearer one lived to the supply the better. This explains why the north side of Tehran—the side nearest to the mountain water supply—has always been more desirable than the south. The same pattern of residence desirability is repeated in most Iranian towns and villages. In northern Tehran, the *joobs* provide a refreshing coolness on the main streets during summer, as well as water to wash the streets. In the poorer areas of south Tehran, the water is still used for domestic purposes, if not often for drinking. In the countryside, where there are no natural streams, the *joobs* flow to various parcels of land at set times, as the water is shared between those who maintain its supply.

A VERY BRIEF HISTORY OF IRAN

As any guidebook to Iran offers a basic historical background to Iran, and there are many recommended books on specific periods and aspects of Iran's long history, I shall confine myself to the briefest outline of the key periods and historical characters. Iran has existed in its present region, although differing considerably in size, since the first Persian Empire was established in the mid–sixth century B.C.

The Achaemenians

Following the collapse of the Assyrian Empire, Cyrus II (Cyrus the Great) led the Persians in the defeat of the Medes, the Elamites, and the Lydians. He ruled from Ecbatana (near modern Hamadan), Susa, and Pasargadae (near Shiraz). He and his descendants ruled over the largest Persian Empire, including much of Turkey, Iraq, Greece, Syria, Israel, and Egypt. Darius I extended the empire to its farthest limits, and Persepolis became its magnificent summer capital. The Achaemenians pioneered efficient communications and a policy of tolerance to local customs and religions.

Alexander the Great and the Seleucids

The Achaemenian Empire met its defeat at the hands of Alexander the Great in the fourth century B.C. Alexander (who died in 323 B.C.) added Persia to the world's biggest ever Empire, but after his premature death, Persia passed to the rule of the Macedonian Seleucus I who Hellenised his portion of the empire, which limped along with weak central control for nearly 200 years.

The Parthians

In the middle of the third century B.C., initially under the king Mithridates, the Parthians established independence and then took over the entire Persian Empire. They held firm against Roman attack and ruled until 226 B.C.

The Sassanians

The Parthians were overthrown from inside by Ardashir I, the leader of the inhabitants of the central province of Fars, the true heirs of the Achaemenians, in A.D. 226. The Sassanians were Zoroastrians, and this became the official religion of the Persian Empire. Noted Sassanian kings were Shahpour I, Ardashir I's son; Bahram V; Firouz; Khusrow I (Anushirvan the Just) and Khusrow II (Khusrow Parvis). Factional fighting and constant war with the Byzantines so weakened the empire that the Arabs were able to conquer the Sassanians in the seventh century A.D.

Islamic Rule

The Islamic Arab armies conquered the Sassanians at Qadisiriya in A.D. 637. The Arab conquest changed the fabric of Persian civilisation more than any other before or ever since. In the words of the twentieth century Iranian writer, Jalal Al-e Ahmad, the Arab invasion acted like a scissors that cut Iranians from their pre-Islamic roots. Most of the inhabitants of the Persian Empire enthusiastically embraced the new, democratic religion, casting aside the feudalistic aristocracy of the Zoroastrian priests and rulers. Small pockets of resistance remained in Yazd, Kerman and in the northern mountains. The logical Arabic script was introduced, and Arabic became the dominant language for

43

literature and learning. Iran was a part of the greater Islamic Empire, ruled from Baghdad.

During this period of Arabisation, many great Iranian scholars, such as the doctor Abu Sina (Avicinna) wrote in Arabic, often leaving the impression in the West that they were Arabs. This is something that modern Iranians find hurtful, and are eager to impress on foreigners that many Western texts do not acknowledge the specifically Iranian contributions to science, astronomy, medicine and mathematics. The fact that many Iranians used Arabic name styles during this period adds to the confusion.

The Seljuks

During the eleventh century, Iran was invaded by Turkic nomads from the northeast, the most successful of which were the Muslim Seljuks, who captured Isfahan in 1051. Until 1220, they ruled an Islamic Empire, presiding over a period of literary, artistic and scientific productivity.

Ghengis Khan and the Moguls

In 1221 the Moguls flooded across the Iranian plateau, leaving destruction in their wake. Ghengis Khan and his son, Hulagu Khan, destroyed much of northern Iran, and Hulagu established Mongol rule in Iran under the Ilkhans, who came to appreciate the need for rebuilding their wrecked dominions. As they settled down, the Mongols appreciated the finer things in life as much as previous Persian rulers, and built magnificent religious, educational and public buildings. Still, for most Iranians, the Moguls are associated with little but destruction and barbarism.

The Timurids

As the Mongol Empire collapsed under poor leadership, a new Turkish invasion in 1380, under Timur-e lang (Tamerlane) took over the empire. Timur was an exemplary leader, but his sons allowed the empire again to degenerate.

The Safavids

Internal order was restored by Shah Ismail in the early sixteenth century, who established Shi'ism as the state religion, probably the second most significant era after the Arab invasion in Iran's history. His almost personal war with the Ottoman Turks under Selim the Grim led to the Turkish capture of Western Persia, and several centuries of border struggle between the Persian and the Ottoman Empires.

The Safavid dynasty reached its peak during the reign of Shah Abbas I (1587–1629), who established Isfahan as his capital and built most of the magnificent buildings that remain today. He also established the famous caravan routes, established relations with the West, and presided over a cultural renaissance. After his death, there followed the usual cycle of decline, until 1722, when an Afghan army captured Isfahan.

The Afshars and the Zands

Nader, a leader of the Afshar tribe, pacified the country over the next eight years, defeated the Afghans, and in 1736 assumed the title of Shah. It was he who invaded India and captured the Peacock Throne and the Koh-e Noor diamond. His assassination in 1747 was followed by a fifty-year struggle for leadership, which was finally won by Karim Khan Zand, who ruled from Shiraz. In his twenty-year rule, Iran saw a rare period of peace and prosperity, followed by another prolonged leadership struggle, eventually won by the Qajar dynasty.

The Qajars

The Qajars are the reason that Tehran remains the capital of Iran, despite its northerly location. The first Qajar monarch was the eunuch Agha Mohammed, who despite uniting Iran and reconstituting Shi'ism as the state religion, was brutal and hated. Under his successors, Iran lost some of its northern territories to the Russians, its eastern territories to the Afghans, and the nation shrank to roughly its present size. Afghanistan was given its independence in 1857. Iran became an area where rival European powers vied for influence, all attempting to limit each other's expansion.

In the early 1900s, oil was discovered in Iran and was exploited by the British, who paid only a token amount of their profits to the Iranian government. A Constitutional Revolution in 1906 forced the Shah to accept an elected parliament. The Russians and the British formally divided Iran into spheres of influence, and Iran was occupied during the World War I, even though she remained neutral. After the war, Britain and Russia both retained a protectorate attitude to Iran, but a 1921 coup détat overthrew the (by then) ineffective Qajar Shah, Ahmad Shah.

The Pahlavis

Reza Khan, the young Cossack army officer who staged the coup, subsequently established a military dictatorship and proclaimed himself Shah, taking the name Pahlavi as his family name. With a combination of Messianic modernist zeal and brutality, Reza Shah Pahlavi dragged Iran into the twentieth century and modernised its economy and social structure. He insisted that other countries use the correct name for Persia, Iran. He is best known for his banning of the *chador*, the brutal pacification of minority tribes, and his attempts to create a centralised European-style modern state, much along the lines of the Turkish Republic.

During the World War II, Iran was officially neutral, but again Britain and Russia controlled most of the country. The Shah's warmth towards the Germans saw him forced into exile in 1941, when he was succeeded by his son, Mohammad Reza Pahlavi. From this time on, Iran was firmly allied with the West, particularly the Americans and the British. Despite the repressive regime, Iran was rapidly modernised, as Mohammad Reza introduced many 'reforms' of land owner-ship, religious matters, family law, women's rights, education, and health care.

Mohammad Mossadegh

There was a major blip in the Pahlavi rule in 1952 when militant nationalists, led by Prime Minister Mohammad Mossadegh, pushed the parliament to nationalise the oil industry, which had previously been in the hands of the Western oil companies. This greatly alarmed the West, and the oil industry almost collapsed under a British blockade. The Shah fled the country, but the American C.I.A. staged a coup détat to overthrow Mossadegh and restore the Shah and his obliging attitude towards the Western oil consortia.

The White Revolution Onwards

Throughout the 1960s and 1970s, social and economic reforms continued—despite some resistance—at a fast pace, largely in the form of the 'White Revolution'. Many of these programmes were thoughtlessly introduced and applied, and there were inevitable conflicts. The Shah also took a harsh line against political dissent, while increased educational opportunities at home and abroad al-lowed Iranians to question why political reforms did not accompany the other strands of reform. The Shah became increasingly autocratic with the support of the Americans, and the 1974 oil boom heralded widespread corruption and an increased gap between the rich and the poor. Development projects were increasingly inappropriate, and the Shah was persuaded to squander much of Iran's new wealth on useless armaments, in his American-inspired role as 'Policeman of the Gulf'.

The Islamic Revolution

There are innumerable accounts of the 1979 Islamic revolution, its origins, and its aftermath. (I have only briefly discussed the revolution

47

in Chapter One.) I would suggest that the reader tackle some of these works, as Iran is now, after all, an Islamic Republic, and everything before the revolution is really history.

The Iran-Iraq War (1980–1988)

Up to a million Iranians and Iraqis lost their lives in this long war, which really ended with no change to the status quo. It is worth remembering that Saddam Hussein—the self-elected, apparently lifelong President of Iraq—invaded Iran in 1980, taking advantage of Iran's domestic chaos. Iraq was seemingly supported by both the West and the U.S.S.R. and was well-armed, but the Iranians had fanaticism, a sense of moral right on their side, an army of volunteers in addition to the regular army, as well as a population three times larger than that of Iraq.

Iran felt and still feels very aggrieved that Iraq was not recognised and punished as the aggressor in the war, despite the fact that Iran refused to make peace when the opportunity presented itself. The 'War of the Cities' saw much of south western Iran devastated by aerial bombing, and Iranians in most cities still shiver at the sound of planes overhead. The exchange of prisoners of war is still dragging on, and the Iranians, with justification, feel that their prisoners were very badly treated. The Iraqis also used chemical weapons against Iranian soldiers, which the Iranians believe were manufactured from Western-supplied materials.

The Iran-Iraq War is referred to as 'the Imposed War', and Iran is scattered with graveyards filled with young soldiers, as well as civilian victims of the war. Behesht-e Zahra graveyard in Tehran has a fountain that runs red as blood on Fridays to commemorate the lives lost. The many disabled veterans, their families, and the families of the 'martyrs' (*shaheedan*) are provided for by the state. Unfortunately, in a parallel to the United States' experience with the Vietnam War, the sacrifices of the 'martyrs' and the veterans are less appreciated with passing time, and their privileges are even resented by the rest of the population, who see the war as a shameful waste of lives and resources. The war was a major rallying point for the revolution, and many of its veterans feel that revolutionary values are now redundant.

POPULATION

Iran's population is still growing rapidly, despite efforts to slow it down. It has now passed the 70 million mark (having been 19 million in 1956) and is predicted to be 110 million by 2015, putting Iran's existing infrastructure under even greater pressure.

When is a Persian not a Persian?

The Fars, or Persian (Farsi) mother–tongue speaking individuals, do not actually comprise a majority in Iran (they represent 45 to 50% of the population), although national integration is fairly successful, if uneven and unequal, and bilingualism is almost the norm. It is unlikely in Tehran that you will meet many non–Persian speakers, although this is a strong possibility in certain provinces. Tehranis of other ethnolinguistic origins are usually pleased to discuss their backgrounds, although few will admit to rural origins, and some admit only to coming from the main centres of civilisation. Many ethnic minorities abandon their mother–tongues after migrating to Persian–speaking cities, but they often retain certain characteristics that define them as non-Persians.

As Iran is very much a multiethnic society, the various attributes of the ethnolinguistic groups that make up the population are part of everyday life. It is useful to be able to understand common perceptions of the different peoples and the ways in which they are stereotyped. Of course this involves some degree of generalisation and stereotyping on my part, for which I hope I will be forgiven. As regional and ethnic jokes are so common in Iran, I have included some typical examples, and I hope these will not be thought of as necessarily reflecting my sense of humour. Of course, many jokes revolve around accent and dialect differences, and these are difficult to translate, so I have avoided them.

The Azeris

Azeris, who comprise 18 million people (roughly 25% of the population), are generally called Turks in Iran, although they may prefer the appellation Azeri, due to the connotations inherent in the word Turk. Azeris speak Azeri Turkish, a Turkish dialect mixed with much Farsi vocabulary. The main difference between Azeris and other Turkic peoples is that the Azeris are Shi'ites, which is probably the main reason that they remain well-integrated within the Iranian state. They are concentrated in the northwest of the country in the provinces of East and West Azerbaijan, and also in Tehran. The capital of East Azerbaijan is Tabriz, the cultural capital for Iranian Azeris. Although many Azeris have relatives in the Republic of Azerbaijan, the long period of border control between the old U.S.S.R. and Iran has weakened their ties, and Iranian Azeris are not generally very involved in the events north of the border.

Azeris have their own publications and limited broadcasting, but many Azeri Iranians have been and remain prominent in Farsi literature. The majority of Azeris have no sense of divided loyalties, and can lay claim to the best cultural and social tradition of both Azeri and Fars culture.

Azeris are famously active in the areas of commerce and in the military. The bazaar in Tehran echoes with loud Turkish cries, as do the bazaars in many smaller towns with mixed populations, such as Hamadan and the Kurdish towns of West Azerbaijan. There are also many well-known Turkish politicians and clerics, and Azeris have been very active in left-wing politics. It is widely accepted that Azeris prefer to marry with each other, and this is often for commercial as well as social reasons. They are often recognisable by their fairer hair, the women are perceived as attractive, capable and artistic, and the men are thought of as well-built and rather macho. They have their own musical and dance traditions, much of which has been absorbed into mainstream Persian culture.

Although the Azeris are an accepted part of the fabric of almost all Iranian life, there is a dark side to Iranians' attitudes to Azeris. 'Turk' can be a pejorative term for someone stupid, naive, stubborn, or all brawn and no brains, and there is clearly some overlap between the perceptions of rural and urban Turks on the part of other Iranians. The words 'Turk' and 'donkey' are often juxtaposed. Azeris usually have distinctive accents, and cannot pronounce certain Farsi consonants and vowels, and this is the subject of much teasing or even mockery. Naive remarks are often attributed to Turkish public figures, as it seems more entertaining that way.

A typical joke might concern a Turkish-accented minister who was approached by a farming delegation concerning the fact that their soil had become salty and unsuitable for cultivation. The answer was that the soil would be ideal for growing salted cucumbers!

The Kurds

The Kurds, numbering 6 million, make up almost 10% of Iran's population, but they have tended to remain in the mountainous western border provinces, especially Kurdistan, and have not traditionally migrated to Tehran or other central cities, unlike Azeris.

Therefore, many Iranians have never met a Kurd, and know very little about them and their way of life. Kurdistan province has the second lowest educational, health, and social indicators of any province in Iran and is thought of as a wild, godforsaken place that no one would visit voluntarily.

What other Iranians know of Kurds generally comes from the coverage of the various civil wars involving the Kurds. Most Iranians are aware that the Iraqi and Turkish Kurds are closely related to the Iranian Kurds, and that they have been fighting for independence or autonomy. The Iranian Kurds have also had their fair share of disputes with the central government, and there was a bloody civil war over autonomy for two years after the 1979 revolution. Although left-wing Iranians largely supported the Kurds in their struggle, many Iranians were disgusted by the loss of Iranian troops, and concerned by the spectre of the break up of Iran. The province is still under military rule, and any signs of ethnic unrest are promptly crushed.

The Kurds have their own language, which they share in various dialects with the other 30 million Kurds across the borders. They also have their own distinctive dress (which is still in everyday use), customs, and religious practices. Most importantly, the majority are Sunni Muslims, and only a few are Shi'ites—mostly in and around the city of Bakhtaran (formerly Kermanshah), where the Kurdish and Persian cultures mingle. Kurds are stereotyped as simple folk, tribal in their social relations, musical, and having a penchant for warfare. The men are thought of as very masculine, haughty, with aquiline features, usually dressed in traditional clothes, carrying a weapon, or astride a horse.

Many other Iranians have a patronising, if benign attitude to the Kurds, seeing their language as a primitive form of Farsi, and their culture as primitive. Iranians are generally reluctant to admit to the distinctiveness of Kurdish identity lest this encourage them to break away from Iran. The government of Iran clearly sees the Kurdish opposition as their most serious threat, illustrated by the attacks on opposition figures in Europe. There has been little serious aim for Kurdish independence on the part of the Iranian Kurds, but rather a desire for cultural, and maybe political, autonomy.

The Arabs

Like the Kurds, the Iranian Arabs have largely tended to stay in their area of origin, the southwest and south of the country, near the Persian Gulf (and close to the Arab states). So despite their relatively large numbers (2.5 million, or about 4% of the population) they remain quite exotic. Unlike most of their Arab neighbours, they are Shi'ites, and thus are generally content to remain Iranian, although they often have close family and business links with the Arab states. They speak Arabic and may wear Arab dress, but in the cities they are usually bilingual. Some still live a tribal herding lifestyle, although they can no longer cross the border into Iraq. Most Iranian Arabs are darker skinned than other Iranians, having some African ancestors, and the women traditionally cover their faces with masks, like the women of certain Arab Gulf states. Most of Iran's oil wealth is concentrated in the Arab southwest, and there have been persistent claims that the indigenous Arabs are neglected in the oil bonanza. Many Iranians refer to Iranian Arabs as *Bandaris* from the word for port (*bandar*), as they live in the port cities of southern Iran. There is a distinct style of music as well as a shimmying dance called *Bandari*.

The Turkomans

The one million or so Turkomans (Turkmen) living in eastern Iran, are the descendants of the nomadic Turkish tribes who once ruled Iran. There are several more million Turkomans living in the Republic of Turkmenistan. They speak a Turkic language and have one of the most distinctive physiques in Iran, being very tall with rather Mongolian features. They wear distinctive, colourful clothes, and on rare visits to cities like Tehran are easily recognised. Most of them are settled farmers, and their abilities in horse breeding and racing, as well as wrestling, are renown. Few Turkomans live outside their homeland—like the Kurds, Turkomans are Sunni Muslims who find it hard to integrate into Iranian Shi'ite society.

The Baluchis

Although there are only 750,000 Iranian Baluchis, they are part of a larger ethnic group spread across the border into Pakistan and Afghanistan. They have a very distinctive culture, their own language, and are often physically identifiable. They live in the southeast of Iran, largely in the barren, arid, and least developed province of Sistan va Baluchistan. Both men and women wear the *shalwar kameez*, a loose, long shirt over baggy trousers—as worn in Pakistan—and headcoverings. Many are nomadic, as the urban centres are few and the infrastructure in the region is massively underdeveloped. The main industry is smuggling—drugs, arms, people, and livestock, and the area has frequent military operations to capture drug running mafias. Baluchis have distinctive facial features, and are very dark-skinned. As their accent in Farsi is similar to an Afghani accent, they are liable to the same prejudices when they venture out of their region.

The Nomads

Successive Iranian governments have waged determined campaigns to settle or control Iran's nomadic population. This has been partly as nomads do not fit in with the government's image of a modern state, but also as they, and tribes in general, are hard to control politically, hard to integrate into the state ideal, and often unpopular with the settled population. Most Iranian tribes have tended to be Sunni Muslims and non-Persian speaking, and thus quite detached from central control.

There are probably fewer than one million nomads left in Iran, although many settled villagers will spend part of the year in the pastureland with their livestock. The two main groups of tribal nomads left in Iran are the Bakhtiaris and the Turkic Qashgha'is, the former living in the provinces of Chaharmahal va Bakhtiari and Khuzistan, and the latter in the central province of Fars. There are other nomadic tribal groups, mainly in the periphery of Iran, and gypsies who travel around offering goods for sale as well as services such as tinsmithing and harvesting. All are gradually settling in the cities and villages of their old nomadic regions. Nomads, particularly women, usually wear distinctive, often colourful, tribal costumes; the women go about unveiled. Tribal Iranians can be seen either visiting market towns, or in their encampments. Foreign guests will most probably be welcomed and invited to stay for tea in the chief's tent.

SOCIAL DEFINITIONS AND DIVIDES

Local and Regional Stereotypes

In addition to the ethnolinguistic groups described above, there are several other groups in Iran who have distinctive cultures and possibly speak named dialects of Farsi that would not really be classified as distinct languages. These groups can be regionally defined, as the inhabitants of certain cities are considered to have distinctive character traits.

As with the ethnolinguistic groups, these regional cultures are often the butt of jokes and anecdotes, and I would again like to point out that I am relaying common stereotypes. In order to participate in social intercourse in Iran, it is useful to be aware of these, but they should of course be taken with a pinch of salt:

- **Rasht**. The inhabitants of the northern Iranian province of Gilan, whose capital is Rasht, are technically known as Gilakis, as is the dialect they speak, but they are more commonly known as Rashtis. They are commonly represented as stupid and naive. The men are characterised as lacking an essential Iranian quality, that of *ghayrat*, or manliness—this means they are both lacking in a healthy libido and also very cowardly. The women are perceived as sexually rapacious, free with their attentions, and scheming either to deceive their husbands or to 'liven them up' with garlic-laced foods. (Garlic is little eaten in the rest of Iran, but is thought of as somewhat of an aphrodisiac.) Jokes abound concerning the Rashti man's relaxed attitude to his wife's infidelity, as well as his general stupidity and innocence. Of all the groups in Iran, it is the Rashtis who are the butt of the most jokes, partly because they have a very distinct accent in Farsi, which is widely imitated. A typical joke might involve a Rashti man complaining to his wife that her lover is waking him up every night. When she points out that her lover is very tall and strong, and thus bangs his head on the door frame whenever he enters, the husband immediately becomes apologetic and suggests putting in taller doors, thus solving both of their problems.

- **Isfahan**. The citizens of Isfahan are reputed to be mean and grasping, much as Scottish people are portrayed by the English, especially towards the many tourists that visit the city. They also have a unique singsong accent, and although sophisticated, are considered prone to religiosity.

- **Tabriz**. The people of the Azeri city of Tabriz are famed for their gruffness and unwelcoming attitude to outsiders, the latter a trait that many Iranians attribute to all Azeris. The men are famed as street toughs who pick fights.

- **Qom**. This is a sacred Shi'ite city, much like a bigger version of the Vatican in Rome. Thus it is reasonable to expect some degree of conservatism and even religious fervour amongst the population, and indeed this is how they are perceived. At least every second person can be assumed to have clerical connections.

- **Shiraz**. Shirazis are considered to be fun-loving sybarites with sophisticated lifestyles who are warm and friendly to outsiders.

This perhaps befits the inhabitants of Shiraz (the resting place of the poet Hafiz), often described as the city of wine and roses.

- **Mashhad.** The people of the shrine city of Mashhad are, of course, famed for their religious fervour, but they are also known for their business acumen.

- **Qazvin.** To the west of Tehran, Qazvin is for some inexplicable reason, commonly claimed to be rife with rapacious sodomites.

- **Hamadan.** Up in the Zagros highlands of western Iran, Hamadan was traditionally an opium-growing region; the Hamadanis are famed for their use of opium, as are the inhabitants of the central cities of Iran, such as Yazd and Kerman.

Refugees

It is little appreciated that Iran hosts more refugees than any other country in the world, with very little aid from the international community. Indeed, Iran has rarely requested assistance with its various refugee crises, and when it has, it is usually with several provisos, making it difficult for the international agencies to be involved. It is estimated that about one-and-a-half million Afghanis live in Iran, and despite persistent attempts by the Iranians to resettle them in Afghanistan, each new wave of unrest brings more refugees back to Iran. The Afghanis generally work in very menial positions, often as construction labourers and domestic servants, and are popularly blamed for most organised and petty crime in Tehran and Mashhad.

During the Iran-Iraq War, over half a million ethnic Iranians fled from Iraq, where they had long been settled, to Iran. Additionally, many Iraqi Arab Shi'ites escaped to Iran, where they were resettled, despite the war-torn economy. Every new twist in the long-standing civil war between the Iraqi government and the Iraqi Kurds brings a wave of refugees into Iran. After the 1991 Gulf War, 1.5 million Kurds flooded into Iran. None were turned away, and yet the West's media attention focused on the events on the Turkish border, where the refugees were treated most inhumanely. Civil unrest in Armenia and Azerbaijan puts Iran's northern borders also under intermittent pressure from refugees.

The Iranian people and government feel quite justifiably aggrieved that the world largely ignores Iran's impressive humanitarian efforts in its stereotypical images of the country.

Rural vs. Urban, Capital vs. Provincial

Perhaps two of the biggest social divides in Iran are between the countryside and the city, and between the capital and the provinces. To be *shahristani*, or provincial, is automatically to be less sophisticated than a Tehrani, however delightful that province, its capital, or its inhabitants. Urbanisation has been an increasingly rapid phenomenon over the last thirty years or so, and the upheavals generated by the 1979 revolution and the ten-year Iran-Iraq War intensified the rate of urbanisation. In a country that traditionally lived off the land, over 60% of the population now lives in cities, with about a sixth of the population (12 million people) crammed into Tehran's massively overcrowded metropolis.

Few urban Iranians admit to rural origins. There is more of a stigma attached to being of rural origin (*dehati*), than being *shahristani*. Jokes about the villager mentality abound. Yet as in most Middle Eastern countries, most urbanites are rather wistful about the life of honest toil in the village. A popular film character of the 1970s was Samed, a naive village fool who often turned the tables on urban sophisticates. He represented much of the Iranian confusion over the economic and cultural role of both agriculture and village life. Although the Samed films are no longer approved for public consumption, the character lives on in the popular mentality, and people often refer mockingly to a situation as 'Samed goes to _____', after the typical film titles, which include *Samed Goes to the City* and *Samed Goes to School*. Rural-urban migration is still enormous; the village lifestyle is under great threat, and any opportunity to visit villages should be grasped eagerly. Villagers may be conservative, but they are usually hospitable and generous, and it is here that you will see what many Iranians consider to be the 'authentic' Iran.

There is also a big divide between Tehran and other cities, most of which lack many facilities taken for granted in Tehran. For example, foreign airline offices are concentrated in Tehran, and they may not take bookings except in person. There is a distinct hierarchy of provincial capitals in Iran, and few, such as Shiraz, are considered to be on any sort of cultural and social par with Tehran. Many people will claim to be from Tehran itself, even when their accent indicates that this is unlikely, and others will claim to be from the nearest provincial capital to their home village or small town.

THE ECONOMY

Iran has an average per capita income of U.S.$4,700, and a very high unemployment rate of up to 30%. The country suffers from underdevelopment, bad management, widespread corruption, and the effects of a U.S. embargo on its exports. Meanwhile, the government is still trying to recover from the estimated U.S.$1000 billion in war damage, as well as the capital flight and brain drain precipitated by the 1979 revolution. Iran lost many of its richest entrepreneurs, brightest students and intellectuals, and most skilled professionals to emigration or to the war. Efforts to persuade Iranians abroad to return have been largely unsuccessful.

Black Gold

Iran's economy is firmly based on its most valuable asset, oil. Despite its current economic chaos, Iran is still clearly an oil economy. Petrol is cheap, as is gas and oil for fuel. Nevertheless, Iranians complain bitterly that these are so expensive, as they remember the days when these things were almost free.

Iran is the world's third largest exporter of oil. Petroleum accounts for over 80% of Iranian exports and contributes 40% of the government's income. Iran produces about 3.6 million barrels per day, of which they export around 2.5 million. Reserves are estimated at 90 billion barrels, enough to last at that rate for another seventy years. Oil prices are the stuff of everyday conversation in Iran, and the currently low world oil prices are a source of great concern. In real terms oil prices are now at 1960s levels, and have been around U.S.$10–11 per barrel for the last few years. As the government's five-year budget is calculated based on predicted oil prices, fluctuations can ruin any economic plans. Most Iranians have a detailed knowledge of the oil markets and can remember the price of oil at key times.

Agriculture and Fishing

After oil and carpets, agricultural products are Iran's largest exports. Iran's pistachio nuts are widely regarded as the best in the world. Despite the immense hardships of farming in Iran, over 30% of the population is engaged in farming, growing mostly cereals, fruit, and cotton. The caviar produced by the sturgeon fish in the Caspian Sea is a very lucrative product for export.

The Rest

Up to 20% of Iranians are employed in industry, mostly the petro-chemical industry, as well as steel manufacture, mining, and car manufacture. There is a small textile industry in addition to carpet manufacture, which is workshop based. The Iranian natural gas reserves are enormous and have recently been exploited in export deals as well as domestic usage. The D'Amato legislation, a U.S. law which penalises foreign firms investing more than U.S.$40 million per annum in Iran, is being ignored by companies who are keen to buy and export Iranian gas. Meanwhile, Iran, in an attempt to lessen its dependence on the West, is looking more towards Central and Southeast Asia for new markets.

ENTER THE TOURIST

The enormous difficulties involved in getting to Iran for most foreigners means that they are likely to undertake only one tour of Iran, and in fact booking an organised highlights-of-Iran tour is the easiest way of getting in to Iran. Tours and tourists generally visit the same areas: the Caspian coast; Tehran; Shiraz; Isfahan; Yazd and the ancient sites of Bam, Persepolis, and Pasargadae.

All of these areas are fascinating, and should be visited by anyone who has the time or opportunity, but all of Iran has something worth seeing and experiencing, often all the more precious as so few foreigners visit off the beaten track. Once you have a tourist or work visa for Iran, few areas are forbidden to you. Only certain narrow border zones, areas of unrest, military zones, and some holy shrines are off limits to foreigners, although journalists may have qualified visas and be expected to travel in the company of a government official on a pre-agreed itinerary. Do not think of Iran as secretive in the way of some other Middle Eastern countries, for example, like Syria. Iran is like a bottle—it has a narrow opening, but once you are in, you can rattle around in considerable freedom. It is also very safe; there are so few tourists that they are not the target of crime or harassment. Rather you will be met with bemused curiosity or welcoming enthusiasm.

Although Iran is now more open to tourists, claiming that 350,000 visit each year, these are mostly from neighbouring states. Probably fewer than 5,000 Westerners visited Iran in 1996, including the Japanese, who are the most visible 'Westerners' in Iran.

THE VISA PROBLEM

Only the citizens of a few countries—currently Slovenia, Macedonia, and Japan—can get almost guaranteed three-month tourist visas, possibly on arrival. For the rest of us, obtaining a visa requires the expenditure of considerable time, energy, and money, with no guarantees offered. The citizens of smaller countries which have good relations with Iran, as well as Australians, are generally welcomed to Iran. Israelis are not given visas, nor is anyone who has an Israeli stamp on their passport. Thai visas are often unpopular, due to its association with sex tourism, and Iraqi or other Arab country visas will require considerable explanation. Americans are now allowed visas, but only on tours or with good reason.

The Tourist Visa and the Transit Visa

Tourist visas of two weeks or one month are generally granted as part of an organised tour package, in which case the tour company will advise on procedure, or to visit relatives. It is theoretically possible to be invited by a friend in Iran, who must obtain an authorisation number from the Ministry of Foreign Affairs in Tehran. This requires patience and time, and possibly personal contacts, and is rather a lot of trouble to ask of any but the most determined and enthusiastic Iranian. Your sponsor will be interrogated at length as to how and why they know you, and the application may well not be accepted. Generally, this method is best avoided. The most common way for foreigners to visit Iran is on a transit visa, which is valid for seven to ten days, and allows you to travel overland in and out of Iran, usually via Turkey and Pakistan.

The Iranian embassies and consulates vary greatly from country to country. Some travellers find that the consulate in a neighbouring country will be more helpful. It can be useful to ring around until one gets at least a hopeful response, and also to keep applying. Single women applying are likely to be refused on safety grounds, although she could always claim to be meeting up with friends along the way. The cost of a visa, along with the application procedure, varies greatly, but is rarely less than U.S.$50, although Australians in Australia do not pay anything. You may be asked for substantial paperwork, including letters from employers, a letter from your embassy if abroad, travel tickets, a planned itinerary, as well as photographs and passport details.

Remember that when attending an Iranian embassy or consulate, men must wear tidy clothes, and should dress conservatively in long trousers and sleeves. Women must wear loose, conservative clothes with a headscarf and no bare legs. All photographs of women for applications must be with headscarf, and smiling in photographs is frowned upon. If possible, adapt one's personal circumstances to suit the application. For example, discard an undesirable profession in favour of something bland—a 'lecturer' is always safer than 're-searcher' or 'writer.'

Extending the Visa

Also unlike the case in many other Middle Eastern countries, the short visa period in Iran need not deter you from visiting. Once inside Iran, all these visas are usually easily extended one or two times, for up to two months in total inside Iran, although offices in provincial cities, especially touristy ones, are generally more helpful than the ones in Tehran. The provincial police headquarters (*shahrbani*) or the provincial government office (*shahrdari*) is usually the place to arrange for a visa extension, but some cities have a foreigners/aliens bureau. You will need two photographs, a completed application form, a stamp from a branch of the Bank Melli (which will also stamp your forms), your passport, and photocopies of your passport and any other documents. You may be interrogated at length about yourself, your planned itinerary, and your views on Iran. It is wise to enthuse about the beauty of the country and its people and sidestep controversial issues. The extension may take minutes, hours or days, and will not usually be given until a few days before the visa is due to expire.

THOSE TOURIST TRAPS

There are no places in Iran that are overwhelmed by foreign tourists, but internal tourism is very popular and focuses on most of the same places that foreign tourism does. Places with a 'touristy' feel, albeit Iranian style, are more relaxed and there will be more facilities for you, but, as I said earlier, there are great rewards in seeing other parts of Iran. If you are living in Iran, you will be urged by Iranians to visit the main tourist resorts, and, as the Iranian weekend is too short for extensive travelling, every holiday period sees a big exodus from Tehran to these resorts.

The Caspian Region

For most Tehranis, this is the place to spend one's short breaks, and many wealthier Tehranis own or rent villas here. The balmy climate, the beaches and the spectacular green mountain scenery make this an area well worth visiting, as it seems so different to the capital city. You can reach one of the Caspian seaside towns such as Ramsar or Chalus within five hours from Tehran, via a spectacular drive over (or via a tunnel through) the Elburz Mountains. Many of the towns here are overdeveloped, the beaches are rather disappointing and the climate is tiresomely humid, but, still, the area has many charms.

As this region was the focus of internal tourism in the 1970s, there are many tourist facilities, although now sadly ill-maintained. People are very relaxed and friendly in the Caspian area, women generally have more personal freedom, and there are many restaurants, cafes and hotels. There is also a tradition of taking in bed-and-breakfast guests, which is a fascinating experience for those who know some Farsi. There are many restaurants specialising in the northern dishes, especially fish, although the local caviar is almost all exported. The beaches are mostly segregated, and there are few beaches where women can swim without full *hejab*. Many people like to rent or borrow a villa with its own pool, so they can swim in peace.

The Gulf Coast and Islands

Although the Persian Gulf is intolerably hot for most people in the summer, it makes an appealingly warm winter resort area, and one that the previous government tried to promote. The present government has developed two islands, Kish and Qeshm, as duty-free zones. Qeshm is not yet well-developed, but Kish has been described as resembling a mini-Singapore or a poor man's California. Kish is very expensive and has a very rather relaxed attitude to Islamic morality laws. There are many shopping malls selling the duty-free electrical goods, some rather nice sandy beaches, and also theme parks for children. Kish is popular with rich Iranians, who feel they can relax here, and airline tickets are heavily booked in winter. Be warned: duty free goods worth more than around U.S.$20 are not importable to mainland Iran without customs formalities, which are long, arduous and often ludicrously expensive.

Shiraz and Isfahan

Most tourists, or anyone staying or living in Iran, will want to see Shiraz and Isfahan, which are rich in architectural gems and delightful places to visit. Shiraz is much further from Tehran and very hot in the summer, but it is the starting point for visiting the important ancient sites of Persepolis and Pasargadae. Both of these cities are the best prepared for foreign tourists, with a relaxed attitude to their eccentric behaviour. All guidebooks on Iran give full details of visiting these cities, and there is even material available in English inside Iran about their architectural wonders. Occasionally, at times like Easter, one can feel a little overwhelmed by German and Japanese tourists, although of course this is entirely relative to the sparse numbers of tourists to which you will have become accustomed. Also, these cities become very overcrowded with domestic tourists at peak Iranian holiday times like the spring New Year, and you may find flights and accommodation scarce.

The Safavid Se-o-Seh Pol Bridge in Isfahan, a must-see for tourists.

Persepolis and Pasargadae

No visit to Iran should exclude its most famous tourist attraction, Persepolis (or Takht-e Jamshid), the ruins of an Archaemenian summer palace complex razed by Alexander the Great in 331 B.C. Usually part of a trip to Shiraz, Persepolis is blisteringly hot in summer and very crowded on Fridays and during public holidays. Nearby (6 kilometres north) lies Naghsh-e Rostam, the site of four imperial tombs, as well as rock reliefs and an ancient fire temple.

Pasargadae is the remains of the earlier imperial city, founded by Cyrus the Great. The awesomely simple tomb of Cyrus is the centrepiece, and it's worth visiting just for that, as the rest of the site does not compare to Persepolis. Persepolis is about 60 kilometres from Shiraz, and Pasargadae is about 130 kilometres away from Shiraz in the same direction.

The Central Cities

The ancient and very typically 'Iranian' cities of the high central plateau are easily reached by rail, long roads, or internal air travel. Yazd, the traditional Zoroastrian centre, has one of the most extensive old cities in Iran laced with fascinating architecture. Wind towers which channel cool breezes into basement pool-rooms in the summer are its most distinctive feature—and also a striking example of indigenous technology. Kashan is famous for its carpets, gardens, and mosques, and Kerman for its Bazaar-e Vakil, a very traditional bazaar. Bam is often the farthest flung destination on tourist itineraries, as the citadel and original city remains are possibly the most impressive archaeological sites in Iran.

The Shrine Cities

Religious Iranians often visit shrine cities, and this is also an option for foreigners, although a few shrines are forbidden for non-Muslims. Most shrines are accessible if you wear suitable clothing (*chadors* are often provided for women), remove your shoes and behave respectfully. They are often spectacularly beautiful. Qom is close to Tehran and a day trip is quite possible. Mashhad is a popular holiday destination, as a sophisticated major city, as well as the site of the holiest shrine in Iran, the tomb of Imam Reza. With a guide, you will probably be allowed to see the shrine precinct, as long as you behave respectfully. Security is very tight in Mashhad after a string of bombings in recent years.

Off the Beaten Track

As suggested earlier, one should take any opportunity to see almost any of the areas in Iran, almost all of which hold many attractions for the slightly adventurous tourist. Iran is quite safe, as long as one respects the law and local customs. Certain areas obviously have fewer facilities and more attendant hardships, and the most extreme example of this is probably the eastern side of the country, where travelling is very hard work. Although it is possible that the *komiteh* in any particular area may take an interest in you, generally the worst that will happen is that you are politely requested to be a tourist elsewhere in Iran. Some border areas show increased security surveillance, and it is worth introducing yourself to the local police headquarters and explaining that you are a tourist. If you flatter them enough, they may give you a letter permitting you to tour around, which could come in useful.

Areas which may prove particularly interesting include those peripheral areas with ethnic minority populations, such as the western Kurdish provinces, eastern Mazanderan province (populated by Turkomans), and the Azerbaijani provinces in the northwest. The area between Hamadan and Kermanshah in the west is known for its archaeological sites, but is now little visited by foreign tourists. Many foreigners have found that the Elburz Mountains offer a wealth of possibilities within easy reach of Tehran.

SOME TOURIST PRACTICALITIES

Price Penalties

Iran has a system of charging foreigners at a different rate for many things. This is often disguised by posting foreigners' prices in U.S. dollars (instead of in rials, the Iranian currency) and insisting on hard currency. (For information on the exchange rates, see Chapter Nine.) This policy applies to tickets for international travel, admission fees to tourist attractions (up to ten times the price for Iranians), and rates for the better hotels. The tourist attractions may charge you the Iranian rate if you have a student card. Foreigners are classified by passport, so some Iranians who have taken foreign nationality will be penalised, whereas foreign spouses of Iranians who hold Iranian passports will benefit.

Hotels

All hotels are regulated by the government, and graded from one to five stars, but these should not be assumed to correspond with European grading systems. Most hotel prices, other than probably the five-star hotels, are negotiable, although possibly only the manager will have the authority to negotiate. You can also try arguing that you have no hard currency, and as the rial price will be converted at the official rate, this will save you some money.

Double rooms are more common than single ones, and single travellers may not get a price reduction. Breakfast is not necessarily included. Filling out the hotel registration forms is mandatory, and you may have to surrender your passport so that the police can inspect it when they visit.

A *mosaferkhaneh* is a lodging house, used mostly by Iranians, but some are suitable for foreigners on a budget. The worst are unimaginably awful and intended for itinerant workers who sleep in dormitories. Many do not take foreigners as the local police object.

A *mehmankhaneh* or *hotel* is a hotel. All hotels with one star or more have private bathrooms and toilets. Hotels vary, especially around different parts of the country, so follow recommendations. Have a look around before booking, and women should especially make sure that the management feels the accommodation is suitable for a lone woman. (The manager will not be shy about answering that question, as he doesn't want the bother of any unsavoury incidents). Four and five star hotels ostensibly have the trappings of luxury hotels, but are often poorly maintained, and the standards of house-keeping and service may be slipshod. Prices are very high, often even by Western standards, and the hard currency regulations are always enforced.

Souvenirs

Iran has many wonderful handicrafts, although unfortunately the standard of these appears to be in widespread decline, as mass-produced items become more popular. Even excellent work is often spoilt by cheap finishing touches, such as synthetic backing to textiles or rough woodwork to mount items. Certain items are the speciality of particular cities or regions, and are often better and cheaper there. Isfahan has a long and venerable tradition as the centre for most traditional handicrafts.

Miniature painting is particularly famous in Isfahan, where examples on camel bone can be found which require a magnifying glass to view the details. Metal work is widely available in silver as well as base metals, and large trays which can be used as tables are wonderful souvenirs. Copper and bronze are less available than they used to be, and tinware, other than the enamelled Isfahani items, is very rare now. Woodwork is often spectacular, although the mother of pearl inlays seen in Arab countries are rare, and often the wood warps after purchase. Marquetry (*khatam*) is the most widespread woodwork form, involving painted and gilt wood, and is used on all objects, especially picture frames and boxes. Ceramics and pottery are often lovely, especially around the Caspian and around Hamadan, but they are heavy and often very brittle, and so hard to transport. Glassware is widely available, and hand blown frosted glass plates, vases and bowls are very cheap, retailing at inflated prices back in the West.

Textiles include carpets, hand block-printed Isfahani cloths, embroideries, and weavings, including Kelims. Care should be taken in purchasing any items that might be antique or carpets, as export restrictions apply. (See Chapter Nine.)

You can post most souvenirs out of Iran, having sought advice from the local customs office, and this may be less trouble than carrying them around and getting them through the airport. The Iranian government runs a chain of shops under the control of the Iranian Handicraft Organisation. All provincial capitals have at least one 'official' handicraft shop, and Tehran has five such outlets. The prices are fixed and reasonable (although they may not be the cheapest), the goods are of high quality, and the selection of products includes most of the major traditional Iranian crafts. These shops have a poor selection of carpets, however, as there are so many private, reputable carpet shops to be found in Iran.

Chapter Three

THE LANGUAGE
OF POETRY AND SUGAR

LEARNING FARSI

Only perhaps 50% of Iranians speak Farsi ('Persian' is a European term unfamiliar to most Iranians who have not lived abroad) as their mother tongue, but it is the only official state language, it is understood by the majority of the population, and all official and almost all written communications take place in Farsi. Unless you intend to live or travel extensively in one of the parts of Iran where Farsi is a minority language, such as Kurdistan, Baluchistan, or Azerbaijan (where attempts to communicate in the local languages will be warmly appreciated), Farsi will be your main language in Iran.

Although compulsory, the standard of English teaching in Iranian schools is generally low, and there is not the same saturation of American and English media found in other Middle Eastern countries. It is only really Iranians who have university level education, or those who have lived abroad, who are proficient in English. Since 1979, there has been no sizeable European expatriate population, and foreign languages have not been considered very useful for Iranians who wish to remain in Iran. In order to live or even travel comfortably in Iran, a grasp of the basics of Farsi is essential. Although in most situations, someone who speaks a modicum of English may eventually be found to help out, it can be very alienating not to be able to communicate at all.

Won't They Laugh at My Efforts?

As so many Iranians speak Farsi with strong regional accents, and possibly quite poorly too, you will not need to worry about your outlandish accent and poor grammar; most Iranians have heard it all before from their fellow citizens, and will not shriek with laughter at your efforts. Although there is a rich vein of humour about regional accents, they exist at all levels of society, and many well-known characters in the government have thick accents and speak less than elegant Farsi. *You* may have trouble with following the colloquial accent or idiom, or the varied accents, but they will probably understand you perfectly.

Written Farsi is standard Farsi, whereas native speakers generally use a colloquial form which shortens some verbs. In Tehrani Farsi, the long *a* sound (pronounced *ah*) is shortened to *oo*, as in 'room'. For example, Tehran would be pronounced *teh-ROON*, not *teh-RAHN*. To some extent this will become normal for you if you live there. Although you may feel you sound bookish when speaking standard Farsi, this is considered charming by most Iranians, and it also aids in reading and writing standard Farsi. It is unrealistic to try to sound like a native speaker, and attempting to speak the language correctly, if formally, will probably minimise misunderstandings.

Reassuringly Simple

Although initially, Farsi may seem very daunting, it is surprisingly logical and one of the easier languages to learn. For anyone who has attempted Arabic, be reassured that as an Indo-European language, Farsi is much more familiar, and less complex than most European languages. The only things Arabic and Persian share are a similar alphabet and some Arabic loan words.

Nouns in Farsi have no gender and even personal pronouns are genderless. Every person, lingually at least, is effectively an 'it'. All verbs are regular bar two—the verbs 'to be' (*budan*), and 'to have' (*dashtan*), and these are only irregular in the present tense. There are fewer tenses than in English, and it is necessary only to know the infinitive and the present root of a verb in order to conjugate it in all tenses. Word order in a sentence is not crucial, although verbs generally come at the end. There is no word for 'the'. Vocabulary is generally less than in English, with one word covering many meanings, and very educated Iranians often draw on obscure Arabic terms for greater precision.

Some vocabulary will be familiar from European languages, and there are only a handful of sounds that are unfamiliar for English speakers. Some of these sounds, particularly the glottal consonants, are difficult for many Iranians too, so you will be in good company if you don't manage them all initially. An effort should be made though, as the difference between the *kh* (as *ch* in the Scottish 'loch') and *k* sound, for example, may alter the meaning of a word, and certainly will make it harder to remember how to write the word correctly. Farsi vowel distinctions can be particularly difficult for North Americans. The difference between the short *a* (as in 'ran'), or long *a* (as in the second syllable of 'Nevada') and the short unwritten *a*, is vital, as it affects the meaning of words. Iranians pronounce Iran as *ee-RAHN*.

Reading and Writing

Some grasp of the Farsi alphabet will be necessary, as only major street signs (and the menus of luxury hotels) are written in English. The Farsi alphabet has thirty-two letters, twenty of which are common to Arabic and Persian, eight are found only in words borrowed from Arabic and Turkish and four are not known in the Arabic alphabet. Farsi is written from right to left, so books start at what most European language speakers would consider the back of the book. There are two kinds of vowels: the short ones (*a*, *e* and *o*, which do not normally appear in writing) and the long ones (*oo*, *ay* and *ee*, each of which is represented by a letter in the Farsi alphabet and also serves as a consonant). The method of writing Farsi is logical, although reading can be trickier, as one has to guess at the unwritten consonants of unfamiliar words. This is all a matter of practice. The only tricky part is that all letters have three forms, depending on whether they occur at the beginning, middle, or end of a word. This is because in Farsi, almost all letters are joined together in a smooth flow, there are no capital letters, and all writing is cursive. Initials rarely stand alone in written Farsi—full names are usually used to avoid confusion.

The Arabic Influence

During the Arab domination of Iran, the modified Arabic alphabet was introduced, and for many centuries, most Iranian scholars in the fields of religious studies, philosophy, science and medicine wrote in Arabic, thus being regarded by the world as Arab scholars. This is very irksome for modern Iranians, who generally hold Arab culture in low regard, and in fact may consider the term 'Arab culture' to be an oxymoron. The works of great writers such as Avicennia (Abu Sina) are all now translated into Farsi, and Iranians are often eager to point out that many of these scholars wrote poetry in Farsi, which was often their mother tongue. The fact that Iran did not lose its national language, unlike other portions of the Arab Empires, is a source of pride to many Iranians and fuels the widespread belief that everything Iranian is superior to everything Arab.

In addition to retaining the Arabic alphabet, certain influences on the language clearly remain. Whenever a word is particularly difficult to pronounce, or write, one can be fairly certain that this is an Arabic loan word. Certain letters of the Arabic alphabet (which in Arabic have a distinct sound) remain in Farsi, but they now sound too much like certain Farsi letters, thus creating spelling problems. In the 1960s and 70s, efforts were made to expunge the Arabic influence in Persian vocabulary and grammar. As most clergymen in Iran have studied extensively in Arabic, such efforts have been abandoned since 1979, and, still, the Arabic influence creates minor irritations for learners of Farsi.

How Will You Learn?

Iranians will generally be eager to help you with your Farsi. Textbooks available outside Iran are probably of better quality and clarity than those inside, although copies of some Western textbooks in Iran. Private tutors advertise in the *Tehran Times* and the *Kayhan International* (two English language newspapers in Iran), but one should chose a same-sex tutor, in case of official misunderstandings. There are classes at Tehran University, which are of dubious benefit. Teaching methods tend to be dated and undynamic, although there are some tutors who are familiar with new techniques, such as T.O.E.S.L., which they apply to Farsi teaching. Your embassy will be able to advise you about recommended classes.

A child's schoolbook will be useful in helping you to learn the alphabet, as well as introducing you to the language. After all, Farsi is a foreign language for many Iranian children.

When It's Best Not to Know Farsi

Iranians are generally eager to impress on foreigners the beauty of their language, but there are occasions when your grasp of Farsi, or even attempts to learn, may be open to misinterpretation. The Iranian

government and its officials generally hold the belief that foreigners would only bother to learn Farsi in order to undertake espionage activities inside Iran. This attitude also occurs in other echelons of society, and there are no foreigners who have spent any time in Iran who have not found to their horror that they are assumed to be an intelligence agent working for one organisation or government or another—and possibly even a double agent.

Please do not let this put you off learning Farsi or taking an interest in almost any aspect of Iran that you find interesting. However, a certain awareness of this current in Iranian society is essential in order to avoid unpleasant incidents as much as possible. It can be helpful to remember that Iran has such a complex history of outside power manipulation that Iranians have every right to treat foreigners' interest in them with suspicion. Also, being an intelligence agent in denial may be a big deal with the government, but many of your Iranian friends will still like you, despite your assumed 'activities'!

When dealing with Iranian officials, it is best to be modest about one's linguistic abilities, unless it is essential to communicate in Farsi. It is generally unwise to attempt to dazzle such people with your Farsi, unless invited to do so, in a clearly sympathetic environment. Never admit to studying Farsi before entering Iran, unless you are sure of your ground.

When making acquaintances, by all means greet them in Farsi, but do not initiate conversations, leave that to the other person. Iranians are rarely shy about conversing with strangers, but may not wish to talk to foreigners. A barrage of conversational questions, however innocuous, especially in Persian, may evoke a suspicious response.

Be very careful about admitting knowledge of other languages in general, especially such suspicious ones as Hebrew or Russian. Knowledge of Iranian minority languages such as Kurdish not be seen as an asset, so again you will have to gauge individual situations carefully before leaping in.

Politeness

Iranians are very polite in speech, and can be very formal. Like French, Farsi has familiar/polite plural forms of the word 'you': in the first case, *to*, and in the second, *shoma*. *To* should be used only with familiars of the same age, children and animals. Even when speaking to social inferiors of the same age or older, Iranians will generally maintain polite forms. The verb ending for the polite form is safest, and does not sound ridiculous if used for *to*, but rather like a safe compromise.

The language contains many formulaic polite expressions, which will begin to trip off your tongue easily, as you learn to be an Iranian social being, using the language as a tool for smooth social interaction. The use of these formulas ensures a pleasant social atmosphere and a feeling of contentment. It soon becomes normal. Many statements have standard replies. Examples of standard formulas include:

- When thanked for something, Iranians will always answer with something like the following: 'it was worthless, don't mention it' (*ghabel nabud*); 'you're welcome' (*befarma' eed*); 'it was no trouble' (*heech zahmat nabud*); or, 'it's nothing' (*cheezi neest*).

- Iranians will always apologise for turning their back to someone, to which the answer may well be, 'A flower has no back' (*gul pusht-eh ruh nadareh*).

- When a guest arrives bearing flowers, the host will declare, 'You are a flower yourself, why did you bring flowers?' (*shoma gul hastid?*)

- When asked if an outing was enjoyable, one replies, 'Your place was empty' (*jay-yeh shoma khalee bud*).

- When someone admires an article, the owner offers it as a gift— *pishkesh* (this is rarely a very serious offer, unless accompanied by definite further actions)—and will be answered in return with, 'Thank you, but it suits you best' (*mamnoon, khoshetan meead*).

- When complimented on one's appearance: 'Your eyes see beautifully' (*cheshm-tan ghashang meebeeneh*).

- After any labour, such as on return from work: 'Don't be tired' (*khasteh nabsheed*).

- After a physical task, such as after cooking: 'May your hands not be tired' (*dast-e shoma dard nakoneh*). This is usually said by guests after eating.

- A most useful expression is *befarma' eed*, literally meaning 'give orders'; it is useful in all social interactions, accompanied by the appropriate physical gesture implying the situational meaning. It can also mean: 'you're welcome'; 'please help yourself'; 'let's go'; 'after you'; or 'can I help you?'

Greetings

Greetings take up rather a lot of time in Iran. Not only does one usually enquire after someone's health, but also after any of their friends and relatives with whom one is acquainted. The standard initial greeting is the Arabic *salaam aleikum*, or more often, just *salaam*. Properly, this first greeting receives the reply *aleikum salaam*, but just *salaam* is fine. Other possibilities include *sobh bekher* ('good morning') or *shab bekher* ('good night'). The most usual health enquiries are *hal-e shoma chetor eh?* (the more casual version is *hal-et chetor eh?*—

79

literally, 'Your health, how is it?') or *hal-eh shoma khoub eh?* ('Is your health good?') The very formal version (*ahwal-e shoma chetor ast?*) uses the plural of 'health' with the formal 'you' and the formal form of the verb 'to be'. The reply can be *khoub-eh* or *khoub-am* ('It's good,' or 'I'm good'), or *bad neest* or *bad neestam* ('Not bad', or 'I'm not bad'), followed by return enquiries.

When you want to ask a question, start with *bebakhsheed* ('Excuse me'). 'Thank you' is actually *mamnoon*, usually qualified as *khayleh mamnoon*, although the French *merci* is universally used, and the Turkish *tashakoor* is common, especially in its verb form, *tashakoor mekonam* ('I thank you').

Behfarma-eed is the polite way to answer the telephone or any enquiry, although *allo* or *baleh* often precedes or replaces it on the telephone. *Allo* is only really used on the telephone.

Iranians are very affectionate people and on greeting, men generally kiss men and women kiss women, at least once on each cheek. When meeting in the street, handshaking is more common, as with officials. Religious people do not shake hands with the opposite sex, never mind kiss them, so no contact of that sort should take place in public unless initiated by the Iranian. Some sophisticated Iranians practice social kissing with the opposite sex, but generally, secular men and women will shake hands with the opposite sex. Bear in mind that some very religious people find physical contact with any non-Shi'ite Muslims polluting, whatever their sex. The safest thing is to be reticent, with both your hands and your lips, until you are clear about the social form. When physical contact is ruled out, a small bow, with one or both hands placed over the heart, generally suffices.

Yes, No, Maybe?

'No' is *na*, or *nakher*, but this is an expression which does not fit the Iranian ideal of polite helpfulness. Thus Iranians may often avoid the word, by using expressions like: 'Not today, maybe tomorrow'; 'Unfortunately not'; or *inshallah* ('God willing'). 'No' may be indicated by a gesture of raised eyebrows, and/or an upward jerk of the head. Shaking the head from side to side indicates wonder or disapproval. You will soon learn to distinguish negative responses by tone and gesture, although Iranian reluctance to disappoint makes this a perennial problem.

'Yes' is *baleh*, or, less politely, *aray*, although other expressions may be used to indicate positive answers—especially ones which indicate a strong agreement such as: *sad dar sad* ('One hundred percent'); *be khodah* ('By God'); *befarma-eed*; *bereem* ('Let's go') and so on. A single nod of the head indicates assent, as does an upwards and sideways movement of the head. Remember that 'yes' does not always really mean 'yes', it may be the answer that is judged to be what you expect.

Calling on God and Other Patrons

Farsi conversations are peppered with references to God, both in the Farsi (*khoda*) and Arabic (*allah*) forms. 'By God' (*be khoda*) is frequently used for emphasis (or as an emphatic positive answer), and expressions such as 'Thank God,' 'In the name of God,' and 'God willing' are similarly used. The Arabic expression *inshallah* ('God willing') is used alone as an answer meaning 'hopefully' or 'possibly', and, coupled with a sentence, as a device to show a certain humility in the face of life. *Alhamdillah* ('Thank God') is used as an expression of pleasure or achievement, as well as a sign of piety, in counting one's blessings. Only pious Iranians will usually declare *bismillah* ('Blessings of God') before undertaking an action.

It is hard to escape the influence of Ali, the son-in-law of Mohammed the Prophet, in Iran. Even in everyday speech, people will call upon him for emphasis, as on God, or use his name as an exhortation—*yah Ali!*—expressing surprise, or meaning something like 'Onward!' Iranians may use the names of other Shi'ite holy figures, such as Imam Jaffar, or that of Husayn, Ali's son, in similar ways. It is fine for Iranians to call these characters by their first names

81

for such purposes—after all, they feel very close to their imams and clerics. It is much more respectful, polite and safer for you to refer to them, when necessary, with the prefix *hazat-e,* or 'blessed', as in *hazrat-e Ali.*

Avoiding the Evil Eye

Mashallah ('As God wills') is a vital device to ward off the influence of the evil eye (*cheshmeh bad*), attracted by admiration, compliments, achievements or good news. Many Iranians seem very diffident about praise or admitting to good fortune. Enquiries will often be met with, 'Not bad,' or 'I am managing.' To boast is seen as bad manners and possibly dangerous. There are two aspects to this danger: that of others' jealousy inadvertently casting the evil eye on the fortunate one, and that of arousing envy and malign behaviour. Many Iranians qualify positive statements with *mashallah!* or *alhamdillah!*—or if it implies a future benefit, *inshallah.*

Compliments are often accompanied by *mashallah!* especially when related to children or very sensitive areas, lest the comment be mistaken for envy. Many charms are in common use to prevent the casting of the evil eye, which is not a deliberate process, but caused inadvertently by jealous thoughts. Some degree of superstition exists at almost every level of Iranian society concerning this, and you should think carefully about how to express admiration or comment on good fortune.

Profanity and Rudeness

Although Iranians commonly tell bawdy jokes, usually in single-sex company, they do not usually pepper their speeches with profanities. There is a venerable historical genre of bawdy poetry which uses them for effect, although these are always deleted in the printed works. The verb 'to do' forms many compound verbs, but when used alone has the usual double meaning. Words for breaking wind and other such bodily functions are considered vulgar, but not particularly obscene.

As Iranians are normally so courteous in speech, rudeness is conveyed by abrupt speech, absent titles and familiar forms of verbs. This, however, is unusual, except on the telephone, for some reason. Incorrect dialling will often be met with extreme rudeness. Officials, particularly minor officials, can be quite rude, but will often thaw to your polite responses. Expressions like 'shut up' are considered very rude, and even complaints are often couched very jovially, so as to seem half-joking. English expressions like, 'You fool,' 'Don't be silly,' or 'Rubbish!' are all very offensive to most Iranians. Such expressions would be incredibly rude in Farsi. Most Iranians are well aware that allowing the opponent to 'save face' by appearing generous or in control is more likely to achieve success.

What's in a Name?

Iranian surnames can be quite complicated. They often are double-barrelled, the last part usually reflecting the place of family origin. The suffix 'ee', implies 'from that place', or 'possessing that quality', and certain suffixes like *zadeh*, mean 'born of'. Many names have a very poetic or comical aspect, with meanings such as 'good-living' or 'happy-faced'. Initially the meanings of surnames seem very literal, but it should be remembered that many Iranians adopted surnames in the modernisation drive of the 1920s and 30s, and that they were often either adapted parental nicknames, or chosen by the registrar.

A Title for Everyone

Iranians are extremely title-conscious; for example, husbands and wives will often refer to each other by their titles in public, and possibly in private. Only amongst young people who are close friends will first names alone be used, and even then, endearments will often be attached to names. The standard form of address for a man is *agha*, which can be used alone—or before or after a first name—as 'Sir', or as the equivalent of 'Mr.' (before the surname) in the form *agha-yeh*. Other possible titles for a man could be *khan*, used after the first name, which is very flattering; *hajji*, used before the first name, which denotes someone who has made the pilgrimage (*haj*) to Mecca; or *sayyed*, also used before the first name, which denotes someone who is a descendant of the Prophet Mohammed. Religious figures may have special titles such as ayatollah or *hojat-ul-Islam* before their last names. When confronted by a very pious-looking older man, always upgrade him to *hajji*; he will rarely demur.

For women, *khanom* is the standard form of address, meaning 'Madam', 'Mrs.', 'Miss' and 'Ms.', and following the same rules as *agha*. More formal is *khanom-eh*, which precedes the surname. Women in Iran do not change their names on marriage, but a woman may be referred to by her husband's surname for social reasons, by prefixing *khanom-e* to his surname. Many westernised Iranians think it is European to adopt the husband's surname, and do so with gusto in social settings. Every Iranian always retains, legally and in his professional life, his father's surname, unless he changes his name by deed poll, which is very rare. All children must bear their father's full surname. An older woman, who appears to have made the pilgrimage to Mecca can be called *hajjieh* or *haj-khanom*.

Professional titles are also commonly bandied about. For example, anyone with a doctorate or medical degree will be referred to as *doktor*, and an engineer (with a degree) called *mohandes*. These titles are usually preceded by *agha-yeh* or *khanom-eh*, and followed by a surname, or possibly a first name, depending on the situation. Confusingly, the female combination could mean the wife of a doctor or engineer. Such combinations can be applied to other professions, for example, *khanom mo'alem* ('Madam Teacher'), or *agha-yeh ranandeh* ('Mr. Taxi-driver'). Titles can be doubled up for added respect, such as *agha-yeh doktor mohandes* (for someone with a doctorate in engineering). An extra polite way or referring to someone is as *janab-e-ali*, or 'your presence', and to refer to oneself as *bandeh* or 'one's slave'. Initially, it is standard practice to use the most flattering combination, which can be corrected by the addressee if necessary.

Within the family, and family-like situations, titles such as father, mother, aunt and uncle are used before the first name. Many middle class urban Iranian children call their parents by just their first names—possibly the only people to do so—but when referring to them in front of others, they will prefix their father's name with *baba*, and their mother's with *maman*. These titles can stand alone, but also can be used with names for people other than one's own relatives. For example, grandmothers, or the mother of a close friend may have their names prefixed with *maman*. Relatives are carefully defined, with distinctions made between maternal and paternal aunts and cousins. Male friends of the family can be referred to as *amoo* (a paternal uncle), and women friends of the family as *khaleh* (a maternal aunt). Older sisters may be titled *abji* and elder brothers *dadash*. Daughters-in-law may be called *aroos*, or 'bride', by all the family. It is important to note that a man has a *zan* ('wife' or 'woman') and his family has an *aroos*, referring to his wife. *Aroos* refers specifically to the bride (i.e., the daughter-in-law), so don't jump to the wrong conclusion if an old man tells you he has several young brides.

It is useful to learn the vocabulary for relatives early on, as there is an implicit order in importance of aunts, uncles and cousins, and such general terms will not enlighten Iranians when you want to describe your family.

Beloved or Just Dear?

In addition to this bewildering array of honorific titles, Iranians use endearments in all but the most formal situations. The two main terms are *aziz* ('beloved') and *jan* (literally 'soul', but like 'dear'), both used after the name or alone. (Note that the Tehrani colloquial Farsi version of *jan* is pronounced *JOON*.) These endearments can be upgraded to 'my beloved' or 'my dear' by the suffix *am, azizam,* or *janam*. There are many husbands and wives who never refer to each other in public or call each other without using one of these terms. When wanting to seem friendly, or even respectful, Iranians may use these endearments even to strangers, such as *agha-yeh doktor* Tehrani *jan* ('Dear Mr. Dr. Tehrani'). Instead of 'Pardon?' Iranians may say *janam?*

Amongst close friends, and within the family, first names with the suffix *jan* are generally an automatic reflex, and it can seem quite abrupt to call someone's first name alone. Although using such additions to names seems complex at first, it soon becomes a habit, and you should not try to force Iranians to address you casually by your first name; and unless they really insist, you should not do it to them. One of the nicest aspects of Iranian society is that people generally even call servants and beggars by proper titles.

Taking It All with a Pinch of Salt

Although Iranians are generally superficially modest, they may lavish others and their abilities with praise—carefully expressed to ensure no suspicion of jealousy. Affection is expressed openly, and you will be adopted by many people as an honorary relative. Iranians are very warm and friendly, and Farsi is a very elegant language for flattery. Initially, a barrage of flattery and personal comments may seem invasive, or at least embarrassing, but you will soon learn to take it all with a pinch of salt, as a habitual style of speech. Simply demur modestly, as Iranians would, and turn the comment around to flatter the other party. You can use the phrase *ekhtiyaar daarid*, meaning, 'You are too generous.'

Excessive dramatic statements are quite normal amongst Iranians. A host may feel a knife in his heart because you can't stay to dinner; a friend may threaten never to speak to you gain if you insist on paying; someone may insist they love you more than their own sibling. All this is quite normal amongst Iranians; you will have to learn to enjoy their effusive warmth, and not to be embarrassed by these excesses. Insincerity is not defined in the same way as in many

Western societies, and a honeyed tongue is a social attribute. Flattery and expressions of devotion are considered speech conventions which should be taken in the right spirit. When concrete actions consistently follow the verbal declarations in a similar spirit, you will know the depth of sincerity involved.

Numbers

It will be very useful to memorise the numbers, in their oral and written forms. It is useful to remember that, although the script is written from right to left, numbers are written in the other direction, as they are in European languages. Dates start from the right, but each section, i.e., the month or year, is written from left to right.

A NATION OF POETS

Poetry has an importance in Iranian society that is probably not replicated in any other country. Of all literary forms, poetry is the most developed and admired. The majority of Iranians, even those with no formal education, show a startling degree of erudition about classical poetry, and are often able to quote lengthy passages, as well as to use verses to illustrate concepts and emotions. Urban Iranians are generally passionate followers of new developments in poetry, as well as the classical poets. Many Iranians pen their own poetry, and much of this is published in newspapers or the many poetry journals. Circles for both writing and reading poetry are widespread. Iranians who cannot write their own poetry still pride themselves on their love of poetry, and the ability to produce the apposite lines for any occasion. The most common type of greetings cards in Iran show poems in calligraphy, which are chosen for their significance to the sentiment of the occasion. The ability to recite poetry with feeling is highly prized, and someone who is talented at this may perform for friends. An appreciation of poetry is essential to someone who wishes to be considered sensitive or cultured.

Whilst much classical poetry is translated into English and French, and it is possible to enjoy and appreciate the translation, any effort to learn small poetic quotations in Farsi will reap dividends in terms of both personal enjoyment and in relations with Iranians. Conversations are often liberally strewn with poetic quotes, as many Iranian poets were philosophers with a talent for versifying their thoughts. It should also be noted that many Iranian poet-philosophers were also religious theorists or scientists, and may have contributed to several fields of knowledge, confirming the Iranian concept of poetry as a necessity of life rather than an abstract art form. Familiarity with some of the more common quotes will delight Iranian friends, who will be enthusiastic guides if you choose to explore Iranian poetry. As most classical poetry is written in a particular script style, reading poetry will take some guidance and familiarity with both the script and the classical conventions. The vocal component of classical Iranian music consists of poetry. For Iranians, there is no clear distinction between poetry and song.

Before the Arab invasion during the seventh century, Iranian poetry was largely transmitted by minstrels, or written in the languages and scripts that preceded Farsi. For about two hundred years, Iranian intellectuals wrote in Arabic, but gradually Farsi reasserted itself, this time through the medium of the Arabic script. The thirteenth and fourteenth centuries saw the greatest flowering of Iranian poetry, which fell into decline between the fifteenth and nineteenth century; it has since re-emerged in new forms. Iranian poetry has profoundly affected the literary and cultural traditions of Iran's neighbouring countries, as well as farther flung areas. Some of Iran's poets are considered without equal in the world.

Who's Who of Iranian Poetry

Many Iranian classical poets were known as Sufis. Sufis seek through mysticism a relationship with God in which they will lose all individual identity, merging with God as one. Their poems often refer to acts forbidden to Muslims, and they express all aspects of their relationship with God—irritation, anxieties, as well as love. Many poems appear to be addressed to a beloved, which can be, and usually is interpreted as God. As Farsi is genderless, the sex of the 'beloved' is unclear, and contemporaneous social norms, as well as biographical details, lead us to discount the likelihood of a female subject. The works of all the Sufi poets can be enjoyed by sceptics at face value, or seen by the believer as a giant metaphor for the love of God. Any perception of homoerotic overtones in many poems will not diminish their beauty, and one's reading depends on personal attitudes and even moods. Certain sections of poems or collected works are generally edited, so that the poems which are decidedly profane or atheistic are removed. Biographical details are widely known, and act as an aid to interpretation.

It is noteworthy that the late Ayatollah Khomeini was reputed to be a Sufi poet, and after his death, published poems attributed to him used the familiar metaphors of drunkenness and intoxication to explain the intensity of the relationship with the lover-like God. This type of poetry is most commonly called *Irfan*, or mysticism.

- **Omar Khayyam** (eleventh century) is the Iranian poet best known in the West. He was a mathematician and astronomer who challenged many accepted principles, both scientific and religious. Favouring quatrains (*rubai*), his most famous work is called in English *The Rubaiyat*. Like many poets, his work protests against the established articles of faith, and contains many possible blasphemies as well as exhortations to hedonism.

- **Saadi** (thirteenth century) is less well-known in the West, but was extremely prolific, producing mostly *ghazals*, or short poems. His most famous works were the *Gulistan* ('Rose Garden') and the *Bustan,* both collections of short stories and verse. His works are alternately ribald and wise and witty. His views on such universals as old age are as fresh now as then, and he expounds a humanistic philosophy. A poem by Saadi, which describes humans as drops of water from the same pool, is inscribed at the headquarters of the United Nations in New York.

- **Jala-e Din Rumi** (thirteenth century) used his poetry to explain Sufism to his disciples. He died in Turkey, where he is seen as the spiritual founder of the Mevlevi Sufi order, and is mistakenly often thought of as Turkish, rather than Iranian. Many of his poems are addressed to his Sufi peer, Shams-e Tabrizi.

- **Hafiz** (fourteenth century) is possibly the most quoted Iranian poet. Every Iranian household possesses a copy of his *Diwan* (a collection of odes), and it is probably considered to be the most admired Iranian volume of poetry. His Sufistic love poetry has fuelled many an Iranian romance. He is noted for his style and elegance of metaphor.

Ferdowsi's Book of Kings

Ferdowsi holds a special place in Iranian literature as the poet who allowed Iranians to express their distinctiveness from Arabs, and to reclaim their pre-Islamic imperial history. Around 1010, he completed his epic, after thirty years of labour, the *Shahnameh*, or 'Book of Kings'. Based on the deeds of real and legendary kings and heroes, drawing on the oldest sacred and historical texts of Iran, most of which are now lost, the poem is exhaustingly long, consisting of 50,000 couplets.

The *Shahnameh* contains a continuous mythological narrative of Iranian history—its rulers and its relations with its neighbouring empires—until the end of the Sassanian period. It is full of demons (*divs*), dragons and mythical creatures. A large part of the work narrates the activities of Rustam, whose life spans the reigns of many kings. The feats of Rustam, a giant hero, and his horse are detailed, ending in two tragedies of Shakespearean hue: Rustam realising that he has slain his own son, and Rustam himself being slain by his half-brother.

The work is intensely gripping, although it is written in an epic style that is initially hard to understand. The stories, or at least large numbers of them, are known to all Iranians, and until recently, they were transmitted by illiterate performers, who learnt whole sections and recited them in teahouses for pay. The characters of the epic and their names permeate Iranian culture totally, and much has been written of the insight into the modern Iranian collective psyche that can be gained from examination of the *Shahnameh*. It is the inspiration for many Iranian arts, especially miniature paintings.

During the reigns of the two Pahlavi Shahs this century, the poem was emphasised as the acme of Iran's non-Islamic, non-Arab identity, and as a vindication of the monarchy ruling the Iranian nation. The work was initially dedicated to Ferdowsi's reigning monarch, Sultan Mahmoud Ghaznavi, and certainly emphasised the dedication of the Iranian people to their rulers. As the work was so firmly identified

91

with monarchism and with the Pahlavi regime, it fell from favour during the initial years of the revolutionary government. Personal names derived from the work were discouraged, and its teaching in schools was banned. Many works of art related to the poem were damaged, as was Ferdowsi's tomb. Recently, however, the regime has reassessed its attitude towards Ferdowsi, and again he is used cautiously to assert Iranian distinctiveness. Only the old guards of the revolution now object to the use of names and tales from the epic. It is possible again to hear recitations of Ferdowsi in certain coffee shops in Tehran.

More Poets than Stars in the Sky

There are so many Iranian poets that it is impossible to discuss them all here. More recent poets of great note were: Iraj Mirza (nineteenth century), whose dry scepticism and heart-tugging pathos are both contained within his *Diwan*; Ahmed Shamlou; and Forough Farrokhzad, a woman whose poems described the suffering of Iranian women. Any Iranian will be delighted to direct towards their favourite poets, both classical and modern.

FICTION AND DRAMA

Writing has always been an important yet hazardous occupation in Iran. Under all regimes, writers have been subjected to censorship and persecution. Writers are generally considered to have a political agenda, even when they are writing fiction. Many Iranian works have been published first abroad, and possibly never legalised in Iran. Generally, educated Iranians revere their writers, and they are avid purchasers of books.

Short stories are an old-established form in Iranian literature. Many old fables and cautionary tales exist, often attributed to mythical idiot savant characters, such as Mullah Nasreddin, known by various names throughout the Middle East and the Islamic world. In the last century, most Iranian writers of short stories have dwelt on social themes and common cultural angst—so using their writing as vehicles of social and political dissent and change. Many of these pre-1979-published Iranian writers have been translated into Western languages, and their stories will allow an easy insight into Iranian society. Well-known writers of short stories include: Jalal Al-e Ahmad, whose explorations of Iranian alienation from their own Shi'ite cultural heritage over thirty years ago are still meaningful; Simin Daneshvar, Al-e Ahmad's wife and the first major Iranian woman prose writer; Sadeq Chubak; Sadeq Hedayat; and Jamalzadeh.

The novel is a fairly new form in Iran, but several excellent ones exist. The novels of Al-e Ahmad and Daneshvar are particularly famous. The majority of these are published in English or Farsi in the West. The first multivolume Persian novel, *Kelidar*, was written in 1985 by Mahmood Dolatabadee.

Iranian writers of the twentieth century also wrote plays, many of which have never been seen in the theatre by Iranians due to their dissident themes. Iranian plays are generally read as novels in text form, although the Iranian urban elite will attend any production that is allowed. Traditional Iranian theatre takes two forms. That of the *tazieh*, or passion play, and the folk theatre of the *ruh hoz* (literally 'over the pond', as this would take place on a wooden stage, erected over a garden pond). This latter type of dramatic expression has fallen into disuse, although characters from the genre remain popular figures, such as Haji Firuz, a clown with a black face.

Sadeq Hedayat:
Social Reformer, Political Ideologue, Existentialist

Sadeq Hedayat committed suicide in Paris in 1951 at the age of forty-nine. He authored over 100 hundred essays, stories and novels. His most celebrated novel, *The Blind Owl* (a terrifying work of psycho-fiction), had an impact far beyond Iranian literature, and drew attention in the West. Many of his short stories give expression to the suffering of the silent—the poor, the dispossessed, the unloved, the lonely, even dumb animals—and are often deeply disturbing, with themes of death and alienation. Hedayat has been compared to the likes of Jean-Paul Sartre, Edgar Allen Poe, and Franz Kafka (with whom Hedayat felt a great affinity).

THE MEDIA

Iran is well-supplied with newspapers, publishing over seventy titles a day, four of which are in English, although none of them are very gripping. The English language titles are *Kayhan International*, *Tehran Times*, *Iran Daily* and *Iran News*. *Kayhan* has more international news, but tends to be extremely turgid. *Tehran Times* has useful small ads and also lifts articles and cartoons straight out of the American press, which seems very incongruous.

A newspaper vendor in Tehran.

Of all the Iranian newspapers, *Kayhan* and *Etel'eat* are the most widely read, and although broadly pro-government, they do not support any particular faction within the government, and thus are often party to some heated debate. New newspapers start up and then fold regularly, reflecting the chaotic Iranian political scene.

The Iranian journal scene is more dynamic—although in English there are only business and trade journals and *Mahjubah*, an Islamic magazine for women. Journals open and are close down regularly, and this is one of the ways in which dissent is expressed within Iran. Many journals are literary journals, publishing new poetry and criticism of existing authors. These journals often print satirical commentaries and veiled criticism of the government and its institutions.

Foreign Journals

In major cities, you can buy international journals like *Time* and *Newsweek*. They will have been censored, mostly for decency rather than political content, which usually goes uncensored. Pictures of bareheaded women will be found to have had black ink headscarves applied by the mysterious people whose job it is to censor these journals. These sort of journals, as international newspapers (available at luxury hotels), are very expensive by local standards, even higher than the cover price. You can also order 'suitable' foreign journals by post, such as *Reader's Digest*, and these will rarely be censored, although they often go missing. Most women's 'glossy' magazines present a problem, as the number of pages that need censoring are so great that they are effectively banned as un-Islamic.

Chapter Four

THE INNER IRANIAN: FAMILY, WOMEN AND CHILDREN

IT'S ALL ABOUT FAMILY

Most Iranians reserve their private selves for their families and very close friends. The extended family is an important source of support and influence, as well as a place of comfort. Even though there may be great rivalry or disharmony, the family always unites against outsiders, and almost no one criticises their family to those outsiders. When asked about your family, it is usually considered quite shocking if you admit to any friction, or not being close, or not particularly missing them. It is best to describe them warmly and imply frequent contact, if only by letter or telephone. Many Iranians are aware of the generally looser family ties in Europe, but they enjoy meeting people whom they feel disapprove of this.

Interrogation about your family, especially parental occupations and education (as well as sibling occupations) allows Iranians to place you within their social context. An eccentric or unsavoury family life is best glossed over. Many Iranians find divorced parents a stigma, and consider such families unstable. Consider carefully before imparting such information, except to your closest friends. Previous marriages are also usually rather secretive matters. You may become very intimate indeed with someone before they will consider sharing any such family secrets with you.

Although it is not unusual to find a wealthy or educated Iranian whose family in fact has poor or uneducated roots, Iranians generally tend to judge a person by his or her family. Although differences in wealth or education can be tolerated without disapproval of someone's family background, one very much stands or falls with the status of one's family. If a family has a black sheep, it is in everyone's interest to try to rehabilitate that character, so that the rest of the unit does not suffer the consequences of social disgrace.

Middle and upper class Iranians are often remarkably mobile, with relatives all over the world. They will generally have close and frequent contact with these relatives, and may travel frequently to visit them. Families who had relatives abroad before the 1979 revolution can generally be assumed to be of the higher social classes, as Iranians at that time generally travelled abroad to study at their own expense. After 1979, many Iranians became refugees abroad, although this is a topic for discussion generally only with one's closest friends. A favourite topic of conversation is the visa situation with regard to various countries, and you will often be asked for your advice and for letters of invitation that will supposedly facilitate or expedite the obtaining of visas.

Favours

As the family is the main financial support unit in Iran, family members often employ each other and consider it their responsibility to find employment or organise advancement for their relatives, even if they are quite distant in kinship. To be the close relative of someone in a powerful position is very advantageous, and not the irrelevance that it may seem to Westerners. Nepotism and simony are not the social embarrassments that they might be in the West but indications of one's devotion to the family. Thus, favours are often boasted of extensively.

Requests for favours for relatives are a constant irritation to anyone in any position of power in Iran. Everyone has a needy relative, many have a veritable plethora of them, and direct refusal of requests are insulting. Deflections and maybes are useful, as the petitioner may feel equally embarrassed at the request, and just needs to be able to justify himself to his family. If you are in a position to grant such favours, consider abandoning your previous scruples about favouritism. If you were thinking of employing a cleaner anyway, then there is probably no good reason not to employ Ali, the chauffeur's sister, as requested. Staff are often best found in this way anyway. Favours are often not difficult for you to grant, but can reap dividends in the form of loyalty, reciprocal favours and good will.

Friends: Part of the Extended Family

Iranians generally expect to share their friends with the family. When you become friends with an Iranian, single or married, you, whether single or married, will generally get to meet the entire family in due course, and certainly will get to hear of them early in the relationship. Siblings often socialise together, and the in-laws become part of the extended family. The husbands of sisters or the wives of brothers are expected to develop close ties and to spend time together. Cousins are expected to play together and often grow up to be very close.

Single people generally live at home at least until they marry—unless they go away to university or to work in another city. Iranians often live in multigenerational families, although richer Iranians will aim for neighbouring apartments. It is not unusual to find that an extended family occupies several apartments in one building or houses in one street. The grandparents are the child-carers of choice for most working women. When you are invited to someone's house, expect that some of their family will be present. Most Iranians enjoy socialising in large groups, and the generation gap is not as fetishised as it is in the West. A good friend and guest should be able to converse across the generations, and not expect to only socialise with their own age group.

As many Iranian families are socially upwardly mobile, meeting the family can offer interesting opportunities to meet Iranians from different backgrounds as well as different regions of the country. You may find yourself sucked into a family who likes you, and this may be pleasant or unpleasant, depending on your personality or the family. It is worth noting, as described below, that Iranians see friendship quite differently compared to most Westerners, and that for Westerners, Iranian friendships can be quite overwhelming and at times quite intrusive. If you wish to function in Iranian society, this is something you will have to get used to, and being bombarded with invitations by your friends' relatives is part of the warmth and close family ties that make Iranian society what it is.

Making Friends

Iranians are warm, friendly, generous people, and although many are suspicious of foreigners, many more are very keen to mix with them—particularly Europeans and Americans. Invitations are bound to be offered, and adoption by whole families is common. Although English language teaching in Iran is truly appalling, many Iranians were educated abroad and love to speak English. They appreciate any effort to speak Persian and are keen to share the benefits of Iranian civilisation with interested foreigners. Iranian friends go to great lengths for each other and consider European relationships to be very cold and unloving.

AN IRANIAN'S INNER SELF

Iranian friendships can seem quite overwhelmingly claustrophobic to those of us who are used to the more casual and distant Western friendships. At the same time, the complexity of Iranian formality and secrecy, at least in the initial stages of a relationship, is also confusing to Westerners, who are generally more transparent in their social relationships. Many foreigners find Iranians somewhat duplicitous and insincere, and there is indeed often a clear gap between effusive statements and the reality of a situation. To place this perceived behaviour in context, some understanding of the typical Iranian 'world view' is useful, as is an understanding of the ways in which Iranians see themselves in relation to others.

A Fragile Social World

For many Iranians, the external world is threatening, always in turmoil, and one must guard against the malignant power of others as well as the burden of obligations. There are two facets to all areas of Iranian social life and identity: *zaher* and *batin*, or external and internal. The external world requires certain standards of behaviour, and only in the private, inner world of family and close friends can a person really relax and show one's true self. Iran has suffered a great deal of political and social upheaval, and, indeed, within living memory, the social fabric of Iran has been rent asunder more than once, shuffling a new social group to the upper echelons of society. It is vital therefore for Iranians to guard against making enemies and to maintain a variety of social contacts, as another's knowledge of one's true self may be used negatively in a changed environment.

Aberu, or honour, is a powerful social force. All Iranians measure themselves to a great extent by the honour they accumulate through their actions and social interrelations. A formalised ritual politeness (*ta'arouf*) exists to allow all parties to preserve their honour in an uncertain world. Ritual politeness makes social interaction like a carefully choreographed dance, which appears elegant, and where there is no danger of anyone stumbling or appearing not to be part of the dance. Chapter Five describes the operation of *ta'arouf* in some detail.

Personal Expression

Narahati are the upsets and unhappiness of everyday life. Iranians usually express such private sadness or unhappiness via quietness, refusing to eat, quiet weeping and in a variety of illnesses, generally typified as 'nervousness'. The public display of *asabaniyat*, or anger, is socially unacceptable, except maybe with workplace inferiors, and even then shows a lack of control, or an immature personality. Due to the possibly serious social consequences, anger is often suppressed, and this is possibly one reason that Iranians seem to suffer from so many psychosomatic illnesses, as well as a fairly high rate of coronary artery disease. *Ghamgini* is grief, which is always respected and openly vented, for example after bereavement. All Iranians, including men, are not ashamed to cry noisily and openly, as well as displaying grief in other physical ways, such as tearing at their hair or clothes. To display grief appropriate for a tragic event is not considered weakness but an expression of honesty. It can also be poetic in quality—for example, tears precipitated by a moving tale or event in which one has no real role.

Personality is a conflict of *zerangiyat* and *hessasiyat*. The former, meaning cleverness (and maybe even cunning), are admirable in certain respects, and necessary in order to negotiate the outside world. The latter, meaning sensitivity, is a very admirable personality trait in the private world, but is a disadvantage in external relationships, as it opens one to humiliation and pain. Being able to confine these qualities to appropriate situations and, thus, stay in control is the key to a balanced person who can interact appropriately. People are eager to display the correct balance in the appropriate settings. For example, sensitivity can be displayed by appreciation of poetry or music; shaking one's head, or uttering *bah, bah!* during the recital shows sensitivity to artistic stimulation.

Naz is usually translated as coyness, but has a much wider meaning in Iranian society. It can be positive in that women are expected to be *nazee*, or modest, in their manners and body language, and this is a good quality in women and girls. However, *naz* can also have negative connotations, in that to *naz* is to be oversensitive to small hurts, or to feign false modesty in order to receive praise. If a person is *nazee*, they may need gentle handling or persuasion, and to *naz* can mean exactly that: to show affection and gentleness to someone. Iranians may say *naz nakon* ('Don't be coy'), affectionately or with some degree of irritation, depending on the situation. You may reply, *naz nemekonam* ('I am not being coy'), when you want to insist that you are not displaying false modesty, or to emphasise that you are not hurt.

The two stereotyped extremes of personality are the *derwish*, who ignores *ta'arouf*, and the *loti*, who lives the ideal social model literally, making it his life's duty to make others happy. Both are admired and despised in equal measure. It is considered that few are in a position to adopt either extreme posture, since those confident or moral enough to do either are rare. The *derwish* is also divorced from material cares, and the *loti* devoted to pleasure. These terms are used to describe people both positively and negatively. To be a *derwish* can be good, as one cares little for trivialities and is pleased with one's lot in life, but implies a certain laziness in social relations. Conversely, the *loti* lives his life through pleasure and the enjoyment of others' happiness, but is probably not very spiritual or capable. Ultimately, the highest accolades to which an Iranian aspires to are, firstly, to support and provide for one's family, and, secondly, to be a good friend.

IRANIAN WOMEN

If you visit Iran expecting a land of veiled women who are submissive and who play no role in public life, you will have your prejudices confirmed only partially on the first preconception, and not at all on the second or third. It is true that Iranian women are forced to wear all-concealing clothes and to cover their heads, but unlike, say women in certain Arab countries, women in Iran do not cover their faces, except perhaps in the Arab south. The *chador* can be used to cover all of the face except for one eye, but this must be held in place, so it is only a transitory phenomena. It is soon very clear that for the majority of middle class Iranian women, the modest dress code is imposed by force, not through choice—this is demonstrated by the many small subversions of the Islamic dress code, from poorly concealed hair to outrageous red lipstick.

Iranian women are generally perceived as more outgoing in public life than the women of their neighbouring states, and also to have more control over family life than might initially be expected. They are to be seen socially in public both with their families and with other women friends. Women drive cars and even travel together on trips. There are many women's organisations, catering for both the secular and religious types, and most women of all classes have active social lives in varying forms. Women in Tehran and other big cities, and especially younger women, are often extremely outgoing, even in mixed company.

Women and the Work Force

Before 1979, Iranian women were active in most fields of professional employment and education, and despite the constraints imposed on women after the Islamic revolution, this remains largely true. In 1998, more women than men entered the university entrance exams. Women were barred from judicial positions and from the offices of President, Prime Minister and Supreme Leader. Other than

Many Iranian women pass the time making carpets, even if only for their own domestic use.

that, they face few legal obstacles in pursuing their chosen profession. Primary school teaching and nursing are almost entirely female professions, and there are many women doctors, academics, lawyers, engineers and other professionals. The necessity of wearing Islamic clothes makes work often an uncomfortable and hot affair, and many women who worked before 1979 find the ideological constraints, as well as the low pay levels in the public sector not conducive to continued employment.

Women and Islam

For many Muslims, Prophet Mohammed was the first prophet to address women's rights specifically, and the period preceding Islam is seen as a dark time for women, before Islam offered them protection and rights. You will hear many times that the pre-Islamic Arabs used to bury baby girls alive, seeing them as worthless. It is the official line that Islam treats men and women as equal but different, with different, not fewer, rights and responsibilities. In Islam, men and women are complimentary to each other (not identical) in their needs and abilities, and these complementary sides are accommodated within the framework of the family, which is the basis of Islamic society.

It is important to remember that Islam is not monolithic—much of Islamic law and practice reflects the traditions of the pre-Islamic cultures. This especially applies to its dealings with women. Veiling was not introduced by Islam, but it is probable that Islamic attitudes to women allowed such practices to persist. Even throughout Iran, the degree to which women are traditionally veiled varies greatly with social class, education and region. For example, the *chador* is almost unknown in some parts of Iran. There is also often a large gap between 'official' Islamic law and its practical application, which may reflect local practices. Do not assume that the law as applied to women in certain Islamic countries applies to women in Iran.

However, despite all this, the law in Iran is fundamentally discriminatory towards women. A woman's testimony in a law court is worth half that of a man's. Women inherit half the property that their brothers can; they are dealt with more harshly than men for adultery; they have fewer rights to divorce and child custody than men; and they are subject to harsher dress laws and more restrictions on their comings and goings than men.

The Subversion of the Official Line

Officially, the Islamic Republic claims a greater deal of gender segregation than exists in public. Women are generally supposed to go out and about with their male guardians, but in reality this is not enforced except in times of high tension, when women may be harassed by the Pasdaran. Buses are officially segregated (women are supposed to sit at the back of the bus), but this is only enforced in very conservative areas, and one sits where one can. In shared taxis, women sit next to strange men if necessary, and seating on planes and intercity buses is assigned regardless of gender. Although some men will automatically reshuffle so as not to sit next to a strange woman, this is not always the case.

Islamic Feminism

There have long been 'Islamic Feminists', although some of these have been male writers, academics and clerics. Many of the women who have been the most fierce advocates of veiling have good credentials as advocates of women's emancipation and rights. Many Islamic feminists follow their own professions and believe that Islam offers them the chance to act as human beings in the world rather than as sex objects. They feel that the *hejab* offers them the chance to work with men equally, much in the way that 1970s feminists rejected the trappings of femininity as part of the sexual fetishisation of women. Women's roles as mothers are protected in Islam, and the husband has a duty to support a woman and her children, although there is nothing to forbid women from working outside the house as long as their family is cared for. A prototype Islamic feminist is Faizeh Rafsanjani, the daughter of a former President of Iran; she is a Member of Parliament, an academic and an Olympic calibre horse rider, as well as the mother of two children.

Shi'ah Islam has always had strong female role models, in particular Zaynab (the sister of the Husayn and the granddaughter of Prophet Mohammed) who defended her family to the last in battle, and Fatima, the daughter of the Prophet Mohammed, who had a reputation for feistiness. Other female relatives of historical religious figures are venerated in their own right. Women preachers and religious figures continue the strong tradition of active participation by women in religious activities. Women visitors to Iran should accept any opportunity to participate in such activities, as it gives an unexpected insight into the traditional roles of Iranian women.

The New Feminism

Islamic feminism does not of course appeal to the secular Iranian women, who have felt very alienated by the regime until recently. In 1997, President Khatami received 80% of the women's vote, having campaigned on a ticket of greater liberalisation. He appointed two women for cabinet minister posts and another for the position of vice-president. The ban on women judges was overturned by the appointment of four women as family court judges. There is a much vaunted, new, upbeat feeling amongst Iranian middle class women, who are comforted by the President's reminders to the Islamic militia that women should not be pestered in public about their dress and companions.

Sports

Women have recently challenged the official line on sport for women. Although women have entered in international competitions for shooting, fencing, and archery, women have been limited in participation and attendance of other sporting activities, mostly due to concerns about revealing sportswear. An Iranian markswoman participated in the 1996 Olympic Games wearing full *hejab* in the humid Georgia summer. When the Iranian football team returned home after successfully qualifying for the 1998 World Cup, more than 5,000 women defied a ban on female attendance, stormed the national stadium and succeeded in securing an agreement that women should be allowed to attend major matches in the future. Girls have insisted on playing football at school as well as more opportunities for sporting participation, culminating in an international women's sporting competition (with only female spectators of course). As football fever swept the country in June and July of 1998, women proved to be as enthusiastic followers of the Iranian team as men.

Gender Roles at Home

The status of Iranian women at home obviously depends on their social class, their level of education, individual personalities and abilities, and their families' attitudes. However, it is probably fair to say that the majority of Iranian women are firmly in control over most aspects of running the home, and often over all aspects. Many Iranian women are quite the equals or even superiors of their husbands, although social convention generally dictates some degree of gender separation and an apparent male superiority.

It is a rare Iranian man who concerns himself with cooking, cleaning or running the house, and few Iranian women seem to want greater spouse-involvement, as they are generally very proud of their domestic capabilities. Men often do the shopping, especially in traditional families, where the women may not go out much, and men are often therefore very knowledgeable about produce, and therefore cooking techniques. This is not to say that they then use this knowledge to cook, but they comment knowledgeably on the food, and are generally great gourmands, like most Iranians. Of course there are some intellectual families where men share domestic tasks, but male domestic work is usually limited in company.

Women who work have little recourse to convenience foods, and often spend long hours late at night preparing food for the following night, as well as lunches for the family to take to work. Most Iranian women prepare their own preserves and pickles, and many make clothes for themselves and the children. Domestic help is not particularly common, and is generally reserved for heavy cleaning tasks, not the daily grind of housekeeping.

Social Situations

When invited to Iranian households, it is the hostess who will probably prepare the food, serve it and clear up, although only in the most traditional families will women sit or eat separately. Generally women sit close to and talk to other women, but this is not true in all social settings, and it is often noted that Iranian women can be rather noisy conversationalists in mixed settings. When you enter a room, unless invited to sit in a particular place, try to sit next to a person of the same sex.

Women visit restaurants and cafes with their families, female friends or, in some areas, occasionally alone. In areas such as central and northern Tehran, this does not merit a glance, but in conservative areas, women and families will be expected to sit in a family section, where lone males and groups of men are not allowed. Some eating places are not equipped to serve women, and it should be clear from the outset if a place is unsuitable for women. This generally includes all teahouses, which are male preserves. Although a foreign woman may receive a warm welcome, no Iranian women would visit unless it specifically catered for them. A polite request from a waiter as the whether you may enter will elicit a refusal or a bemused assent, but be prepared to be the object of intense scrutiny.

Although women can travel alone or in groups, some hotels, as well as eating places, are unwelcoming, and again one should expect some curiosity from others. There are whole areas in Iran where women are publicly invisible; conversely, in certain places, such as north of Tehran, women are free to go almost anywhere. Foreign women will soon develop a feel for where they can hang out and where they should hurry through purposefully. Particular areas, such as parks in Tehran or stylish shopping malls, are known as pick-up joints, and women alone may be pestered by Iranian men, although this will not be the threat that it might be in a more conservative area. Generally, women are quite safe in Iran, as long as they dress appropriately, and do not mislead men with confusing signals. If in doubt, do not talk to strange men, avoid eye contact and do not smile back. This is not rudeness; it is normal behaviour for most Iranian women.

MARRIAGE AND SEXUALITY

The vast majority of Iranian women marry and have children, whatever their profession, as do the vast majority of men. Homosexuality is illegal, socially stigmatised for men and barely conceived of for women. There is no word for 'lesbian' in Farsi. There is no possibility of a gay lifestyle in Iran, although a discreet relationship is certainly possible. Many male Iranian poets, writers and artists were known to be homosexuals, but homosexuality is still generally seen as a perversion with entirely sexual motivation, rather than emotional.

From 1967, Iran introduced probably the most progressive (at least in Western eyes) family law in the Middle East concerning divorce and child custody. After the 1979 revolution, family law again fell under the jurisdiction of religious courts, and reverted a more traditional Islamic interpretation of women's rights, although this change of jurisdiction did not totally abandon women's advances. (One major exception: the court's legalisation of early marriage.)

The Islamic interpretation of marriage is that it is essential for all men and women, and that it is a civil contract, whereby a man and woman supply each other's sexual needs, they agree to have children, and the husband agrees to support his wife and the children of the marriage. They do not share their property; the woman can maintain her financial independence and has no financial obligations—only an obligation to care physically for her husband and children and the house.

A woman can marry only one man at a time, and must wait for three months after divorce or childbirth before remarrying. A man can marry up to four wives, as long as he can care for them equally; he may also enter unlimited temporary marriages (*sigheh*), an institution recognised only by Shi'ites. This sort of marriage can last anything from a few hours to many years, as stipulated by the contract, and can fulfil many functions, not only sexual needs. Both polygamy and *sigheh* are generally limited to the traditional clerical and landowning classes, and are infrequent in the wider society, although *sigheh* can be practised either as a form of prostitution, or as a way to circumvent various restrictions on associations between men and women.

Divorce

According to Islam, a man can divorce his wife without any particular reason simply by declaring his intention three times. Certain restrictions apply, such as her pregnancy or young age. He must then give her the dowry agreed to in the marriage contract, and he gets automatic custody of the children (after they have reached a certain age). Women have the limited right of divorce if a man refuses to support her or is impotent. However, in Iran, and according to Shi'ite law, things are not this straightforward.

Men have to register their divorce with a court to validate it, and generally, the judge will attempt to reconcile the couple as well as try to ensure that a woman is provided for if considered blameless. It is possible for women to insert clauses concerning their rights to insist on a divorce in certain preset circumstances, but this is usually the preserve of upper and educated classes who have the family status to request such clauses. For women who married between 1967 and 1982, their marriage contracts automatically stipulated that they have the right to insist that their husbands divorce them under certain circumstances, such as taking a new wife. After 1982, new contracts were introduced. These allow the wife the right to half the family wealth if the divorce is not her fault. This is decided by a judge. There are also various clauses which allow a woman to petition for a divorce, although officially, as before, the husband divorces the wife—not the other way around. All of these clauses require signature by the husband at marriage to validate them, but a judge can still in practice apply them even if the man did not sign. A man's taking another wife is not considered grounds for divorce (unless he is unable to support them both), nor is the man's entry into a temporary marriage or marriages. Adultery is a criminal offence, dealt with by the criminal courts, and not simply grounds for divorce. A man may be punished for adultery, but his wife may still not receive a divorce.

For most women, the fear of losing their children is generally the major deterrent to divorce. Custody of boys over two years and girls over eight years is generally awarded to the father, although some fathers may not want their children—or the judge may decide that the father is an unsuitable carer, thus awarding custody to the mother. This is a dreadful gamble for the woman, as the father (or upon his death, the paternal grandfather) may re-petition the courts at any time and possibly have the ruling overturned. Women will find it difficult to support their children, and men are reluctant to marry a woman with dependent children. The wicked stepmother is a potent spectre in Iranian popular mythology, and only truly desperate women will risk abandoning their children to the care of a new wife. Most younger divorced women lose contact with their children, and the social stigma of divorce is great, except possibly in certain social classes which have allowed greater freedoms, such as the landed gentry.

CHILDREN IN IRAN

Iran's population is a young one—over 40% of the population is under the age of fifteen. This is partly the result of the period following the

1979 revolution, when large families were encouraged and contraception outlawed. Once the economic impact of uncontrolled population growth was fully appreciated, this policy was reversed with a vengeance. Iran now has an impressively low rate of population increase (1.8% in 1998), and most educated Iranians are happy with one or two children. Contraception is widely available and free. An abortion is also relatively easy to obtain, at least in major urban centres, despite the legal requirement that the mother's life be at risk.

Children are universally loved and welcomed throughout Iran. Despite lax public safety standards and the absence of children's clubs or activity centres, Iranian children feel safe and comfortable outside their homes. The idea that adults pose any danger to children is largely an alien one. Strangers feel free to pet children, and one really need not worry about leaving one's child in the care of strangers whilst visiting the toilet, for example.

These seven-year-old schoolgirls have begun a life of public conformity to the Islamic dress laws.

Pampered Princes and Princesses?

Although one can find Iranian families who follow the Western model of child-care, where the child follows a set routine, sleeps early in the evening and does not participate much in adult social activities, this is rare. Most children lead what appear to be fairly chaotic lives until the age of six, when they start school, although, for some, school doesn't affect their lifestyle habits at all. Children are included in almost all adult entertainments (dinner party invitations rarely exclude children), and they can be seen playing in parks in the summer until after midnight. They sleep when adults do, supplemented by afternoon naps, and often doze off in public places or in other people's houses. The majority of Iranian children are well socialised, adept at polite comments and comfortable with strangers. In fact, they can be very precocious; girls are often encouraged to dance for guests, and boys are often asked to display their scholastic abilities.

There are few organised entertainments for children; they have fewer toys than their Western counterparts and are expected to play with their siblings, cousins or friends for amusement. Children in public are encouraged to play with other children and to share their toys and sweets. Formal mother-and-toddler groups do not exist, but as Iranians are quite gregarious and friendly to strangers, no one with a child need be lonely. Parks have playgrounds, but these are rarely well maintained, and often are quite dangerous. Fun fairs are often equally alarming, with poor safety standards. Children routinely sit in unsecured in the front of cars or on the back of mopeds. Riding a bicycle anywhere except in the park is probably quite dangerous.

Of course, many Iranian children are very deprived, and work long hours in family businesses or at home. The carpet-weaving industry makes extensive use of children's labour, as they have small, nimble fingers. These children are often to be seen playing in the streets in dirty clothes or peddling goods in public places. By contrast, the majority of middle-class children are pampered, fussed over, petted, showered with expensive toys and clothes, and dressed like dolls—

particularly by their devoted mothers. The children are wrapped up excessively in winter and kept indoors in inclement weather. Their mothers cook them elaborate meals from an early age, spoon-feeding them until an advanced age, pleading with them to eat the last morsels. Iranian parents enjoy dressing their children like miniature adults, and it is not unusual to see a small girl with make-up, nail polish and jewellery, or a small boy in a suit and tie.

Few Iranians seem to be concerned about dental decay, and children are often fed large amounts of sweets and sweetened tea or milk. However, as most Iranian adults are very concerned about their own health, this is extended with interest to their children. Great concern is expressed over the children's eating or toilet habits, and generally at the first sign of any illness, they are bundled up and rushed to a doctor, who generally prescribes antibiotics and anti-fever medication at the parents' insistence. (Moreover, most Iranian parents will have a refrigerator full of medications at home.) Parents also follow folk medicine practices, which may involve preparing special soups or avoiding certain foods, such as ice cream.

TEENAGERS

There is no common word for teenager in Farsi, other than perhaps *nojavanha*, which means 'new young people'. There are an awful lot of teenagers in Iran, and the phenomenal unemployment rate means that many of these are totally without aims in life. Even for the middle classes, university education is no guarantee of gainful employment, and many teenagers and young people are very disaffected with the state's response to their predicament. Most middle class teenagers spend a year or two preparing for university entrance exams (concour), but are unsuccessful due to the sheer number of entrants, the ideological screening, and the system that reserves places for the war heroes and their offspring. Only the truly wealthy can afford to study abroad, although fantasising about a new life in Europe or America is rife. Many working class teenagers enthusiastically join the enforcement of Islamic standards, relishing the chance to harass the wealthier classes.

Entertainments, other than sports, specifically for teenagers are almost nonexistent, and boys and girls are discouraged from socialising together. Schools are segregated, and university students sit separately. Even the most innocent of social contacts is viewed with concern by the authorities, and the *komiteh* are often on the lookout for such activities. This means that most teenagers spend an inordinate amount of time trying to get to know members of the opposite sex, with the added frisson of possibly being caught and punished. This is achieved by random telephone calls; cruising in cars along Tehran's boulevards; hanging around shopping malls, parks and cafes; and attending illicit parties. Unless you are living in a very conservative provincial town or a village, it will not be long before you see quite blatant teenage flirting and pickups in public. There are many urban legends about the sordid activities of Iranian middle- and upper-class teenagers, and it may be true that sexual experimentation is rife in an atmosphere that lends a sexual charge to social contact that Western teenagers take for granted. Drug-taking is increasingly common amongst wealthy, bored teenagers, and the stigma attached to such activities, as well as the danger of arrest, deters parents from seeking help for their addicted children.

— *Chapter Five* —

THE OILED WHEELS OF IRANIAN SOCIAL ETIQUETTE

If thou art aware of news that will grieve a hear, remain silent that others may convey it,
Nightingale! Bring tidings of spring, leave bad news to the owl.

> —Saadi, 'Rules on Conduct for Life', *Gulistan*

THE IRANIAN SOCIAL HIERARCHY

How to Explain?

Iran presents a very diverse society. Iranian, Islamic, Middle Eastern and European culture and values are fused in a very heterogeneous system of class and outlook. The existence of an influential class who feel that they adhere to Western values further complicates the picture. Conversely, many Iranians of all social classes have been involved in the rediscovery of their Iranian roots, both in the 1970s and over the last decade. Many Iranians will, at least in the presence of foreigners, appear to conduct themselves in the manner of Europeans, although the generalisation involved in any Western model of social behaviour indicates the strangeness of the situation. 'European', for many Iranians, means a fusion of mainly American, British and (amongst older, educated people) possibly French culture. For the irreligious youth, America provides the model for behaviour, aided by Turkish satellite television with its diet of popular culture.

Social Mobility

Iranian society is intensely hierarchical, but a large degree of unconventional social mobility exists, of which Reza Shah was a good example. A semiliterate soldier, he progressed through a good marriage, military valour and political acumen to being Prime Minister and, ultimately, the Shah of Iran. The Iranian elite is always in flux, and it changes with political and economic events, although a certain stratum always seems to manage to stay in evidence throughout. Society revolves around multiple patron-client relationships and reciprocity of favours. Bribery exists, but it is more common in the socially acceptable form of exchanging mutual favours. Family and friends are expected to use their power and influence, and to call in outstanding favours in times of need.

A Quick Who's Who in Iran

Iranian social groups include: the *taghouti* (literally 'idol worshippers'), or pleasure-seeking wealthy, many of whom have emigrated; the mullahs or *akhounds* (religious conservatives and clergy), who are allied with the *bazaaris*, or merchant class; the modernists, who tend to admire Western values; the *roshanfekr*, or intellectuals, who come in many guises; the new elite (such as the new entrepreneurs and technocrats), who may or may not be pro-regime; the middle classes, most of whom are office workers or professionals; the *basijan*, or war heroes, and the families of the war dead who are awarded preferential positions, especially in education; the *daneshjoo*, or students, who are well-respected and, hence, potentially powerful; and the masses, both the mobilized and the apathetic. The very devoted supporters of the Islamic regime are known as *hezbollahis* ('members of the party of God'). This latter group can usually be recognised by their clothing, beards and extreme religiosity.

In the official rhetoric of the Islamic revolution, the masses are the *mostazafeen*, or 'downtrodden', in whose name the revolution was successful. The *taghouti* are the hated remnants of the old ruling class, who turned away from Islam and favoured drinking, gambling and the pursuit of other immoral pleasures, with complete disregard to the needs of the masses. As to the *mostazafeen* themselves, only a minority remain mobilised; the rest are largely busy scrabbling around for a living in Iran's economic mire.

FOREIGNERS IN IRAN

Foreigners hold a curious position in Iranian society, especially since the 1979 revolution. Iranians generally hold strong views about foreigners, their merits and negative qualities, and many of these views are diametrically opposed but held simultaneously by the same people. Iran's unfortunate history of economic, political and social interference by foreigners has undoubtedly coloured Iranian views of foreigners, but it would be a serious mistake to think that foreigners are perceived entirely negatively, at any level of society.

Foreigners are roughly divided into two groups: Europeans and North Americans—although smaller groups of Australians and other 'white' semi-Europeans are acknowledged. Those not covered in these main groups are viewed largely in disparaging terms, especially those from 'Third World' countries such as India. Very few Iranians can be bothered to distinguish between India and Bangladesh, for example, and it is not considered that such countries have much to offer culturally. Iranians do not usually consider holidaying in such countries, and those Iranians who study in India or other 'Third World' countries are acutely aware that this is not highly thought of in Iran.

Non-white citizens of 'white' countries present Iranians with a dilemma, as they often cannot accept such a possibility, and may assume that one is lying about one's origins. The concept of naturalisation is not widely understood, and people generally retain their natal nationality for life in the Iranian scheme of things. Postrevolutionary Iran has close links with Japan, and Iran sees many Japanese tourists and business travellers. This can be confusing, as all foreigners may now be thought of as Japanese, which can be a strange experience for a Westerner.

Love of the West

Iranians historically have been very open to European culture, absorbing many words, concepts and ideas, as well as lifestyle changes. This was recognised in the 1960s by one of Iran's most famous writers and intellectuals, Jamal Al-e Ahmad, who described the Iranian condition in a book called *Gharbzardagee*, inelegantly translated as 'Westoxification' or 'Weststruckedness'. The theme of the book, which struck a chord with most intellectuals, was that Iranians were almost chameleon-like in their ability to adapt to Western ways, favouring such ways over their own culture, which was becoming increasingly degraded. Al-e Ahmad favoured a return to Shi'ite culture, as a unique manifestation of 'Iranianness', as the pre-Islamic culture was as alien to modern Iranians as Western cultural values. He blamed intellectuals and the wealthy for the Westernisation of Iranian culture, predicting that only the peasants would retain an Iranian identity in the future, the rest of society becoming an imperfect replica of all that was bad in Western societies.

Being a Westerner in Iran

Most Iranians will happily criticise the West and, in particular, the governments of the West, who are held responsible (with some justification) for all of Iran's problems. Despite this, they will generally be most generous with praise for the West's perceived advantages and even superior attributes, and will be alternately boastful of Iranian superiority and apologetic about Iranian shortcomings. This schizophrenic attitude is quite normal and will seem commonplace after a time. You should be careful initially not to unintentionally denigrate Iranians' culture and values.

Even during the height of revolutionary fervour, with regular chants of 'death to the West' and anti-Western graffiti commonplace, most Iranians distinguished between the individual and the government, and were usually unfailingly polite to stray Westerners. Intriguingly, a claimed neutral nationality like Irish citizenship is less enthusiastically received on the ground than being, say, British. This is because Iranians have generally a limited idea of world geography and can more easily relate to what they believe they know, so don't be shy, unless you are Israeli (and even then, middle-class Iranians will probably be eager to know you). Westerners are usually afforded V.I.P. treatment in Iran by all but hard line *hezbollahis*.

Foreigners are referred to as *kharaji*, and this is a useful expression for when you need help, as most Iranians feel a collective responsibility to help foreigners and be hospitable. Another expression is *ferangi*, from the old word for a Frankish crusader. This latter term only refers to Westerners.

121

COMMUNICATING IN IRAN

Ritual Politeness

Iranian society revolves around the concept known as *ta'arouf*, which consists of formalised ritual politeness, involving verbal and nonverbal forms and cues. It is a ritual display of vulnerability, which the other participant knows not to abuse, invoking a sort of noblesse oblige. Iranians appear to belittle themselves in order to seem humble, but a clever Iranian knows that this is a form of politeness and does not press any advantage, but rather responds in kind. There is no assumption of status in the Iranian etiquette system, which reflects the reality of frequently changing social relations. No one wants to alienate the apparently humble civil servant who may later provide a gateway to a powerful personage.

Small talk on all occasions is mandatory for Iranians, and oblique approaches to business matters and the imparting of less than pleasing news is normal—as in fact is its complete avoidance. Imparting bad news is always a task to be avoided. Indirect approaches to subjects are useful, so the initiator can avoid asking an outright question or favour, and the recipient of the query can avoid answering with a blunt 'yes' or 'no'. Always couch answers to requests in terms of your desire to do something, rather than ability or even actual willingness.

A good rule to follow is that of 'three times'—that is, always offer three times and decline three times before accepting anything or finally refusing. If your offer is sincere, press past the third time. If the person offering you is insincere they will usually drop the offer at the third refusal and face will be saved by both parties. If you admire any possession of an Iranian, they will try to press it upon you, and you must also be prepared to offer an admired possession. The rule of three times allows this to occur without undue embarrassment, although be warned that not all Iranians play by the rules all the time, and greed may overrule *ta'arouf* on occasion.

The Language and Gestures of Ta'arouf

There is a physical and verbal language of *ta'arouf*. The former consists of such activities as jostling to be the last through the door, seeking a humble seating location, or standing to attention on the arrival or departure of other guests. Verbally there are prescribed self-abasements used which can confuse a Farsi learner. For example the use of the word *bandeh* ('slave') instead of 'myself', as well as expressions such as 'you ordered' rather than 'you said'. A very common form of *ta'arouf* is referring to people as *ghorbon* ('sacrifice'), meaning that you are at their disposal. All gestures and utterances are open to interpretation and symbolic meanings sought in all utterances, gestures and actions. This partially explains why conspiracy theories abound in Iran and are perhaps the most complex in the world.

One should take care when refusing favours, such as food and hospitality, as the host may believe that you do not feel welcome enough to accept. Often Iranians who are not hungry are forced to eat anyway, as the host seems distressed by the social consequences of a guest not eating. The constant use of *ta'arouf* means that it can be difficult to establish the truth of a social situation. Should you believe that an unexpected guest really has just eaten dinner? Or are they just being polite? Exceptionally *ta'aroufi* people may continue their stance beyond the three-times rule, and so may be hungry but deny it. Equally, a host may be insisting that they were just about to serve dinner, whereas the proverbial cupboard is bare. Gauging the veracity of these competing claims is a matter of experience and intuition, and even Iranians get it wrong sometimes. Many people tell anecdotes about such experiences, where they got it wrong and were forced to go hungry or forced to eat two dinners in one evening, but all this is considered a necessary price for the social convenience of *ta'arouf*.

Although you may find *ta'arouf* maddening, you will gradually adjust to this model of behaviour, and indeed if you don't, you will find Iranian society unbearable. A useful expression is *be ta'arouf*, or 'without *ta'arouf*', which indicates your sincerity. Of course this ploy can also be used as a tool of *ta'arouf*!

Polite behaviour also generally consists of showing your consideration of others in your behaviour—for example, listening politely, not interrupting, preceding statements with 'in my opinion' or 'with your permission', sitting to attention rather than slouching, rising when others enter or leave, praising the food and hospitality, or asking after others' family and mutual acquaintances.

Getting angry in public is considered very bad form, and rarely achieves anything anyway. It demonstrates a loss of control that is the opposite of an ideal personality as well as evidence of a poorly managed situation.

Small Talk

Small talk is vital to oil the wheels of Iranian social proceedings, and it precedes most matters. Expect to discuss family, impressions of Iran, your home country, traffic and the weather (not as much as in Britain). In general, discussion of religion and politics should be confined to noncommittal responses and should not be initiated. Money, earnings and fertility are not the taboos they are in most European societies. In same-sex groups, sexual matters are often discussed frankly or joked about. Even apparently sophisticated, secular Iranians can be very sensitive to what they perceive as criticisms of Iran or their religion. A feeling of deja vu may be experienced as you appear to have the same conversation again and again, often with the same people, but remember that conversation is seen as a means of putting someone at ease, and is not necessarily intended to impart new ideas or news.

VISITATIONS

When is an Invitation not an Invitation?

The answer is possibly quite often in Iran. It will take a little practice to always differentiate between a genuine invitation and one offered as a result of *ta'arouf*. If a firm date is given or suggested, it is probably sincere, but vague invitations may be simply a means of showing goodwill. In this case, no firm answer is usually necessary. It is not dissimilar to Europe or America, where people often comment that, 'You really must come over some time,' without anyone actually getting out their diary to fix a date—however, Iranians usually sound much more committed. The majority of invitations in Iran are to meals; invitations to 'tea' (*chai o shirini*) are rarer, and are usually imposed on the host by the potential guest, who might suggest that they call round between meal times.

Impromptu invitations are not as likely to be insincere as they are in some other countries. Iranians are quite used to providing meals at short notice, and an invitation on impulse should be put to the test by the three-times rule. Some invitations are clearly polite ones, such as when you bump into someone who is just leaving their house to go to an appointment, or entering their house heavily laden with shopping. You can invent a convenient prior engagement on these sorts of occasions that will save everyone's face. White lies are an essential part of *ta'arouf* and are socially responsible, rather than dishonest.

Punctuality

Punctuality should be observed by yourself, but never expected from your Iranian guests. Guests frequently arrive late (maybe with other guests in tow) or even cancel at short notice. You are expected to understand their social pressures, as they would if you cancelled or arrived late. You can express great disappointment at such changes in the programme, but not really anger.

GIVING AND RECEIVING GIFTS

Guests almost always bring small gifts. These are generally candy or flowers. Both of these will be appreciated all the more if they are wrapped elegantly. A foreign guest can endeavour to bring a souvenir from home, ideally something with novelty value. Small gifts for the children of the house are another alternative. The guest usually offers the gift diffidently to the host, apologising that they couldn't find better, and the host usually expresses their delight, claiming that it was totally unnecessary, and then will often not open the gift until the guest departs. In more traditional households the gift may be deposited silently, spirited away, and not mentioned again. It is a very new phenomenon for gifts to be opened in the guest's presence, as the tradition being that this would seem greedy, because, after all, the guest is the real gift. If the gift is not flowers or chocolate, thanks will be offered at a later meeting. Please do not take your host's apparent indifference to your offering at face value, but understand that they want you to feel that you would be equally welcome whatever you brought, even if you came empty handed. Arrival without a gift needs an apology, after which the host's response will be that you are a gift yourself.

Beware Iranians Bearing Gifts

Gift exchange is a major aspect of *ta'arouf*. Many social events are marked by an exchange of gifts, and these are usually dictated by a general agreement on the nature of the appropriate gift. Gifts are given as part of hospitality, on returning from a trip, to mark personal and business successes, to mark holidays, and in return for services. Gifts are often subsidiary to the practice of ritual visits, which are expected on various occasions.

For major life events such as engagement, marriage or the birth of a child, formal gifts of gold coins or money are common. Gifts of money are given to servants or anyone who has provided a service on certain holidays. It is appropriate to ask the advice of others as to the appropriate amount for such offerings. When one passes an exam, gets a new job or promotion, or achieves a major success in life, it is normal to treat one's friends, family or colleagues to cakes or sweets. A common expression is that you are looking forward to when someone buys the sweets, meaning that you wish them success. A person may also chide a successful friend in a good-natured way, asking, 'Where are my sweets then?' The successful person may also buy small gifts for their nearest and dearest to share their good fortune. This is especially true if there was a financial reward. An invitation out, for which the successful person pays, is also common. Conversely, although less commonly, well-wishers may buy gifts to celebrate the success of another person.

Birthday gifts are less common than in the West, and only really routine within the family, mostly for children and amongst educated urban families. Announcing that it is your birthday is more likely to mean that you should buy the sweets rather than that you expect to receive gifts. Housewarming gifts can be something for the house, flowers, a potted plant or the ubiquitous candy. The most traditional of all gifts upon moving house is a cone of loaf sugar, which indicates that the house will see a sweet life within. People who have returned from a long trip abroad, and particularly from a pilgrimage to Mecca (*haj*) must be visited and given a small gift of flowers or candy. In return, you will usually receive a gift from the trip.

This custom of bringing gifts from trips is widespread, and a major headache for Iranians, especially ones who travel abroad. It can seem that everyone you know expects a gift (*soghat*), and many Iranians spend their entire vacation shopping and worrying about the number and quality of gifts. One is expected to bring gifts for one's boss, maybe one's colleagues and neighbours, and certainly for one's friends and family. The most usual gifts are souvenirs typical of the area or country visited. For example, anyone visiting Isfahan usually brings back boxes of the local candy, *gaz*, or the local handicrafts as gifts. When visiting overseas, almost anything can be a gift, from medicines to clothes to foreign magazines.

When someone is ill, it is customary to visit, even if you can only see the family rather than the person who is sick. Apart from flowers and candy, *compote*, or preserved canned fruits, are a traditional gift for a sick person—or any food which the person particularly likes or which may be considered beneficial (for example, honey).

Unwrapping your gift in front of its bearer will only occur in certain circles, as it is considered rude to seem eager to examine a gift. Gifts are always offered with an apology for its inadequacies, and accepted graciously but with insistence that it was unnecessary. Thank-you letters for gifts, as for hospitality, are almost unknown, but for gifts other than candy or flowers, it is expected that you display your gratitude at a later date, ideally by using the gift, indicating your pleasure in it.

Gifts can be a form of bribery, and expensive gifts from your inferiors or petitioners should be handled tactfully. It is rarely necessary to refuse a gift, although if it is very expensive, you may have to. You can try indicating your surprise at such generosity and explain that Westerners are not comfortable with such displays, and that it could strain your relationship, which of course would pain you greatly. Remember that the majority of such gifts are not bribes, but simply attempts to demonstrate respect and generosity in order to engender good will. Business contacts routinely exchange gifts, and this is part of normal business etiquette. Foreign businesspeople should come prepared with some appropriate gifts from home (souvenir trays, traditional handicrafts, pens, etc.) and expect to receive such gifts.

During the 1998 World Cup, the Iranian football team arrived on the pitch at the start of each match bearing flowers for each of the opposing team members, and gifts of an Iranian metalwork tray and candy for the captain. This was typically Iranian.

Beware Admiration

Compliments on possessions may generate the obligation to offer that item as a gift. Usually this is done in a clearly ritualised manner, with a token gesture and gift (*pishkesh*). Refusal is in the form of a further compliment such as, 'It suits you more than me, but thank you.' Sometimes one becomes obliged to accept the gift, when polite refusal is ignored and the giver is sincere. In such cases accept graciously and offer a small token gift in exchange either then, or at a later date. If you are in the position of offering the *pishkesh*, decide if you are sincere beforehand, and remember that more than three refusals means they probably regret the compliment, and you should desist.

Loans vs. Gifts

With Iranians, the distinction between a loan and a gift can be very indistinct. Whenever you lend an item, be aware that you may never see it again. If this really bothers you, find a polite way to avoid loaning the item in the first place. This is in itself difficult, but you could claim that you yourself have borrowed it, or that you have promised it to someone else already but will tell your friend when it is returned. Never suggest loaning something unless you are prepared to lose it, as this is often a face-saving way of giving a gift.

Iranians generally see lending or giving items between friends as a way of increasing closeness and cementing ties. To make free with each other's possessions is an indication of your closeness, and as you adjust to the Iranian way, you will begin to see Iranian generosity as positive and to realise that you too must relax your attachment to your own possessions.

Returning the Dish

It is not unusual to offer someone a special dish to try. For example, a neighbour may prepare a special dish and offer a portion to a neighbour. A guest may be given a portion of a dish they enjoyed to take home, or for an absent friend or relative. If it is known that you enjoy a certain delicacy, a friend may always remember to bring you some of it whenever it is made. When returning the dish in which it was presented, it is customary not to leave it empty, even if this is a few sweets or biscuits. This shows your appreciation of their generosity.

THE IRANIAN HOME

Iranians generally love their homes. If an Englishman's home is his castle, an Iranian's home is the haven for his or her inner self, away from the outside world. Iranian homes are generally very comfortable, clean and well cared for. They are all equipped to be comfortable for guests, and it is in the home that the Iranian really enjoys dispensing hospitality and socialising. The best Iranian food is served at home, and eating in restaurants is considered a poor substitute for eating comfortably at home. Single men who live alone are generally pitied at being unable to aspire to the standard of comfort of a family home. This reflects the pivotal role of the Iranian woman in the home, whatever her social status. Single men very rarely invite friends to their home to eat, and almost never invite couples or families. If they want to repay hospitality, they generally invite friends to a restaurant.

Foreigners in Iran are very likely to be invited to the homes of Iranians, and, as long as you observe basic rules of politeness, you will be enchanted by the warmth of your welcome. For advice on eating at home, as well as in restaurants, see Chapter Seven on eating and drinking.

The Inner and the Outer House

Traditionally, Iranian houses were divided into inner and outer quarters. The outer quarters (*anderooni*) were for men and their guests, whereas the inner quarters (*birooni*) were reserved for women and close male relatives. From this division originated the concept of the *harram*, or harem, of Western imagination, which simply means 'forbidden'—the area forbidden to outsiders. You may see such houses in rural or provincial areas, or even in Tehran, although such strict division of space by gender is rare now, except perhaps in the houses of the very traditional clergy. In such houses, men and women will be entertained separately, or Western women may be treated as honorary men. Older houses still show signs of this division, with two entrances and identical sets of rooms. The inner quarters, which include the kitchen and the courtyard, have only one corridor to connect them to the outer ones.

The Modern Shoe Dilemma

In most modern Iranian homes, there still exists some division of space into private and public areas. This is often reflected in the furnishings. Although traditional Iranian homes are simply furnished with carpeted floors and cushions around the walls, most houses in Tehran have at least one room with European-style furniture, which may be used exclusively for guests. In traditional homes, everyone takes off their shoes at the door and pads around in their socks, keeping the carpets clean, and enabling them to sit comfortably on the floor. In modern homes, there may be a traditional room which the family uses to relax or watch television, but the main 'public' areas will be shoe-wearing areas, at least for guests. This can be tricky for you.

Generally, if the floors are marble, the furnishings are European, it is safe to assume that they do not want you to de-shoe, unless it is raining or muddy outside. A safe compromise is to ostentatiously begin to remove your shoes slowly, whereupon the host will insist that you do not. You will have to judge from their response their true feelings on the matter. They may offer you slippers as a compromise. You can also copy other Iranian guests. Iranians seem to be very caught up in what is sophisticated behaviour, and personally I think it a great shame that they are willing to abandon a hygienic and comfortable custom for the sake of vanity, and generally point out when possible that I think de-shoeing a splendid custom, and their carpets are much too precious to bear my dirty shoes.

You will be told where to sit in the guest room, and will be served with titbits, many of which are left ready in fancy, covered dishes in anticipation of guests. The guest-sitting room will generally have the best of everything in the house, and will contain everything for your comfort. Meals with guests will generally be eaten here, and many Iranian homes have dining tables to sit ten or more people. If you are a very close acquaintance, you may be invited into the family room and possibly to dine on the floor in there.

BATHROOM HABITS

Many people in Tehran have European-style bathrooms (*hammam*) and toilets (*dast-shwee*, literally 'hand wash'), but almost all provincial houses have traditional 'hole in the ground' squat toilets and shower rooms. In some households they have both types, and you may be offered a choice. Public steam baths are becoming increasingly rare, but they offer a useful and enjoyable service when you're travelling. Public baths generally cater to men and women at separate times of the day, although they may have two separate sections. Friday is the most popular day. You will be welcomed as long as you copy your fellow bathers and are prepared to be the centre of some attention. Good behaviour includes never walking around naked (you will be given a loin cloth), not letting your dirty water run near anyone else, and cleaning up after yourself. There are now public baths of the individual cubicle type, although an assistant can usually be hired to scrub and massage you. Towels, soap and razors (best avoided) can all be hired. Traditional Iranian men and women remove their pubic and underarm hair with foul-smelling potions or by shaving. At the *really public* public baths this takes place in a special cubicle. A foreigner's pubic hair is a source of huge entertainment—or possibly outright disgust—in such settings.

As far as the home bathroom is concerned, Iranians only use the shower, never a bathtub full of water, for bathing. In the traditional bathrooms, a small stool is provided to sit on and scrub one's feet, and a rough wash mitten (*keeseh*) is used to exfoliate one's skin. The idea is to replicate the steamy atmosphere of a Turkish bath at home, and this takes some time. You may be offered help from friends to wash your back and so on. Remember that complete nudity is generally unacceptable, so, if you're not alone while bathing, keep your underpants on. A selection of bowls and jugs may be provided for soaking and rinsing, especially if there is just a wall faucet and no shower head. Iranians often distinguish between taking a shower (*doush*) and having the longer experience involving exfoliation (*hammam*), which is a weekly or biweekly experience.

Muslims wash completely after sex, so going out with wet hair can cause some ribald comments, especially on Friday mornings, as Thursday night is the traditional night for 'getting close'.

A need for the toilet is generally indicated by a request to wash one's hands, although if shown to the sink only, this requires further negotiation. It is usual to wash one's hands shortly after arrival anywhere that food is to be eaten at all, as well as in restaurants. Although toilet paper may be provided in certain households, it is not usually available in public toilets (of which there are few in Iran—try a restaurant, or a mosque if desperate). In any case, all Iranians wash themselves with water, using the hose, jug, or tin can provided, and their left hand. Paper is just for drying off. This is where you see the advantage of hair removal. It is best to learn the Iranian style of using the toilet early on; as it becomes routine, you will see that it is most hygienic. It does mean that the toilet floor is generally rather damp, and a special pair of plastic shoes are provided in all homes for toilet use, which should not be worn outside the toilet.

When using a toilet with no nearby faucet, check there is water in the jug before using the toilet. Flush traditional toilets are rare, but it is usual to run some water after use. Your host will generally check that you are provided with water and soap for washing your hands afterwards. When travelling, bring your own soap everywhere. Iranians often prefer to keep their towels for individual use, so check that you are not using the host's face towel for your ablutions. Although Iranians do not generally eat with their hands or observe the left hand taboo as markedly as some Muslims, it is good to get into the habit of using the left hand for washing and the right hand for taking proffered food. This could be useful for your own health as well as your etiquette.

Many toilets in public places have inadequate or even no locks, so it is customary to tap on the door twice before attempting to enter. If you are inside, simply tap back to indicate that the cubicle is occupied.

A Note on Noses

Blowing the nose in public is considered revolting. You should leave the room to do so, and if forced to sniff noisily, apologise immediately. Many Iranians do elaborate and noisy nose-clearing manoeuvres at the bathroom sink in order to avoid having to blow their nose in public. Putting dirty handkerchiefs in one's pocket is also considered disgusting. When Iranians offer a tissue on request, they will always offer the box, never an individual tissue, even between close family and friends.

THE SMOKING CULTURE

For those accustomed to the smoke-laden atmosphere of social intercourse in Turkey or many of the Arab countries, Iran will prove restful on the lungs. Attitudes to smoking in Iran are ambivalent, and the practice of smoking is not nearly as widespread or socially acceptable (or perhaps essential) as, say, in Turkey. Cigars are very rare, as are pipes. The government takes a general anti-smoking line and tries to dissuade the public from smoking by a combination of health education and even religious edicts, as smoking has associations with irreligious values. Many public places and offices observe smoking bans, as do domestic flights and city buses; smoking in taxis is very rare, and intercity buses are rarely smoky. Restaurants also are not the lung endurance test found in the rest of the Middle East. In such public places, anyone expressing a dislike of smoke, or an allergy to it, will be sympathetically received, and smokers will usually desist or relocate.

There is a direct relationship between smoking and educational or social level, in that smoking is more common in social situations amongst middle and upper class Iranians (who are often heavy smokers). It is very rare that smoking will be prohibited in households in these circles, and ashtrays will always be provided. As the guest reigns supreme in Iran, permission is never refused to a smoker, although the politest guest would not of course suggest it unless the host smokes. If you really have asthma or some allergic condition, you can try explaining this to your smoking guest or host, but Iranians are generally willing to endure unpleasantness for the sake of friendship or politeness.

— Chapter Six —

RELAXING IN IRAN

A book of verses underneath the bough
A jug of wine, a loaf of bread and thou
Beside me singing in the wilderness
And wilderness is paradise enow

—Omar Khayyam, *The Rubaiyat*

Most relaxation for Iranians consists of spending time at home with family and friends, and the importance of this has already been looked at in the Chapter Five. Although Iranians often have very active social lives, Iran is not the place to be if you are deeply attached to the sort of social life that involves cultural activities. There are no symphony orchestras, opera or ballet companies, and most Iranian performing artists have an uneasy relationship with the Islamic Republic. Although you may fall into a crowd that organises wild parties with drink (and possibly worse) this will all take place in an atmosphere of anxiety and fear, and if you are the type of person who enjoys such activities, you will probably pine for nightclubs and bars.

HOME ENTERTAINMENTS

Most entertainments are home-based. This includes: seeing friends; video-watching; playing cards, chess and backgammon; listening to music and dancing; watching television, satellite channels and listening to the radio. Of all of these, the video runs second to seeing friends. Many Iranians cannot contemplate an evening without seeing friends and family, and close friends and family arrive unannounced (or possibly after a telephone call) on many evenings).

Television, Videos and Hidden Satellite Dishes

Officially, satellite television is banned, or at least only available to those with a government permit (which clearly means that there are government apparatchiks who watch it themselves, maybe in their role as guardians of the moral of others). Nevertheless, most middle class Iranians in the major cities have access to satellite TV. The dishes are hidden on the flat roofs of apartment buildings, carefully positioned behind sheds or water tanks, or hidden under painted covers to blend into the background. The Turkish channels seem to be most popular, probably because they offer a diet of semi-clad women, cabaret and heart-rendering soap operas. Turkish pop stars are very popular in Iran, aided by their frequent appearances on satellite TV.

137

Having been banned for years, video players and recorders are now permitted. Videos are allowed if 'approved', but of course no one watches these. New Western films are soon available in Iran, but the quality of the picture is often dreadful. Films may be watched in any language, even a film in Greek is better than Iranian TV, although occasionally a series has a loyal following, usually a dubbed and ancient British or Japanese saga. Watching videos of social events such as weddings is a popular entertainment and these may be watched repetitively.

Iranian television has five channels, but all of them are equally worthy and dull. The provinces have local programming on one channel, often in local languages. The children's programming in quite good, and there are an awful lot of wildlife documentaries.

For many Iranians, social life takes place in the alleyways of their neighbourhood. These Kurdish women wind wool, chat and care for their babies in the street outside their houses.

Foreign programmes are limited because of the dress restrictions, although historical dramas often get through as the women have hats. Football and other sports are often shown live, even in the middle of the night. Religious holidays are ghastly with nonstop religious programming. There is news in English, usually read by a woman, at around 11 p.m. on channel 4.

The Radio

Iran broadcasts in several local languages, plus in foreign languages, but few Iranians seem to listen to Iranian radio. Many Iranians are avid users of shortwave radios, and have great faith in the Persian services of other countries, including the Voice of America, the BBC World Service and even Radio Israel. There is no official attempt to jam these broadcasts, though people listen to them in private, and there is a rather furtive feeling to tuning in.

VENTURING OUT AND ABOUT

Going to restaurants is the most common 'outdoor' leisure activity, the details of which are described in Chapter Seven, which looks at eating in Iran. Walking in the parks is also quite common, especially in the evenings. Shops stay open late, so there are many shopping centres to stroll around. Many parks have entertainments, such as boating or fun fairs. Driving around aimlessly is popular with young Iranians, and traffic is often bumper to bumper in parts of Tehran late into the night.

Music

Music is also a valued art form in Iran and worth some effort to understand. The popular music scene is mostly illegal, and thus originates now from overseas, especially the United States. The names of the popular singers are still largely those who were famous twenty years ago. Many classical musicians stayed put in Iran, although women cannot sing to men in public. Instrumental classical music is 'approved' and is usually accompanied by sung poetry rather than specific song lyrics. Western classical music is largely acceptable, but not very popular. There are concerts of all of the approved forms of music in major cities, and there are also music festivals marking holidays, which often allow one to experience regional musical traditions. Turkish and Western popular music is smuggled in on a large scale, and is played quite openly in cars.

Iranian Classical Music

There is no difference between a song and a poem in classical terms. Iranian classical music consists of poetry sung to musical accompaniment or unaccompanied music. Most Iranian classical music is played on stringed or percussion instruments. The most popularly used is the *tar*, a pear-shaped, six stringed instrument that is played with a bow. The *seh tar* has three strings, and is plucked with the fingers. The *ud* is a lute; there is also the *kamancheh*, a violin-sized instrument which is held vertically like a cello and played with an arched bow. Percussion instruments include the *dahol*, a large drum played with two heavy sticks; the *diareh* or *daf*, which is a large shallow tambourine-like drum (sometimes with jangling rings) struck with the hand; and the *tonbak*, which is held under one arm and played like a bongo. The *santoor* is something like a zither or xylophone; it is played with a plectrum or struck with two small sticks. The enormous range of sounds created by these instruments is often supplemented by Western instruments such as violins and pianos.

There are many famous musicians in Iran, and now that the restrictions on classical music have been loosened, they actively tour the West, perform concerts in Iran, and produce new live and studio recordings. Of the vocalists, Shahram Nazeri and Mohammed Reza Shajarian are perhaps the most renowned, whilst a group of musicians called the Kamkar brothers are well worth seeking out. Made up of seven or so brothers, one sister and a nephew, all from the Kurdish city of Sanandaj, the Kamkar brothers play a wide range of both Kurdish and Persian music.

The Cinema

Iran has an admirable filmmaking tradition, despite the many years of restrictions. Iran produces over fifty films a year—all on very low budgets. Perhaps these constraints have meant that only serious and dedicated artists have persisted in their activities, and it is refreshing to see a film tradition free of pulp. Several Iranian films have received critical acclaim in the West and have been released abroad in subtitled versions. These include *The White Balloon* (directed by Jafar Panahi and written by Abbas Kiarostami), *The Taste of Cherries* (directed by Kiarostami), and *Marriage of the Blessed* (directed by Mohsen Makhmalbaf). Any films by these directors are worth looking out for, especially as they often handle controversial topics.

There are also plenty of home-produced films (mostly about the Iran-Iraq war, which are often very violent and very popular) and imported martial arts films (also very violent and popular). These types of films are more commonly shown than art house films, especially in the provinces outside of Tehran. Iranian films are not subtitled, and the occasional foreign film will be poorly dubbed. In north Tehran, you can sometimes find European and American films, although they will be heavily censored and extensively edited. The annual international film festival takes place in Tehran around late February.

SPORTS

Sports are numerous and popular in Iran. The government actively encourages sports as 'wholesome', although they are strictly segregated, and some sports are forbidden for women. Football (soccer) is the national game; rugby, American football and baseball are not played, and cricket is played mainly in the south of Iran. Skiing facilities are good, as are those for water skiing, tennis, horse riding, fencing, volleyball, martial arts, wrestling and swimming. Hotels offer segregated swimming, and many people belong to private health clubs with pools; wealthy people often have their own secluded swimming pools. There is a tennis club in north Tehran as well as an eighteen-hole golf course. Both of these have women's sessions. It should be noted that women can only attend women's sports, and men can only attend men's sports, except for certain football matches which have recently provided segregated seating for women.

Skiing

Skiing is surprisingly popular with the middle classes of Tehran, Tabriz and Hamadan. The skiing season is long, with plenty of powdery snow, and costs are very low. Most of the resorts are at an altitude of around 2000 to 3,000 metres. The best skiing is within two hours of Tehran. The Elburz resorts are active from January to the end of March, and are very busy on Thursdays, Fridays and holidays, especially the March New Year holiday. The three main resorts are Darbansar Resort, which is for beginners; Shemshak; and Dizin Resort, the most fashionable, at the village of Shaleh. A ski pass costs as little as U.S.$2 a day, and equipment can be hired in the resorts for around U.S.$3 a day. Accommodation at all the resorts is quite expensive and foreigners will be charged in U.S. dollars.

At these resorts men and women are expected to ski on different slopes, but inexperienced skiers can find their own unmarked slopes or even try cross-country skiing, for example, around Damavand. Women have to wear a baggy jacket that falls below the knee and a scarf or hat that covers the hair and neck. Tourist ski packages are available in Tehran (paid in U.S. dollars for foreigners), and the agencies simplify the whole business for beginners.

Just to the north of Tehran on Mount Towchal are three ski slopes (with snow for almost seven months of the year), none of which are segregated.

Walking in the spring snow of the Elburz Mountains, north of Tehran. Women in chadors pass a fashionably attired group on a similar outing.

Climbing and Walking

Climbing and walking are popular activities in Iran, especially in the north of Tehran, where many people spend every Friday climbing or rambling in the mountains. Always take a sweater, water and a map or compass. If hiking alone, tell someone when to expect you back. Trekking in remote areas is possible, but requires preparation and the appropriate guides. Prior permission from the local governor's office might also be useful to obtain.

Mountain climbing in Iran offers many exciting possibilities. The Elburz range alone offers seventy peaks of more than 4,000 metres. The most climbed mountain in Iran in Mount Damavand (5604 metres), a volcano to the northeast of Tehran. Huts are provided at the base camp, but bringing your own tent may be necessary; the ascent takes around seven hours, and the descent between four and five hours. Most areas of Iran offer climbing opportunities, especially around Hamadan and Azerbaijan. As most Iranians are more into

143

hiking than climbing, there are few specialised climbing gear shops, and even fewer hire facilities, except in Darband in northern Tehran. Luckily, there is an excellent Mountaineering Federation of Iran that can offer advice on all aspects of climbing. The Federation can be contacted at: 15 Varzandeh St., Motaffeh Ave., Tehran; P.O. Box 15815/1881; tel: (21) 8839 928.

Ball Games

Football is the king of sports in Iran, with a fanatical following since Iran's admirable performance in the 1998 World Cup in Paris. The national championship season lasts from October to June. There are games all over Iran on Fridays and some evenings, and in Tehran, ten stadiums offer football matches, as well as other sporting fixtures. The Azadi Stadium in West Tehran seats up to 100,000 fans. Football is commonly played in the streets or on any patch of waste ground that can be found.

Other Sports

Sports-seekers in Iran can also try scuba diving off Kish Island, hang-gliding near Larijan (midway between Tehran and Amol), and sailing/water-skiing off the Caspian coast or at the Amir Kabir Dam (north of Karaj, about ninety minutes from Tehran). Both women and men must wear appropriate clothing, which makes all these activities potentially difficult.

TRADITIONAL FORMS OF ENTERTAINMENT

The Zoorkhaneh

The *zoorkhaneh*, or 'House of Strength', is found only in Iran, and serves as a gymnasium and clubhouse. A youth usually joins the *zoorkhaneh* as a novice and progresses through several grades of expertise, under the guidance of a master, until he becomes a *pahlavan* (champion), who can himself lead the exercises. The system is somewhat akin to a Masonic Lodge, and is shrouded in mystery and tradition, with similarities to the European medieval chivalric traditions. Imam Ali is the patron saint of the *zoorkhanehs*, and all exercise sessions begin and end with a prayer.

The exercises follow a ritual which is accompanied by the chanting of verses from Ferdowsi's *Shahnameh* whilst a drum and bell are beaten to mark time. The exercises consist of whirling heavy Indian clubs, wooden shields, clubs and chains, as well as press-ups and weightlifting. This all takes place in a central pit, so that spectators can observe. It is easy to locate a *zoorkhaneh* in a small town, as the rhythmic chanting and hollow bell carries clearly beyond the building's walls. Wrestling displays are also put on at the *zoorkhaneh*, to which any man is welcome. In Tehran, the Bank Melli Iran Zoorkhaneh has become a well-known tourist attraction.

Wrestling is popular in its modern form also, and Iran is proud of its achievements in the fields of wrestling and weightlifting. The first official invitation to an American sporting group after the Islamic revolution was to a wrestling team in 1998. The sports stadiums in all main cities host international wrestling and weightlifting contests and festivals.

Teahouse Recitals

The recital of poetry is the most traditional of all Iranian entertainments, and it has always been centred on the *chai khaneh*, or teahouse. The most common recital—told from memory—is of parts of the Ferdowsi's epic, *Shahnameh*, and staged before a painted backdrop. The recital may continue over several sessions, leaving the audience in suspense each night. Traditionally, storytellers and bards were also regular visitors to teahouses. The art of storytelling has been in decline for many years, and it can be difficult to track down a performance. One has a better chance of catching a poetry readings or storytelling outside Tehran; ask the regulars of the local teahouse if they know of a planned recital. In Tehran, the Sofreh Khaneh Sonnati Sangalag in the southern end of Tehran's Park-e Shahr has been made over into a traditional teahouse featuring regular readings. Women are allowed to attend.

Traditional Theatre

Iran has some traditional forms of theatre, in addition to the Shi'ite passion plays. Traditional theatre is known as *ru hoz*—literally 'over the pond', as it was performed in the courtyards of private houses, on top of boards set up over the courtyard pond. The entertainment was something like a farce with a moral, involving set characters, such as the black-faced Haji Firuz, who also appears in the Now Ruz (New Year) celebrations. *Ru hoz* has practically died out, although you may be fortunate enough to be invited to a private performance; some acting groups stage revival performances of *ru hoz*.

ILLEGAL LEISURE ACTIVITIES

Games

Chess (*shatranj*) was forbidden in Iran (as a form of gambling) from 1979 until 1989, despite the fact that the game was possibly invented there. (It has certainly has been played there for more than 1,500 years.) Although Ayatollah Khomeini lifted restrictions on chess in 1989, backgammon (*takht-e nard*) and playing cards remain illegal. Nevertheless, backgammon is extremely popular, as are card games, although inside the house only. Being able to play backgammon will cement many a friendship in Iran. Card games are fairly simple to learn (usually involving four or more people) and can be very raucous.

Videos and Reading Materials

The possession or viewing of un-Islamic videos or reading materials (a potentially wide-ranging definition) is a serious offence, and although the penalty for a foreigner found in possession of the latest Kevin Costner flick is unlikely to be too serious, I would avoid any contact with pornography or really controversial films, such as any film with a screenplay by Salman Rushdie. Even watching such films at other people's houses is likely to be fraught with danger, and keeping pornography in your house is not a good idea. Bear in mind that pornography is defined quite differently in Iran compared to other countries.

The Party Scene

Parties in which alcohol is consumed, men and women mix without appropriate Islamic dress, or—horror of horrors—men and women dance together to 'un-Islamic' music, are all *very* illegal. People who hold such parties usually hire a lookout utilising a system of signals, at the first sign of which all illegal activities are covered up. You may well attend such parties, which are reputedly common in certain social milieus and amongst the foreign communities. You may even enjoy the frisson of excitement generated by activities that used to seem quite mundane at home, but you should always be aware that you are running the risk of arrest (and possibly worse). Being stopped outside in the street whilst smelling of alcohol is a serious hazard, even if the local *komiteh* are just looking for a payoff.

Socialising for Singles

Contact between unmarried members of the opposite sex are limited by law, as well as custom. There are widespread rumours that certain areas function as pick-up joints and that there is a swinging singles scene in cities like Tehran. This is probably true, but again you should be fully aware of the risks you run if you become involved. For a foreigner, deportation may be the lightest penalty, but, for the Iranian party, a lashing or worse could be on the cards. If one of the parties to a 'fornication' is married, this is a more serious crime, with the ultimate punishment being stoning. Although all acts of fornication theoretically need to be witnessed in order to be charged, the old adage that 'when a man and a woman are alone, the devil is the third person present' seems to usually provide adequate evidence of wrongdoing. Unmarried women caught in compromising situations are often subjected to 'virginity tests', and the inability to prove that they are virgins can be used as evidence. A man can be forced to marry a woman with whom he is accused of having sexual relations, and this is especially true if the woman herself accuses him of abusing her or if she is pregnant, in which case he must marry her, even if already married. It should be additionally noted that sexual contact between non-Muslim men and Muslim women is forbidden in itself, and a man must convert before he can marry a Muslim woman.

Prostitution is illegal in Iran, but flourishes in certain areas under the guise of 'temporary marriage' (*sigheh*). Children issuing from such a liaison are the man's responsibility. Homosexual activities are illegal, although there is a traditional social tolerance of discreet homosexuality, at least on the part of a 'manly' man who uses habitual homosexuals as surrogate women. This tolerance, however, does not pass down to the 'feminine', habitual homosexual party.

Drugs

Of course, you know that alcohol is banned, and that you are taking a risk every time you come into contact with it. What you may not realise is that drug abuse is quite widespread in Iran. Although there is a long established culture surrounding opium smoking—which is almost socially acceptable in certain areas—it remains illegal, and you should be wary of indulging.

The opium (*teriaki*) culture is typically widespread amongst older, wealthier men, and in the poppy-growing areas. The opium is smoked in a pipe, which is heated by hot coals held in a small brazier. Opium addicts are typified as slothful, constipated and muddled, and there are many jokes about them. Some older addicts are registered with the government, and are allowed to continue their habit.

Other drugs are much less socially acceptable, and are increasingly used in Iran, especially young people, including marijuana and heroin. The government is very keen to stamp out these activities, and there are frequent public executions of drug smugglers, dealers and users. Avoid, avoid, avoid.

CULTURAL HOBBIES

Architecture

Anyone with an interest in architecture will be well rewarded in Iran, where there is a wealth of sights to see and much to learn. Many Iranians are quite casual about their architectural heritage—probably the most magnificent of all Iranian art forms—and much of it has been lost despite preservation efforts. Beware trips with Iranian friends who do not want to waste time on dusty old museums and heritage sights, as old is not always valued in Iran.

Literature

Persian literature plays an important role in the lives of Iranians. Even illiterates are aware of the great national poets and some of their works and conversations are peppered with literary quotes. An appreciation of poetry is considered essential for a sensitive person. Poetry readings are common, and poetry is recited in a practised style. Reading and familiarising yourself with some of the great works will be helpful in conversation and social mixing, and will no doubt become an absorbing interest for you. Many translated works are available, and, however imperfect, they give an indication of the poets' philosophical underpinnings.

Fine Arts

The study of Iranian fine arts gives plenty of insight into Persian culture and history. Carpet-weaving and miniature art are especially important as art forms which survived the Arab domination of Persia. Foreigners can enroll in miniature painting classes or approach specific artists for private instruction. Collecting artwork in Iran can be rewarding, but there are many export restrictions and increasingly few authentic bargains to be found, so all purchases should be approached with caution.

Many people have warned that Iranian carpets are seriously addictive, and a knowledge of carpets can considerably aid one in sniffing out a bargain. Of course, a vast carpet collection amassed whilst in Iran is likely to be problematic on departure due to customs. The same applies to antiquities or rare books and manuscripts.

Chapter Seven

EATING AND DRINKING

Mullah was once asked: 'When is a good time to eat?'
He answered: 'For the rich, always, and for the poor,
whenever they find food!'

—*The Tales of Mullah Nasreddin*

THE TASTE OF HOME

Anyone dependent on restaurants for sustenance in Iran is unlikely to be aware of the diversity and sophistication of Iranian food. Although there are many good restaurants in Iran's major cities and hotels, Iran does not have a well-developed restaurant culture. Iranians tend to eat out only out of necessity, such as when travelling, or to have kebabs, which are difficult to barbecue at home. A number of restaurants only serve kebabs with rice and might have one other dish on the menu.

Most socialising takes place in the home, and this is where the real delights of Iranian cuisine are to be experienced. As Iranians are extremely hospitable, it is unlikely that any foreign visitor will have to forgo the delights of Iranian gourmandising for long. Iran is a very food-obsessed country, and the people are rightly proud of their cuisine. Although women do most of the cooking, men are usually very interested in food and often prepare kebabs or selected dishes. Anyone who wishes to learn how to cook Iranian food is sure to be offered much help and guidance from Iranian friends.

HALAL VS. HARAM

All meat in Iran is *halal*—i.e., Islamically acceptable animals slaughtered in the approved Islamic manner. Pork products are not available in any shape or form, and there is no demand for them. (Beef and lamb sausages and salami-type products can be found, however.) No food products in Iran should contain pork derivatives, although Iranians eat imported foods, such as biscuits, without examining the product ingredient information. The question of forbidden food does not arise, as it is assumed that all food available in Iran since 1979 is *halal*. Seafood is not officially considered *haram*, or forbidden, although it is only along the Persian Gulf that Iranians really eat shellfish. No food contains alcohol. Game meat is available, especially in the north of Iran, and it is assumed that the hunter recited the correct Islamic formula as he killed it.

A DISTINCTIVE CULINARY TRADITION

Iranian culinary traditions are quite distinct from those of other countries in the Middle East or Asia. Many well-known dishes are unique to Iran, although Iranian cuisine also shares some common dishes with Turkey and the Arab states. Iranian meals typically consist of rice with thick meat or chicken and vegetable stews (*khoresht*), often with a sweet (*shirin*) and sour (*torsh*) combination of flavours. This is an inheritance from Zoroastrian concepts of dual forces competing to create a harmonious result.

Iranian food is never very spicy, other than possibly some southern regional dishes. Chilli is not used, and garlic is used only in northern dishes as a pickle. Most Iranians dislike spicy hot food, such as Indian cuisine, preferring sourness or the natural flavouring of the ingredients. The kebabs use little flavouring other than salt and pepper and a scattering of lemon pepper (*sumagh*); cooks rely on the quality of the meat for a distinctive flavour. Ingredients such as dried limes, lemon juice and pomegranate syrup are used to achieve the typical Iranian flavourings. Fruits, especially dried fruits, are used in many dishes to add the sweet counterbalance. Tomato puree is an ubiquitous ingredient.

Dishes often use immense quantities of fresh or dried herbs, which are eaten as vegetables rather than as simple seasonings, as in Europe and America. One dish might contain several hefty bunches of fresh herbs, such as parsley, dill, mint, coriander and fenugreek. As the herbs are usually sold as vegetables with attendant mud and stray weeds, and only wealthy households have food processors, this involves many hours of laborious washing and chopping by Iranian cooks. Common *khoreshts* include: *fesenjan* (poultry in ground walnuts and pomegranate syrup sauce); *bademjan* (fried aubergine and meat in tomato sauce); *ghimeh* (ground meat and tomatoes, garnished with fried potato chips); *aloo* (meat, prunes and spinach); *ghormeh sabsi* (meat in a sauce of several chopped herbs with dried limes and kidney or black-eyed beans).

Herbs (sabzi) are sold and bought in large quantities in Iran, as they serve as an integral part of the cooking, not just as garnishes.

Meat is nearly always lamb, or most likely mutton, from a variety of sheep which drag their fat around in their tails, thus having less body fat. Meat is not generally sold in specific cuts, but rather as slices or cubes for specific purposes, such as stews or kebab. Chops or joints are uncommon. Offal is popular, but mostly in the form of grills and, particularly, as street food.

Vegetables are rarely cooked alone, but rather in meaty combinations, with eggs or in soups. The omelettes (*kookoo*) are oven-baked and very substantial, something like Spanish tortillas. Salads are usually similar to garden salads and are served with a mayonnaise-based dressing. The most common Iranian salad is a bowl of sprigs of mixed herbs, including parsley, tarragon, chives, wild garlic and mint, served with radishes and spring onions. This can accompany meals or, with bread and cheese, be a refreshing meal or appetiser. All Iranian houses have the ingredients at all times for this combination, which is considered very healthy, and a good digestive aid. The Russian salad (called *salad olivieh*) of chicken, peas, potatoes and mayonnaise is an essential of Iranian grand entertaining. Other salads consists of yoghurt mixed with ingredients such as beet-root or spinach. Yoghurt (*mast*) is also served plain, both as an accompaniment to meals and as a snack (with bread), and Iranians are probably right to think that it both aids digestion and prevents many stomach upsets.

An ingenious variety of pickles and relishes (*torshi*) accompanies many dishes. Iranians generally make their own pickles in huge glass jars, which are frequently the cause of unpleasant incidents on flights out of Iran, as the parents of expatriate Iranians attempt to bring numerous oversized jars of pickles to their offspring abroad.

Soups

Soups are both an everyday food for the masses as well as elegant first courses for the wealthy class. In Farsi, the words for 'cook', 'cooking' and 'kitchen' are all derived from the word for 'soup'. Many idioms and proverbs derive from lore associated with soup, and it is often the chosen dish for someone who vows to make and distribute a food in return for the granting of a wish. The staple dish of Iranian manual workers, *abgoosht* (literally, 'water and meat'), is made by simmering together meat, pulses and vegetables in proportions depending on season, taste and economic status. The cooked ingredients are then removed from the pot and mashed into a paste, which is eaten with bread, whilst the broth is served separately. This dish has a certain cult following amongst many Iranians, who may visit restaurants or cafes where they serve individual dishes of *abgoosht*.

Bread

In the past, rice was a luxury food and bread (*nan*) was the staple diet (which it still is for poorer Iranians). Iranian bread is excellent and everywhere. For every few streets there will be a bakery where you can purchase fresh bread daily, often with lengthy queues in the early morning, before breakfast. No bag is provided for your purchases—Iranians can be seen with armfuls of hot, fragrant bread, possibly wrapped in newspaper, on the way home. Some of the newer housing complexes and neighbourhoods built for foreigners in Tehran do not have bakeries.

There is a variety of Iranian bread. *Lavash* is flat, floppy, thin, circular bread that keeps well in a plastic bag or in the freezer. During a meal, folded flaps of *lavash* are spread around the table; between meals, pieces may be stored inside the folded tablecloth. *Sangak* is a thicker, oval bread that is dimpled because it is baked on a bed of stones (take care for any lingering stones). *Taftun* is crispy and round, with a ribbed surface. The most admired bread is *barbari*, which is a deep, oval loaf, possibly up to two feet long, with a scored, crispy crust.

Bread is prepared early in the morning in the tanoor *(oven).*

French-style *baguettes* are probably best avoided, as they can be very disappointing. Iranians buy such breads only for the crust, discarding the doughy centre. Increasingly, this type of bread is factory-made and sold in supermarkets or shops, and it has none of the taste and texture of the wonderful traditional breads.

Bread is very cheap—just pennies per round—and a basic element of all Iranian meals. The standard breakfast is bread with feta cheese, jam, honey or butter.

The Caviar Mystery

It is possible to spend years in Iran and never taste one of its most famous food exports: caviar. The industry is a state monopoly, and the bulk of the catch is compulsorily exported to Europe and North America. Even inside Iran, caviar is phenomenally expensive (from U.S.$100 for a 100 gram tin). It is just possible that some Iranians in the northern fishing regions still eat caviar with hard boiled eggs and bread (the way Iranians are reputed to have eaten it in the past), but this is unlikely, especially when the export market is so lucrative. Caviar is sold in Iran Fisheries Stores and in chic shops in north Tehran. Personal export of caviar is forbidden, except when purchased at the airport duty-free shop. The stewards will refrigerate your purchase whilst on the plane.

Twice as Rice

In most parts of Iran—and all cities—rice is the staple food, served in prodigious quantities that often defeat the appetites of European visitors. Iranian restaurants familiar with European tastes often serve their European guests with smaller rice portions, balanced by additional vegetables. Iranians rightly consider themselves the world's greatest connoisseurs of rice, which, in Iran, is always white and long grain. In addition to producing a very superior long grain rice (*domsiah* or 'black-tailed rice'), Iranians import much of Pakistan's

157

Rice is the centre of all Iranian feasts, prepared in a huge pan called a dig.

basmati rice crop. Rice preparation involves washing, soaking, parboiling and steaming, which produces a mound of fluffy, white rice—every grain separate and perfectly cooked—and a delicious crusty layer of rice, potato or bread from the bottom of the oiled pot (*tah-dig*). The pervasive aroma fills every Iranian house, and, once cooked, the rice can be mixed or garnished with many ingredients. In its simplest form, rice is known as *chelow*; when garnished with yellow saffron rice, it becomes the basis of the national restaurant dish, *chelow kebab*, or rice with meat kebab. In the north of Iran, where most of the rice crop is grown, rice is eaten three times a day, cooked in a wetter style, like Japanese rice.

Many Iranian rice dishes, or *pollos*, contain of meat or chicken and vegetables and form a complete meal. Other rice mixtures are served with meat or fish dishes. Common *pollos* include: *sabsi pollo* (rice with fresh herbs), *baghali pollo* (rice with dill and broad beans), *addas pollo* (rice with lentils and meat), *reshteh pollo* (rice with noodles, meat, and dates), *albaloo pollo* (rice with chicken and sour cherries), *zereshk pollo* (rice with barberries and chicken), and *loobia pollo* (rice with tomatoes, green beans and ground meat).

Sweets, Puddings and Patisserie

Most streets have several fruit juice sellers, who also sell ice cream in the summer. Iranian ice cream is excellent, made with cream and flavoured with saffron, rosewater and nuts. An iced rosewater sorbet containing noodles (*faloudeh*) is extremely refreshing, as is ice cream doused with carrot juice. Italian style ices and commercial ices on sticks are also available.

Patisseries (pastry shops) generally offer only water or soft drinks—not tea or coffee—with their wares, except in European-style coffee shops, which are found in the hotels and upmarket areas of major cities. Patisserie consists of very sweet, but dainty, Iranian specialities such as *baklava* (layers of wafer pastry and nuts, soaked in rosewater syrup); *bamieh* and *zeloobia* (fried pastries in sugar syrup); an enormous variety of cookies; and French-style gateaux and pastries, usually made with synthetic cream, such as choux buns and palmiers (called *napoleans*). Few people make sweets or cakes at home. Instead, the sweet-tooth stricken prefer to eat out or purchase desserts to take away. For Iranians, sweets are generally eaten as snacks at any time—they are rarely saved for after meals like the usual convention.

Certain sweets, including a variety of rice puddings, are associated with specific religious or secular events. The most famed of these is *sholezard*, a yellow, milk-free rice pudding flavoured with saffron and rosewater and decorated with almonds and cinnamon. It is made as part of a vow, especially throughout the sacred Shi'ite month of Moharram. A type of soft fudge, *halva*, has similar associations; it is always made to mark a death, and eating it on such an occasion has a religious significance. Iranian puddings are not considered childish treats or after-meal fillers, but as delicacies in their own right.

There are a huge variety of Iranian sweets, many of which are regional specialities, and often given as gifts by people who have returned from trips to other cities. These include a type of nutty nougat (*gaz*) from Isfahan, wheels of honey-almond brittle from Qom (*sohan*), small pastry crescents filled with ground almonds (*ghotab*) from Ardakan, candyfloss (*pashmak*) and nut-brittle. European-style candy bars and chocolate are expensive and considered luxury items. The cheapest are the Turkish brands, and the European and American brands are more expensive than back home, putting them beyond the reach of most Iranian consumers. Gifts of foreign chocolate and candy are greatly appreciated. Most Iranian households have tables spread with varieties of sweets, pastries and cookies for guests to nibble on with tea. Children are rarely forbidden to eat such treats (most children have appalling dental decay), and if they are, the extent of the ban is only to leave enough sweets for guests. An iron will is required not to overindulge in Iranian households.

After most meals, Iranians eat seasonal fruits rather than desserts. These are almost always wonderful, and there are many varieties, usually served in an elaborate arrangement on platters. The host usually presses fruit upon the guest, piling his or her small plate with choice items. All guests are given a knife, a plate and (often) a fork, and most fruits are eaten peeled, although one can be sure that the fruit was washed thoroughly. The host may take the initiative and prepare the guest's fruit artistically. Seasonal fruit is cheap; out-of-season and imported fruits are extremely expensive. To be offered non-Iranian fruit, such as pineapple, is a great honour. In Iran, small cucumbers, peeled and sprinkled with salt, are eaten as fruits, especially in the hot summer.

SNACKING

In the cities, fast foods such as pizza, fried chicken, burgers and sandwiches are popular. Confusingly, burgers are usually called sandwiches. These foods vary in quality, and although many outlets may superficially resemble American chains, the food does not always faithfully represent the European or American originals. Street vendors sell liver and other offal kebabs (best avoided in the summer), broiled corn cobs dipped in salt water, and baked potatoes. Iran does not have the diversity of street foods found in some other countries.

Iranians have a passion for dried nuts, seeds (*tokhmeh*) and fruits, known collectively as *ajeel*, which are all excellent. Favourite nuts and seeds include roasted hazelnuts, almonds, chickpeas, watermelon seeds, pumpkin seeds and even such delicacies as pear seeds. Pistachios are justly famed, and are surprisingly expensive, especially for the premium varieties destined for export. Dried fruits include figs, apricots, peaches, raisins, mulberries, prunes and currents. They are sold by the kilo, individually or in mixes; they are also sold in paper twists to eat in the street or at public events. Such mixtures will be offered in all Iranian houses—especially after meals—and public transport, parks and the seating areas of sporting venues are often ankle-deep in discarded shells. Eating the seeds is a skill that foreigners must master. Iranians use one hand to direct an endless supply of pumpkin seeds at their front teeth, cracking the shell, extracting the seed and retaining the casing in one fluid movement, much like a parrot. Throughout this, the conversation flows smoothly. Most Iranians are happy to demonstrate the technique, although newcomers may have to resort to a clumsy and combined oral and manual extraction of the kernels. When offered a large bowl of the things, it is polite to serve oneself a portion onto a proffered individual plate, using the spoon provided, although in informal settings, rummaging in the shared bowl is fine. Men in particular pass many hours in conversation over *ajeel* and tea.

REGIONAL SPECIALITIES

Iran's culinary tradition is surprisingly monolithic, with most of the same dishes being available throughout the country, although the central parts of Iran (Tehran and Azerbaijan) are probably the home of the most typical dishes. Azeri cooking—that of the Iranian Turks, centred on Tabriz—is considered to be very good indeed, and from this repertoire come forth several elaborate dishes such as *kofte* (meatballs stuffed with prunes, whole eggs or other meats) and *dolmeh*, or stuffed vegetables. The north of Iran, along the Caspian Sea, offers more dishes using fish and fresh fruit than elsewhere, but these dishes are familiar, if less common throughout most of Iran. Northern cooking also makes use of garlic, a flavour abhorred by many Iranians. The southern regional cuisine, found along the Persian Gulf, is known for shellfish and for being the spiciest in Iran.

A NOTE FOR VEGETARIANS

It is difficult to follow a vegetarian diet in Iran, and, in fact, the concept is alien to most Iranians, who may be vegetarians by economic necessity, but rarely from choice. Meat is associated with wealth, hospitality and celebration— its absence with poverty and miserliness. Some educated Iranians who are concerned with their cardiovascular health rarely eat red meat, eating chicken in its place.

There are few Iranian dishes which do not involve meat, although it is possible to live on egg and yoghurt dishes, rice and bread. The word for vegetarian (*geeyah-khar*) is one borrowed from zoology, meaning ruminant, and may not evoke instant recognition in a restaurant or home. Vegetarianism will seriously curtail your social and culinary life. Only a few upmarket restaurants and cafes will cater to you, unless you eat fried eggs in roadhouses. Iranian hosts may be genuinely unable to think of a suitable dish to offer you, so be prepared to suggest a suitable meat-free dish you like. It may help to remind educated friends that Sadeq Hedayat, the celebrated author, was a lifelong vegetarian.

MEAL TIMES

Breakfast is usually eaten early, starting at 7 a.m.; few restaurants will serve breakfast after 9 a.m. Lunch usually starts at 12 p.m. and is finished by 2 p.m. Dinner is eaten any time between 6 and 8 p.m. Most restaurants close early for the night, although expensive hotels might have late night facilities. These meal times do not really represent those kept at home. Many Iranians, especially in the bazaar, or in the provinces, survive on snacks until they finish work in the early afternoon. They then go home for a large lunch. Dinner will then, especially in the summer, be eaten later. Eating habits depend greatly on location and occupation. Modern Tehrani professionals might follow European eating patterns, whereas in the provinces, or for manual workers, life might revolve around lunch.

FILLING YOUR CUP

The Demon Drink

Iran is a 'dry' country. The importation, manufacture, sale and consumption of alcohol is forbidden, unless for religiously sanctioned purposes. Curiously, the Armenian community can still manufacture cherry brandy, which is only for sale to foreign embassies. Before the 1979 revolution, upper-class Iranians routinely drank alcohol, and alcohol sales were open, although it was mainly Christian Iranians who were involved in its sale.

There is an assumption in Iran that Europeans are all alcoholics. Hosts often offer whiskey, *arak* (vodka), or dubious homemade 'hooch' to foreign guests, and it can be difficult to admit to teetotalism or an indifference to alcohol, when (amongst a certain class of people) this has come to symbolise submission to the Islamic regime. Remember that the consequences of imbibing can be serious, and Iranians also need to learn that not all foreigners are inveterate drunks. Many expatriates develop an obsession with alcohol whilst in Iran, and much expatriate lore concerns apocryphal tales of trying to buy or manufacture it. Wealthy urbanites certainly drink alcohol and offer it at parties, but widespread consumption is probably confined to a narrow social strata.

Thirst Quenchers

Fruit juices are very good in Iran, especially carrot and melon. All are made to order in the numerous juice shops and stalls, along with fresh fruit milkshakes. The commercial cartons of juice, supplied with a straw under the brand name Sandiz, are also very good. Ice-watered, salted yoghurt (*doogh*) is popular and safe in the summer; it is offered in all restaurants and often drunk at home. *Doogh* can be garnished with mint, dill or rose petals, and it is available in bottles (in carbonated and uncarbonated forms). Carbonated soft drinks are limited in variety—basically cola and orangeade, both of which are manufactured in Iran under the Parsi-Cola label, but referred to as Pepsi, Coca-Cola, 7-Up or Fanta indiscriminately. They are sold mostly in returnable glass bottles and delivered by the crate to the house. Diet sodas are not available, and all sodas are expensive by local standards. 'Islamic beer' is alcohol-free lager which tastes reasonable, and it is reputedly often used as a mixer with strong alcohol.

Tap water is safe to drink in all cities and most rural areas, and bottled water is not a familiar item. Although sparkling water is used to make a yoghurt drink, it is not sold alone, except possibly in very upmarket establishments catering to Iranians who have lived abroad. Tehran is reputed to have particularly fine tasting water, drawn from the aquifers of the Elburz Mountains. Certain cities like Qom have slightly salty water, but it is still safe (if unpalatable) to drink. In the south of Iran, where it can be very hot, ice is best avoided due to unsanitary storage conditions. Generally the cleanliness of the utensils, not the water, is likely to be problematic in Iran.

Tea: A National Institution

Tea (*chai*) is ubiquitous and really the national drink of Iran. Although Iran grows its own tea, most tea is imported from Ceylon. The clarity, colour and aroma of tea are appreciated as much as its taste, and it is always served black and in a glass. Tea is drunk through a chunk of lump sugar, held between the teeth, and very rarely sugar is added to the tea, except at breakfast or for children. Iranian tea is drunk after all meals and frequently between meals. It is extremely addictive; some Iranians may drink up to forty glasses a day! By a curious paradox, Iranian tea is warming in the winter and yet cooling in the summer. Tea is safe to drink in the meanest hovel of a teahouse, as the hot tea sterilises the glass, and there is no milk added.

Tea lubricates not only social occasions but also business transactions, and anyone embarking on business or social calls should have a strong bladder and no sensitivity to caffeine. Often one's glass will be constantly replenished; a useful manoeuvre is to lie the glass on its side on the saucer, indicating no desire for more. Tea can also be refused (after drinking the initial serving) from circulating trays, but you still may be pressed upon one. If all else fails, leaving the tea untouched will probably decisively indicate that you really have had enough.

Iranian tea is brewed with the aid of samovars (initially imported from Russia), and a constantly hot samovar is an essential item in any home, office or even shop. Strong tea in the pot is diluted to taste with the water from the samovar, which also provides the hot water to rinse the glasses. The samovar set of urn, teapot, jug, slop dish and tray (often with matching tea glass holders, sugar bowl, tray and spoons) can be lavishly decorated and are wonderful, functional souvenirs. The old-style, brass, coal-powered varieties are now rare antiques, however.

Coffee is uncommon in Iran, and the *qaweh-khaneh*, or coffee-house, is a misnomer, as they serve only tea and simple snacks. Coffee is available in some restaurants, cafes and sometimes offered in houses, especially during the winter. It is usually instant coffee, known collectively as 'Nescafe with milk'. Turkish or Arabic coffee is very rare. The teahouse (*chai-khaneh* or *qaweh-khaneh*) is an all-male preserve, and, in villages and traditional neighbourhoods, it is the centre of all social activity. Although the poetry recitals and bardic delights of old are now rare outside rural areas, the *chai-khaneh* is still the place to come to chat, smoke a hubble-bubble pipe (the tobacco is purchased from the teahouse), listen to the radio, or even watch television. Strangers will be met with curiosity, but if they behave discreetly they will probably be welcomed and even adopted as a regular. This is a good place to practice your Farsi and to hear the views of ordinary Iranians. Simple meals may be served, especially at breakfast time.

RESTAURANT OUTINGS

Although most entertaining is done in the home, restaurants are a popular outing for couples and groups of friends. Only the most sophisticated Iranians would appreciate being invited to a restaurant rather than your home. An exception to this is when a single man feels that he cannot accept any more hospitality from a family without reciprocating. Single men are not expected to entertain family groups at home, as it is assumed that they lack both the skill and the equipment.

The host—i.e., the one who suggested the outing—always pays, ignoring often dramatic protests from companions. Prolonged tussles of this sort can occur over the bill; a clever host will try to pre-empt scenes by seeking out the waiter discreetly before his or her companions can protest, presenting them with a *fait accompli*. It is common for older and wealthier friend to always pay, although this should not be taken for granted. Bills are almost never split, as this would seem mean and unfriendly. It is always assumed that there will be another opportunity to treat one's companions, even if you lose the battle to pay this time. If you meet up with friends by chance in a restaurant, a joint party is often formed, so a diner should always take extra cash to cover such eventualities.

The restaurants in the former luxury international hotels and foreign restaurants (for example, Japanese) are most expensive, and the food is not necessarily commensurate with the price. There are French restaurants in north Tehran, as well as Polynesian, Indian and Chinese. Kebab restaurants serve the national dish of *chelo kebab*. An old-established restaurant in the Safavid Bazaar, opposite the Mellat Park, serves supposedly traditional Iranian food, with booths of rug-covered platforms where food is served on the floor in the traditional style.

Restaurant appearances can be deceptive, and indifferent decor can conceal very good food; conversely fancy decor might just be a facade. Traditionally, restaurants were not places to linger, and, although this was changing in the 1970s, the current requirements of behaving decorously in public and conforming to *hejab* make eating out generally less fun than eating in. In traditional neighbourhoods, as well as in some provincial cities, restaurants are segregated into areas for single men and areas for women and families (usually upstairs, or away from the windows). Although men may eat with their women-folk in such places, they should avoid looking around them too much.

Mixed cafes exist in certain neighbourhoods and in parks. Foreign women may be able to enter a traditional teahouse, but no Iranian women would. Terraced tea gardens in the northern suburbs of Tehran are lovely places in the summer, with running streams, trees and carpet covered platforms and cushions on which to relax. Local advice should be sought by women who wish to visit such places without men, as the atmosphere varies between such establishments, and some are known to function as illicit pick-up places.

EATING AT HOME

Food preparation in Iran is more arduous than in Europe, although modern supermarkets are now offering ready-to-serve items. Iranians eat with a spoon and fork, and, as meat is always well-cooked, a knife is unnecessary. As a foreign guest, you may be offered a knife to make you feel comfortable. Communal dishes and eating with the fingers are rare, other than bread and dips. Although many Iranians, especially the middle classes and the wealthy, eat at elaborate tables, traditionally, food is served on a cloth (*sofreh*) laid on the floor. Unless visiting a very traditional family, you will probably not be invited to eat on the floor, unless you are very intimate with the hosts. Sitting cross-legged around the cloth takes practice, lounging around or spreading out one's legs is not really acceptable, although Iranians will probably understand if you find it difficult at first.

Guests will be urged to eat more, and often served extra helpings by force. It can be difficult to refuse, and a hearty appetite is a compliment to the cook. A small portion left on the plate shows that you really are full. Compliments on the food are appreciated, although the cook will modestly demur and strenuously apologise for the

An Iranian family finishes dinner at home. For the average Westerner, eating on the floor isn't as easy as it looks.

inadequacies of the food and hospitality. Before and after dinner, tea will be served unless you decline by covering your glass and refusing politely. Save space for the fruit, which will be pressed upon you. Dried fruits and nuts will finish the meal. Although a first course, such as soup, may be served, most Iranian meals are served with all dishes set on the table at once. If tea is brought late in the evening, after a long absence, this may be a sign that you should be ready to leave. Guests never enter the kitchen or help with clearing up, although you can certainly offer on an informal occasion with close friends.

FOOD AND HEALTH

Iranians are generally quite health-obsessed, and this is reflected in their attitudes to food. Certain foods, such as yoghurt, are considered healthy, and eaten regularly. Additionally, there remains from the once dominant ancient Greek humeral system of medicine, a pervasive belief that all foods are 'hot' or 'cold', that people have either hot or cold temperaments, and that certain illnesses have hot or cold properties. Thus, certain combinations of foods are advised, for good health, equable temperament and during an illness. Certain combinations of food are unhealthy, particularly when very hot foods are combined with very cold foods, such as fish and yoghurt, or tea and watermelon. Although few young people follow such strictures in detail, older people will often feel free to comment on your diet, and to suggest changes. At times of illness, or for example after childbirth, certain foods will be taken for medicinal purposes. The many herbs and spices in Iranian cooking are considered to be part of a sophisticated system of health preservation, as well as for flavouring.

Chapter Eight

A TIME TO CELEBRATE, A TIME TO MOURN

Into this universe, and why not knowing, Nor whence like water willy-nilly flowing,

And out of it, as wind along the waste, I know not whither, willy-nilly blowing.

—Omar Khayyam, *The Rubaiyat*

RITUALS OF BIRTH

In the cities, most babies are born in hospitals; in villages, women are usually attended only by traditional midwives. Traditional Iranian rituals surrounding childbirth have been largely supplanted by a medical model in which women often acquiesce to having planned Caesarean deliveries—considered safer and more lucrative by doctors, and more dignified and prestigious by most educated, younger women.

One tradition that has not died out is the collective effort by the family of a new mother to ensure that the baby not be left alone for the first forty days of its life. This stems from the old belief that a *jinn*, or spirit, named *Aal* steals unattended babies and replaces them with changelings. New mothers are usually well supported (and cosseted) by relatives and neighbours, who take care of all the maternal household duties. A woman who has no mother or sisters will be meet with much pity as well as sympathy.

Men are not expected to play a big part in the care of small children, nor are they likely to visit new arrivals unless accompanying their female relatives. Close relatives, friends and female acquaintances should visit the new baby within the first forty days. Remember that any admiring comments pertaining to the baby should be prefaced or at least suffixed by the exclamation, '*Mashallah!*' ('Thanks be to God!') Traditionally, this would deflect the evil eye that would otherwise be attracted by boastful comments. Even non-traditional families tend to be wary of openly admiring anything as precious as a new baby without invoking this deprecatory remark.

Baby gifts of clothes or nursery items are becoming common, although a small piece of gold jewellery is more traditional. For boys, this is usually a *plaak* (pendant or medallion); for girls, items such as earrings, rings, chains or *plaaks* are all acceptable. Any jeweller will stock an appropriate selection. These items are often worn from early infancy, and medallions with blue stones or religious connotations are usually pinned to the child's clothing to ward

171

off the evil eye. Alternatively, a guest may leave a gift of money under the child's pillow.

Circumcision

This is not the big event in Iran that it is in other Islamic countries. It is rare to hold a party, but if invited, the guest should bring a small gift of jewellery or money for the child. Circumcision for boys is universal and can take place either in the hospital just after birth or in the first few years of life. It is usually performed by doctors, except possibly in villages and amongst the families of the clergy.

RITUALS OF DEATH

Most Iranians would prefer to die at home, surrounded by their families, as in life. If someone is terminally ill, all efforts are made to reunite the family before the death. Few Iranians await the death of a loved one stoically, and grief is almost always a public and impassioned display. This may reach its apogee immediately after the death, when, especially if the death is particularly tragic (for example, that of a young person), the mourners may become hysterical and injure themselves in their frenzy of grief.

If an outsider finds him or herself involved in such a situation, this can be very frightening. The mourners may be impervious to pleas for restraint and may scream and shout, tearing at their hair, clothes and faces, drawing blood. This behaviour can occur in large sectors of the population when a religious figure dies, and the visitor to Iran is advised to avoid public places immediately following the death of a well-known religious figure, or on the declared days of mourning.

Children are usually excluded from the grieving process; often, they are taken away to a kind neighbour's house until after the funeral. As the majority of Iranians are Muslims, I will describe the events following the death of a Muslim.

172

The Funeral

The body of a deceased Muslim is immediately taken to the cemetery of the local mosque, where it is are prepared by undertakers, possibly with the help of same-sex relatives of the deceased. After being washed and shrouded according to Islamic rite, the body is buried within twenty-four hours of death. Muslims are never buried in a coffin, although they are carried in one to the burial site. Men dominate the proceedings—only close female relatives attend, and they must follow the procession separately. If passed by a funeral cortege in the street, passers-by should stop, bow their heads and recite the *fatihah*, the Islamic prayer for the dead (a general muttering will do, if you don't know the words). If the death was unexpected and the deceased lived far from his or her family, it is possible that the family will be unable to attend the funeral. Thus the events following a funeral are often the real focus of mourning.

The Memorial Service

A gathering known as the Majlis-e Khatm (Meeting of Mourning) will be held on the first, and probably the second and third, night after the funeral. It may be held at a set time, say from 8 to 10 p.m. Notices of such gatherings are often posted in neighbourhoods and in apartment buildings. For important people, the *majlis* may be advertised in newspapers; it may also be delayed so as to accommodate the vast number of mourners. If the person had a wide social circle, the gathering will be held in a mosque or other public place. One should call the house of the deceased to enquire about the arrangements of the *majlis*, as it is unlikely that invitations will be issued. Everyone who knew the deceased is expected to attend, however briefly.

On arrival at the Majlis-e Khatm, one is greeted at the door by a receiving line of (usually) the family's male relatives, with whom one commiserates. One is then shown to a reception room, which is almost always sex-segregated. If the guests are seated around the periphery

173

of a room, as in a private house, they will rise to greet each new arrival, and usually all will recite the prayer for the dead with the newcomer. Upon being seated, it is customary to enquire from one's neighbour about the circumstances of the death, or the situation of the bereaved ones. Conversation may continue about other topics, but always on a sober note. Tea is served with *halva* (a fudge made from wheat flour, oil, sugar, rosewater and saffron), which is cooked and eaten as a kind of offering for the departed one's soul. A useful expression is, '*Inshallah ravan-esh shaad bashaad*,' which means, 'God willing, may his/her soul rest in peace.' If the *majlis* is in a public place, there will be speeches and a Koranic recital, and at the clear end of the event everyone leaves. In a private home, however, you must decide when to leave. If unaccompanied, and feeling rather conspicuous, ten to fifteen minutes should be long enough. On taking leave of one's neighbours, it is necessary again to offer condolences to the hosts and leave. Sympathy cards are only really sent over long distances, and flowers are taken to the grave.

The Mourning Rituals

It is important to know about the etiquette surrounding mourning, as it pervades so much of Iranian culture. Typically, the mourners wear black clothes and do not wash, shave, or wear scents or cosmetics. They do not eat sweet foods, take sugar in their tea, or indulge in any 'frivolous' activities, such as watching television, listening to the radio, or reading (unless it is of the Koran). Bystanders should not undertake any of these activities within earshot or sight of mourners without permission. Women always wear black when attending a *majlis*; the same routine usually applies when visiting a family in mourning. Men wear sober clothes. Although many bereaved people ignore some of these restrictions, they do conform externally to the image of a mourner. The wearing of black clothes, or being unshaven, acts as a useful marker of a bereaved person, so that others can commiserate and behave tactfully. Many events are cancelled or postponed due to clashes with periods of mourning. For example, someone may be unable to hold a wedding party as a result of a series of deaths in the extended family. Iranians respect grief after death, and this sentiment might be considered much healthier (and kinder) than one that represses and refuses to acknowledge grief in times of sorrow. Mourning is everybody's business in Iranian life, and it is considered shocking not to offer condolences even if the acquaintance is slight.

Forty Days and Nights

Although mourning continues for a minimum of forty days, men will probably shave after a few days, and efforts at personal hygiene are rarely looked at askance. On the fortieth day or night after the death, the *chele-ee* (fortieth) will be held, which follows the same pattern as the Majlis-e Khatm, only, hopefully, there is less of the raw grief in evidence. Up until the *chele-ee*, the family and close friends of the deceased will visit the grave regularly; after the *chele-ee*, visits become less frequent, and the activities of daily living are gradually resumed. Bereaved women will continue to wear black for some time. In the case of a widow or a mother or daughter of the deceased, a year of unrelieved black attire is not uncommon. (During this time, invitations to parties or weddings are not accepted and no festivities take place within the family.) On the next *eid* (holiday) following the *chele-ee*, or possibly on the *eid* nearest to the first year anniversary of the death, a close friend or relative will give the woman a gift of a coloured item of clothing to signal the end of her mourning weeds. Some Iranian women, especially widows, will continue to wear black for the rest of their lives. It is the role of others to acknowledge the grief of a mourner yet also to tactfully steer the bereaved towards a return to 'normal' behaviour after an appropriate time period.

Anniversary of a Death

On the year anniversary of a death, there may be another gathering known as a *saal-ee*. If someone close to you suffers a loss, it is a good idea to note the dates in your diary, as your remembering this date will be very much appreciated. Mourning may erupt again on this day, but with much less intensity. The first holiday period without the deceased is a particularly poignant occasion.

MARRIAGE: THE FIRST HURDLE

For an Iranian, opportunities for meeting the ideal soul mate are limited. If you have a yen for your neighbour, cousin, or the best friend of your brother or sister, and the feeling is reciprocated (and the potential in-laws get on you), then you are lucky. In the years prior to the 1979 revolution, only very conservative religious families, peasants and social misfits arranged marriages between complete strangers. Nowadays educational and social facilities are all sex-segregated, which makes it difficult for potential couples to find each other. Men and women cannot sit next to each other in university classes or libraries. It is impossible to socialise in mixed groups, and it's actually dangerous to be caught in a potentially compromising situation with a person of the opposite sex.

Although stories abound of opportunities for illicit sex, the question on the minds of most Iranians over the age of twenty is how to find a marriage partner. Iranian men, and certainly some women, usually divide their active love lives into two distinct eras: premarital and post-marital. It is accepted in large sections of Iranian society that unmarried men have sexual needs which can be satisfied either by other men ('passive' homosexuals are seen as perverted and are thus despised), prostitutes or 'loose' women, usually typecast as divorcees. A great many men, despite boasts to the contrary, are undoubtedly chaste, if only due to lack of sexual opportunities. In elite sections of society it is more acceptable for women not to be virgins when they marry, but the word for 'girl' or 'unmarried woman' also means 'virgin' (*dokhtar*), whereas the word for 'wife' and 'woman' are the same (*zan*). There is no equivalent for men; the terms for 'boy' (*pesar*) and 'man' (*mard*) are used in relation to age, and 'husband' (*shohar*) is entirely another word.

Marriage is the ultimate condition for everyone. The single life is not chosen; moreover, it is considered a curse, as is childlessness. Anyone who is single in Iran is subjected to much banter and serious matchmaking suggestions. For men, the decision to marry is usually related to financial solvency; for women, it is related to age and completion of education. Apart from physical appearance, requirements for marriage usually focus on material matters such as occupation, income and education or family background. The economic hardships endured in Iran in recent years have given added kudos to a match that entails living abroad. For men, the profession of a doctor or engineer has always been top of the marriage stakes. For women, a good disposition, beauty and the 'appropriate' level of education are big attractions.

Of course, in this society, men are expected to seek a partner, not the other way around. All a woman can do is to indicate her availability to her family and close friends, hoping that either one of them will be approached by or on behalf of a suitor, or that they will approach a suitable man, probably indirectly. Approaches to men are usually very oblique, and third and even fourth parties are almost always involved in marriage negotiations, as they can help to save face if things don't progress smoothly.

Courtship and Engagement

An approach is usually made to a close relative or friend, enquiring whether there is any reason that someone has not married or if they wish to marry soon. (Engagements rapidly follow agreements and are almost always short in duration.) Further enquiries will be made about the person, their family and their background. Usually photographs will be sought after, unless the subject has been sighted at a wedding or other occasion. If the man likes what he knows and sees so far, a meeting will be arranged. Ideally this will be an occasion ostensibly with another purpose, as this is less embarrassing. For example, a mutual friend may invite both families to a wedding or dinner and introduce them; or, a sibling may invite their friend around for a family meal. This will be followed in any case (hopefully) by a more formal meeting. The man, or his third party or his parents will call upon the girl's family one evening or afternoon. The man's family may bluntly state that they wish to consider her as a bride, in which case the suitor (*khastgar*) will be coming for *khastgaree*. Remember, the vast majority of unmarried people live with their parents. If the girl's family agrees to the visit, they are in principle open to the idea of a match. These are deeply embarrassing occasions for all concerned, especially the young couple, unless they have already agreed to marry, in which case the *khastgaree* is a mere formality. Traditionally, the girl should be very subdued, show coy behaviour (*naz*) and should serve tea and display her domestic or other abilities. Her parents usually indulge in an orgy of boasting about their offspring and enumerate the many other marital possibilities that exist for their daughter.

The negotiations may end there if the prospective in-laws don't appeal to the other family, if there is an obvious wealth or social disparity between the families, or if there's no attraction between the *khastgar* and the *dokhtar*. Alternatively, a sort of date may follow where the couple goes out for a walk or a meal. In less sophisticated families, this stage will not be possible, and, amongst wealthy Tehranis, this dating can go on for some time. Due in part to the difficulties entailed in dating, and also the prevailing moral codes, the couple will usually decide to become engaged. This will be requested in a formal *khastgaree*. The engagement (*namzadee*) may be celebrated by a party, but more often the close family will gather to eat sweets and cake, and the couple exchange and receive gifts of jewellery. Engagements can be broken, but this probably will have a detrimental effect on the woman's future marital prospects. Men who become engaged more than a couple of times are also considered bad prospects. The affianced are known as each other's *namzad* (fiance/fiancee).

Once engaged, unless from a very conservative family, the couple can spend more time together. The engagement may even take the form of the official Islamic wedding ceremony, so that the marriage is entered onto their identity cards and they can go anywhere alone together. The wedding ceremony may in any case take place some time before the official wedding party, i.e., the public display of the marriage, without which the couple is not considered to be really married. The ceremony can be held with a proxy bride or groom if one of them is abroad; there may then be a series of parties held in both countries.

The Wedding

The marriage ceremony (*akht*) may be very private, or it may precede a big reception (*aroosee*) held in an adjoining room. It is most often held at the groom's house, in the afternoon preceding the reception. The morning will be spent at the barber shop or at the beauty parlour, where the groom (*damad*) will collect the bride (*aroos*) with a gift of flowers in hand. They will be driven in a car beautifully decorated with elaborate flower arrangements and ribbons. A great deal of horn-honking, headlight flashing and noise accompany the cortege of decorated cars, and the *aroos* is the subject of much public scrutiny. This is just about the only time an unveiled woman can be seen in public, and her appearance is much commented on.

The marriage ceremony consists of the traditional Zoroastrian ceremony, overlaid by the Islamic, Christian or Jewish religious rites. The couple sit before a *sofreh* (cloth), richly decorated and spread with several essential items, including: lit candelabras and a mirror, which are gifts from the groom to the bride and may be silver or gold;

a dish of honey for a sweet life; a needle and thread to symbolise industry and the sewing shut of the mouths of interfering in-laws; bread and cheese for sustenance; sweets for a happy life; eggs for fertility; fresh flowers; and rose water and sugar cones for use in the ceremony. The couple will hold a copy of the Koran. Throughout the ceremony, female friends and relatives hold a white silk cloth over the bride and groom, over which they grind the two sugar cones together, eventually tipping the sugar into the bride's hair. They chant rhymes and place some stitches in the cloth, which is then kept for the bride. The religious figure of the ceremony asks if the bride is willing to marry the groom for an agreed *mahr*, a sum of money to be paid to the bride in the event of a separation. (The *mahr* is now most often a token gold coin, but may be the subject of protracted premarital negotiations.) The bride will not answer until the third repetition, lest she look too eager; her attendants will say that she has gone to the garden and so on. The bride may cry, maybe genuinely, as she will be leaving her family. The couple will feed each other with honey and sweets as they are announced husband and wife. They sign the very decorative marriage contract together, having specified any conditions on the marriage in writing. Rings will be exchanged if they haven't been already. Prenuptial agreements have an ancient pedigree in Iran. All of the ceremony is reflected in the large mirror at the back of the *sofreh*, so the guests behind can see everything and the couple can see each other without eye contact. The guests will pass their gifts to an attendant, who will announce their provenance and drape the bride with the items of jewellery, the most usual wedding gift.

Wedding receptions tend to be big affairs, and there is always room for more guests, so you may be invited at short notice, even by third parties. Such invitations are almost always very genuine, as a well-attended wedding is a good omen for a happy married life. If you find yourself meeting the bride and groom for the first time at their wedding, this is neither unusual nor undesirable. They will be happy to welcome the guest of a guest. Everyone knows that few Iranians

An Iranian bride and groom seated before the sofreh-ye akht, *whilst a happily married woman grinds loaf sugar onto a cloth over the couple's heads.*

181

would decline to meet a friend due to a prior engagement—rather they will invite the friend or friends to accompany them. As Iranians are proud of their lovely weddings, they are likely to invite foreign acquaintances anyway. Dress is formal, meaning your newest, most stylish outfit, and take time out to visit your hairdresser or barber; women usually wear heavy make-up for the occasion.

Very big weddings will be held in public places such as hotels or function gardens, but as there is the risk that sex-segregation will be enforced or music and dancing prohibited, a private residence is preferred. Of course there are traditionalists who prefer a segregated state of affairs. It is appropriate, if you are part of a couple, to ask of your hosts what form the celebration will take. Few Iranians can countenance a wedding without music and dancing, and you will be expected to demonstrate your abilities in that department. It is very usual for groups of friends to practice their dancing together before-hand. Even very sedate matrons will dance, often displaying a hidden elegance and skill. A lively wedding reception is a memorable event in Iran: they are noisy, rumbunctious occasions where singles hope to sight a future partner. Double entendres may abound in conversation, and, if the social circle is one where alcohol is imbibed, there may be some quite louche stories to be heard.

The bride and groom rarely appear to enjoy themselves at their own wedding. They usually sit on a platform throughout the party, preserving their decorum and dancing only when pressured to do so. The bride may appear downcast, as this is a form of *naz* in that she should not look too eager to be married.

Photography—especially video filming—are rife at weddings, and the bride, groom and guests will be asked to replay key moments, pose unnaturally many times and to be willing to be filmed at all times throughout the reception. The videotape, once edited and jazzed up with childhood photos, music and special effects, will be replayed for many years and distributed widely.

All couples aspire to offer a full, hot meal to all the guests at the wedding reception—ideally as a seated serving, or possibly in the form of a buffet. Fruit, pastries or ice-cream will also be served, as will cold drinks, and possibly tea. Small bags of *nogle* (candied slivers of almond) are given as favours to the guests. Sometimes, economic constraints may mean that the reception is given after a private dinner; make sure to check your invitation to find out what exactly you've been invited to attend.

Guests at the reception who were not at the ceremony should approach the bride and groom with their present. If it is jewellery, then an attendant will open it for the bride to wear; otherwise, the present will usually be opened in private. Thank you letters are not very common, so, if you don't receive one, don't feel slighted or that your gift was not appreciated.

The departure of the bride and groom for their honeymoon or wedding night destination is an occasion for much merriment. The couple will leave the reception driving a decorated car, which will then be followed by a convoy of horn-honking, headlight-flashing cars. The couple will then attempt to escape their pursuers. This usually happens in the early hours of the morning, and everyone will know the cause of the disturbance. Even if the couple is returning to the groom's home, the site of the reception, the chase will usually take place. Only in very conservative or rural families does the evidence of the bride's virginity play any role in the proceedings.

A New Life Begins

In the weeks following the wedding, all families present at the wedding are expected to invite the couple for a meal, expressing their wishes for a happy life together. The bride (*aroos*) will always be an *aroos* to her in-laws, including their extended family, and she may be called affectionately by that title for the first months or even years of marriage. The man will always be referred to as a 'groom' (*damad*) by his in-laws, but this is less used as a term of endearment than *aroos*.

Remember, a wife is never her husband's *aroos* (she is his *zan*), and a husband is never his wife's *damad* (he is her *shohar*).

Within a year, if the couple are not in possession of, or expecting a child, most people will be openly asking why not. This can be a fraught year for those couples who either fear infertility or who wish to postpone this stage of their lives. Thick skins are an asset.

Polygamy

Polygamous marriages are not very common in Iran. They occur mostly in religious, conservative families and in rural areas. They may also occur when a brother dies, leaving behind a widow with children. Were she to marry outside the family she would lose custody of her children to them. Infertile first wives may prefer to accept a co-wife role than be divorced. In rural areas, there may be too much work on a farm for one woman, and polygamy may be a mark of wealth and social prestige. The first wife is always of elevated status. Second or more weddings are not usually occasions for much celebrating, and few people really approve of such behaviour. You may find men who are polygamously married to their one-time mistresses out of fear of the Islamic morality laws. Co-wives will only be likely to live together in villages. If it becomes apparent that an acquaintance has an unorthodox marital life, avoid intrusive questioning and appear nonchalant when the details are revealed.

THE ZOROASTRIAN LEGACY OF FESTIVALS

Now Ruz (New Day)

Despite initial attempts by the Islamic regime to stamp out Iran's ancient Zoroastrian feasts, at least one of them, Now Ruz ('New Day'), remains the principle holiday in Iran. Certain traditions have been discouraged or even abandoned, yet they survive in images or stories. The New Year commences as the astral year ends at the vernal equinox, one of the only two times during the year that the day and night are of equal length. This is always on or within a day of March 21, the first day of spring, and it's a logical time to for a country of farmers to celebrate a new year and new life. On the Islamic solar calendar used by Iran, Now Ruz falls on the day Farvardin 1.

Many legends explain the first celebration of Now Ruz, which is celebrated by all Zoroastrians, Iranians, Afghanis and Kurds, with fairly similar customs. It is only Iranians, however who celebrate with such a wealth of fixed ritual.

Preparations begin weeks before Now Ruz, with annual spring cleaning and renovations, and the purchase or manufacture of new clothes for all members of the family. Lentil or wheat seeds are germinated on a damp cloth to provide a sign of nature's renewal. Sweets and pastries are prepared. Friendships are renewed and animosities forgotten. The occasion provides a valuable opportunity to repair relationships, often with the help of a mediator who will appeal to the parties' seasonal goodwill. All financial affairs should be concluded before the holiday and not left unresolved for the next year. This is a good time to exchange house contracts or to finalise a slow business deal.

Holiday destinations are heavily booked around Now Ruz, as many people travel to spend the holiday with relatives or at a resort. Travel plans need advance planning and booking. Remember that there is no transport on the day of Now Ruz, and only reduced services run in the following weeks. Only the most essential services operate on Now Ruz, and many businesses close for the entire thirteen-day celebration. All schools and universities close for at least three weeks. The first four days of the month and the thirteenth day are all public holidays.

On the eve of the last Wednesday of the year (Shab-e-Chahar Shanbeh Souri, or literally, 'The Eve of Red Wednesday'), bonfires are lit and people jump over the flames, shouting, '*Sorkhie to az man o zardie man be to!*' ('Give me your red colour, take away my sickly pallor!') Fireworks are also set off. Many people aim to stay awake all night, as this is traditionally an inauspicious night when evil spirits abound, paralleling Halloween (which in Celtic culture was once celebrated with almost identical traditions). Children dressed in shrouds may go trick or treating—without the tricks but with a lot of banging of pots and pans in some neighbourhoods. This night may of course fall up to a week before Now Ruz itself. Since 1979, celebration of this night has been particularly discouraged, but has recently seen a revival.

In the streets, clowns with blackened faces, known as Haji Firouz, may cavort with tambourines, heralding the new year and taking advantage of seasonal generosity. The time of the vernal equinox (*tahvil*), is announced frequently on the radio and television and also written in the newspapers. This exact minute when the New Year begins, may be in the middle of the night, but traditional families wish to be awake in order to observe the ceremony.

As in Christmas in Europe and the United States, commercialization takes over the Now Ruz holiday season. Shops and stalls selling the ceremonial necessities abound, often at exorbitant prices. The tradition of adults giving a new coin (nowadays a bank note, or *aidee*) to the children of the houses they visit over Now Ruz has been supplanted by a gift-giving orgy in more sophisticated homes. Holiday special offers in shops are common and the necessary new clothes are more expensive than usual. Greeting cards, except for those friends and relatives living abroad, are a fairly new concept, and not as widely sent as our Christmas cards. Nevertheless, corporate versions exist and an array of traditional and modern designs are available for personal use.

This is the time when employees expect bonuses and cash gifts. Anyone who has performed a service for you throughout the last year expects a tip. This should be in the form of a new bank note, or a gold coin if the person is exceptionally deserving of reward. The acceptable amount increases annually and is usually ascertained by enquiries to similarly placed persons about the size of their intended *aidee* gift. Although *aidee* are given out on other holidays as well, the tradition is most commonly observed on Now Ruz. There is usually a run on the banks for new bank notes, so try to stock up in advance, as you will need a supply for when you go visiting families over the holiday, or if any families with children visit you.

The Sofreh: Centrepiece of Now Ruz

As on most Iranian ceremonial occasions, during Now Ruz, a cloth (*sofreh*) is spread out on the floor (or maybe on a table) and decorated with certain items. For the New Year, *haft sin*, or seven items, are laid out on the *sofreh*, and the Farsi name of each one begins with the letter *sin*, or 's'. These items are *sabzeh* (sprouted seeds), *sib* (apple), *sonbol* (hyacinth), *sir* (garlic), *senjed* (the jujube fruit), *somagh* (lemon pepper), and *sekan* (vinegar). Seven is an ancient auspicious number, and represents the seven good angels. Additionally, the sofreh displays the following things: a bowl of painted eggs (for fertility), a goldfish in a bowl of water (Pisces), a bitter orange floating in water (the cosmos), coins (prosperity), lighted candles (fire), a mirror to reflect the candlelight, the holy book of the family's religious faith, possibly a book of the poetry by Hafiz, and sweets or other sweet/scented objects. Photographs of absent loved ones may also be displayed. The *sofreh* is lighted on the New Year's Eve, traditionally to guide ancestral spirits who may see their children's prosperity and happiness.

On Now Ruz, the family will bathe, wear clean clothes and sit at the *sofreh*, awaiting the transition to a new year. Once this moment has passed, family members congratulate each other, and the parents give presents or gifts of money to the children. To be holding a gold coin is considered auspicious. Then begins a round of visits to family, friends and neighbours, where vast quantities of sweets and pastries will be consumed. There is a pecking order to visits; children should first visit their parents, and less socially important people should pay the first visit to their superiors. If distance is a problem, then seasonal greetings by telephone follow the same protocol.

Undoubtedly you, as a foreigner, will be invited to many houses for *chai o shirini* (tea and pastries) or for the big Now Ruz meal. You should have plenty of time to visit all of your acquaintances over the first two days of the new year, unless you plan to holiday away. Declining all except one (or two, if you have an iron stomach and can eat a lavish lunch and an almost identical dinner) of the meal invitations will need all of your tact and ability to flatter. Of course you would *love* to come, much more than you wish to dine at the competing host's house, but unfortunately you promised him or her (in a moment of weakness), and now you can't back out, as the household may not have any other guests, etc. However, assure your erstwhile host that as soon as you can decently escape you'll dash round for *chai o shirini.*

The meal is usually the same, although in some regions the host will serve whatever the local dishes are. The first dish served is *ash reshteh* (noodle, bean and green herb soup); unravelling the noodles is symbolic of unravelling life's difficulties. Then there will be *sabzi pollo ba mahi* (green herb rice with fish), *kookoo sabzi* (green herb omelette) and perhaps *reshteh pollo* (rice with noodles). The menu is, of course, heavily redolent with the symbolism of astrology, spring and new beginnings.

In addition to all your usual good behaviour, you should not forget to praise the beauty of the *sofreh* and take pains to look as if you are learning something new when the significance of the elements are explained. It *is*, of course, the most artistic and, in a more sophisticated household, the most novel, *sofreh* you have ever seen. As at most social gatherings, you may be expected to pose for photographs—this time, with the *sofreh.* The annual Now Ruz family photograph is a major institution. You may be treated to a recital of poetry or a musical recital. Don't forget the *aidee* for the children. You can hand it in person or leave it on the *sofreh.* The usual offering of pastries or flowers for your hosts is also in order. If you feel very close, or, if you are eating at the hosts' home, you may bring presents for the children.

This is one occasion where pleading that you must now call on someone else will be acceptable. Although as a foreigner you are in an ambiguous position in any social hierarchy, you should try to at least telephone as many appropriate people as possible to wish them a happy New Year over the following few days. The expression *sel-e now-etan mobarak* ('wishes for success, happiness and prosperity') can be offered. Now Ruz is one of the few times that wishes for successful ventures can be offered without worrying about that wrathful evil eye.

Sizdar Bidar (The Thirteenth Outdoors)

The twelve days following Now Ruz are like an extended St. Stephen's or Boxing Day. The festivities are now over and there's nothing to do but eat too many sweets, visit the houses of those who didn't rank high enough for the first day's round, and watch the accessories on the *sofreh* wither up. But on the thirteenth day, *sizdar bidar* ('the thirteenth outdoors'), everyone finally deserts his house for a picnic in the open air. The overgrown green sprouts are taken too, and once they are tied in a knot they are cast away, ideally into running water. This task is often performed by unmarried girls who recite a rhyme hoping for a husband and a baby in their arms by this time next year. Obviously, both parts of this spell are supposed to work quickly! It may be necessary to rise early to secure a spot to sit, and umbrellas and blankets may be needed. If you live in an area close to a park or in a small town, you will be able to 'table-hop' all day. Otherwise, you will probably be forced to commit yourself to one or two invitations. Remember that it may be difficult to find your hosts if you don't arrive with them.

Shab-e Yalda (Rebirth Night)

The winter solstice, occurring on December 21 or 22, is the longest night of the year. Within the Zoroastrian cosmology of a constant battle of light and good versus the forces of darkness and evil, the winter solstice is a very unlucky and inauspicious night. Traditionally, in order to protect themselves, the people stayed awake to keep their hearths afire all night until morning. Although few people now remain awake all night on *Shab-e Yalda* ('Rebirth Night'), they often light candles, gather around the fire and talk (reciting poetry and stories) until late. They will eat *ajeel* and fresh fruit. In the past, and possibly now in rural areas, summer fruit was hoarded for this night, after which there would be no fresh fruit until late spring. You may be invited to a late gathering, a traditional recital or a party with music and dancing, depending on your social circle.

ISLAMIC HOLIDAYS

As the Arab-Islamic calendar is a lunar one, the dates of Islamic holidays change each year on the Gregorian calendar, moving backwards by about eleven days per calendar year. Thus, Islamic holidays may clash with Iranian civil or traditional (non-Islamic) festivals. This may cause friction when the 'serious' Muslim holidays clash with the joyous pre-Islamic Era holidays. Yet they are all national holidays. The following holidays are shared with all Muslim countries; dates are indicated according to the month and day of the Islamic calendar year.

Ramazan

Ramazan (Ramadan) is the ninth month of the Islamic calendar. Although many Iranians don't observe the complete abstention from food, drink, tobacco and sexual relations from sunrise to sundown during Ramazan (as the Koran recommends all Muslims should), most Muslim Iranians will fast for at least part of it. The fast is imposed on all residents and visitors to Iran, although what you do behind the closed doors of your house is your business. A few restaurants may open to serve travellers, who are exempted from fasting, but they are often screened off from the street; some towns may close all restaurants that are not located inside hotels. Ramazan is not a good time to travel, as even drinking water in public may be considered inappropriate, unless the person is obviously infirm. Others exempted from the fast (in addition to travellers) include pregnant, nursing and menstruating women; anyone unwell or taking medication; and the elderly. Those exempt are expected to make up the missed days later, and not to flaunt their status during Ramazan.

Many people enjoy this time of the year, as the rigours of fasting are compensated for by nightly feasting, family gatherings and late nights. Fasting Muslims eat two meals each day: one in the evening, just after sunset, and one early in the morning, just before sunrise. In some areas, the eating times are announced by drums in the streets. Although little work gets done in Iran during Ramazan, those people who are forced to work find it a trying time, especially when Ramazan falls in the summer, in which case local tempers may be short. Other infringements of Islamic laws, such as possessing alcohol or (especially) being caught in a compromising situation with a person of the opposite sex, are dealt with harshly at this time. Pasdaran are more likely to be on the lookout for such behaviour. Many people, especially foreigners, leave Iran during Ramazan.

Eid-e Fetr (Festival of the Breaking of the Fast)

Lasting the first three days of the month of Shavval, Eid-e Fetr ('Festival of the Breaking of the Fast'), is a joyous celebration that marks the end of the month-long fast of Ramazan. Although the holiday is fixed in advance for many practising Muslims (and officially all Muslims in Iran), the sunset at which the Eid begins isn't known until that very night, when the new moon is officially sighted by the town clerics. As many Muslims like to give alms at this time, there may be an increase in beggar activity. Remember, to be penniless at this time is akin to someone not being able to afford a Christmas lunch. Children will expect *aidee* from adult visitors, and it is customary to greet people with the phrase *eid-et mobarak* ('happy festival') and to enquire afterwards if they enjoyed their holiday.

Milad-e Hazrat-e Mohammad (Birth of the Prophet)

Milad-e Hazrat-e Mohammad, occurring on Rabi ol-Avval 17, is the birthday of the Prophet Mohammad. No real celebration, more a day of contemplation for the religious.

Eid-e Ghorban (Feast of the Sacrifice)

Eid-e Ghorban, the 'Feast of the Sacrifice', falls on Zi-Hajeh 10. This marks the end of the *haj* (pilgrimage to Mecca) and commemorates the willingness of Ibrahim (Abraham) to sacrifice his son. The Islamic version of events differs from the Old Testament in that Ismail was the proposed sacrifice, not Isaac. As with other doctrinal points, you are advised in any discussion to accept graciously that the Koran recorded the true version of events, despite any personal beliefs you may hold. The feast is celebrated by the sacrifice (*ghorban*) of an animal, ideally a sheep, and its distribution amongst the needy. The streets may well be full of live sheep in the days prior to the feast, and littered with blood, gore and sheepskins for a day or so afterwards. This is not a good holiday for those concerned about animal rights, nor for squeamish vegetarians. Sophisticated urban types often agree to share out the best parts of their beast, rather missing the point of the offering. You may be included in one of these 'syndicates' at work, and it is bad form to refuse participation. You may receive beggars asking for a share of your animal, in which case, unless you did purchase one, it is appropriate to donate money or dry food such as rice.

Waf'at (Death of the Prophet)

Waf'at (Rabi ol-Avval 17) commemorates the death of Prophet Mohammed. This is a day of contemplation, and not as important as in other Islamic countries

Maba'th (Mission of the Holy Prophet)

Maba'th (Rajab 27) celebrates the Prophet Mohammed's ascent from Jerusalem.

SHI'ITE ISLAMIC HOLIDAYS

There are several feasts and many more mourning occasions which are really observed only by Shi'ite Muslims. As Shi'ism dominates Iran's unique culture and government, all these events are public holidays. The main celebratory occasions are:

- **Imam Ali's Birthday**, Rajab 13.
- **Twelfth Imam's Birthday**, Sha'ban 15.
- **Imam Reza's Birthday**, Zi-Qa'deh 11.
- **Aid-e 'Qadir-e Khom**, Zi-Hajeh 18; the day on which the Prophet Mohammed supposedly appointed Ali to be his successor.
- **Imam Sadeq's Birthday**, Rabi ol-Avval 17; shared with Prophet Mohammed's Birthday.

All of these occasions are public holidays, but you may not notice anything going on other than the closure of government offices. Celebration of these holidays can be very enthusiastic, as in the case of Imam Reza's birthday in Mashhad, home of his tomb, or very subdued, as in towns where Sunni Muslims predominate. The Twelfth Imam's birthday is marked by a dramatic number of weddings, as it also precedes two months during which weddings are not considered appropriate: Ramazan and Moharram.

Festivals of Mourning

The other group of holidays, some of which affect daily life profoundly, are the occasions for mourning, which in a religion with such a strong central martyrdom theme, are legion. Shi'ism and, indeed, Iranians' relationships with martyrs and the glorification and re-enactment of their suffering, can be compared with the pre-eminence of the theme of Christ's Passion in Southern European Catholic countries during the Middle Ages. These are very visceral attachments for most Iranians, and even very sophisticated and seemingly blasé Iranians can become very distressed if the sacrifices and sufferings of their heroes are belittled, even implicitly. The occasions for mourning are:

- **Ruz-e Qatl**, Ramazan 21; Imam Ali's Martyrdom.
- **Imam Sadeq's Martyrdom**, Shavval 25.
- **Ta'asou'a**, Moharram 9.
- **Ashura**, Moharram 10.
- **Arba'in-e Hosseini**, Safar 20; the fortieth day after Imam Husayn's martyrdom.
- **Imam Hassan's Martyrdom**, Safar 28; shared with the Death of Prophet Mohammad.

Moharram

Whilst most occasions for mourning are marked with a subdued day of limited activity, a trip to the mosque and maybe a moving sermon that reduces the audience to tears, it is throughout the month of Moharram that the symbolism and practice of mourning reach a crescendo. The month will begin with a decrease in social activities. Provincial cinemas may close for the whole month, television and radio broadcasts will be subdued, women may wear more subdued clothing, and there will be no wedding celebrations. Religious households and those with money or status will invite mullahs to perform at *rozeh-khanehs*, or recitations of the lives and untimely martyrdom of the family of the Imam Husayn in Kerbela. These are occasions of great pathos, as they offer an opportunity to weep for all sufferings as well as for the martyrs. If invited, it is worth attending such a gathering (which can be mixed or sex-segregated), as the skill of the speakers can be awesome. Expect a cathartic experience that crosses the bounds of religion and culture.

Water tanks appear outside businesses during Moharram so as to offer the water denied to Husayn's family during their suffering. These tanks are decorated with the common motif of a hand, representing that of Hazrat-e Abbas, whose hands were severed when he tried to obtain water for the Holy Family. Obviously the degree to which Moharram is in evidence depends on where you are in Iran, but even if you're in an elite suburb of north Tehran, where the locals are not especially religious, you will notice a difference. Furthermore, a trip to the bazaar, that bastion of religious conservatism, will really bring it home to you.

During the month of Moharram, guilds, neighbourhoods and assorted organisations will be preparing for the passion play (*tazieh*) and processions to be held on Ta'asou'a and Ashura—the ninth and tenth days of the month—which mark the anniversary of the martyrdom of Imam Husayn and his family. In the two days prior to this climax, there may be orchestrated processions of men who will, at the very least, beat their breasts rhythmically and probably lash their backs with chain-link flagellums or cut their heads with swords, whilst chanting lines of praise for Husayn's family. Expect blood to flow. The processions are accompanied by mournful music and may overwhelm the spectators with emotion. Refrain from whatever activity you were doing when they pass. Appear respectful and do not photograph them. Better still, stay indoors, as emotions will become further inflamed over the following days.

On Ta'asou'a, the mourning will reach its peak, and rage at the sufferings inflicted on Shi'ites in general may boil over into demonstrations and acts against 'infidels'. No sign of pleasure in any activity should be openly exhibited. On the morning of Ashura, the *tazieh* will be enacted. In this play, the events of Husayn's martyrdom are re-enacted by ordinary people—often with great realism and possibly with references to present-day events. In this way the martyrdom appears to have occurred so recently that the dreadful events seem very fresh and tragic, as indeed they were when they originally happened. Key events are always replayed and the audience relives them many times. The unlucky man chosen to play Shemr, the arch villain who administered the death blows to Husayn, runs the gamut of a frenzied audience filled with hatred for what he represents. Incidents of confusion have arisen, when the unfortunate actor was himself slain. The *tazieh* had been almost abolished by 1979, but is now controlled by local authorities to avoid rioting and casualties. They are more likely to be authentically performed in the provinces, although the Tehran bazaar organises a major procession each year. Foreigners are unlikely to be able to observe one safely, unless invited along.

The story may also be shown on television. All places of entertainment remain closed during this time, and sweet shops may not open. Special foods such as *halva* and *shol-e-zard* (rice pudding with saffron) are prepared and eaten.

Forty days after Ashura, another day of mourning, Arba'ain-e Hosseini, is marked with widespread *rozeh-khanehs*. Gradually the black flags of mourning disappear and life returns to normal.

NATIONAL HOLIDAYS

Until you read this section you may have wondered why Iranian civil servants have a fairly short annual leave entitlement. In addition to the major Muslim holidays and Now Ruz, there are several 'bank holidays' and extra holidays are sometimes announced at short notice. The holidays may be moved or extended to increase the weekend. For the following list of established holidays, the dates are indicated according to both the Gregorian calendar and the Islamic solar year calendar.

- **Piruzi-ye Shokhumand-e Enghelab-e Islami-ye Iran** ('The Magnificent Victory of the Islamic Revolution of Iran'), February 11 (Bahman 22); the anniversary of Ayatollah Khomeini coming to power in 1979.

- **Ruz-e Melli Shodan-e San'at-e Naft** ('Oil Industry Nationalisation Day'), March 20 (Esfand 29); the anniversary of the 1951 nationalisation of the Iranian oil industry.

- **Ruz-e Jomhuri-ye Islami** ('Islamic Republic Day'), April 1 (Farvardin 12); Iran's national day—the anniversary of the establishment of the Islamic Republic in 1979.

- **Rehlat-e Jangodaz-e Rahbar-e Kabir-e Jomhuri-ye Islami-ye Iran** ('The Heart-Rending Departure of the Great Leader of the Islamic Republic of Iran'), June 4 (Khordad 14); the anniversary of the death of Imam Khomeini in 1989.

- **Salruz-e Gheyam-e Ommat-e Mosalman-e Iran** ('Anniversary of the Iranian Popular Uprising'), June 5 (Khordad 15); the anniversary of Khomeini's arrest in 1963, following his speech urging the world's Muslims to rise up against the superpowers, which sparked widespread anti-Shah demonstrations.

These holidays are celebrated with varying degrees of fervour and appropriate observation may be enforced on the day, depending on the political scene. Avoid planning any activities not in keeping with the solemnity of the day. Be aware of the significance of the holiday in case you are approached by any zealots. If there are demonstrations, avoid going out, as emotions concerning foreigners may be heightened.

In particular, on the anniversary of Khomeini's death, displays of joviality are inappropriate, and even ordinary activities like eating out and listening to the radio might be open to misunderstanding. Public buildings, offices, shops and even taxis are likely to display the black flag of mourning. Remember, Iran takes mourning seriously, and for those who rejoiced at the loss of this particular leader, there are many others who still feel they have lost their father. There are often power cuts on such days, rumoured to be deliberate attempts to stop people enjoying their enforced day of leisure.

AND THAT'S NOT ALL

The religious minorities in Iran have their own festivals, and these may be evident in the districts where members of these minorities live. Minority workers may take time off work for key holidays. Foreigners interested in observing Christian or possibly Jewish holidays should contact their embassy for advice on the location of places of religious observance.

Chapter Nine

LIVING AND WORKING
IN IRAN

AM I ALONE?

There are very few Westerners actually living in Iran. Most of these are women married to Iranian men, and they hold Iranian passports. Dual nationality is technically illegal for Iranians, but in effect it is ignored by the authorities. Westerners working in Iran are usually recruited from overseas for very specialised jobs in industry. Western women married to Iranians are free to undertake any employment they wish, but most either teach English or run their own businesses catering to other expatriates. These types of jobs are advertised in the

Tehran Times classified section. Casual labour is not an option for Westerners in Iran—tourists are unlikely to stay long enough, wages are laughably low, and it is illegal. There are some Asian (particularly Japanese) engineers and doctors working in Iran, but foreign currency regulations have made this increasingly rare.

The embassies generally have small staffs and rely on local employees to fill the clerical posts. This is another area in which the spouses of Iranians can sometimes work. Whether working for a company or a diplomatic mission, most of one's practical problems would be taken care of by the employer.

Working Visas

Business visas are usually issued through the Ministry of Foreign Affairs in Tehran, often after strenuous efforts on the part of your business contact in Iran. They are issued for periods between two weeks and one month, and may be extended inside Iran, even if you want to stay for tourism reasons. There are regular international business fairs in Iran, and your Iranian Consulate can advise you about these and how to go about exhibiting at one.

ARRIVING IN IRAN

If you travel on Iran Air, you will be requested to dress appropriately. If arriving by land or on another carrier, you will witness a sudden transformation—particularly in the women passengers as they scramble into Islamic dress. For women, a below knee coat, headscarf and socks are essential; men should dress conservatively, with long trousers and sleeves.

Iran Air is a curious airline, in that the standard of service on board seems to depend on the crew on duty, the degree of overcrowding and the day of the week. Although the food is fine, do not expect the same standard of service offered by other carriers. However, Iran Air offers an opportunity to acclimatise to Iran before even arriving, and it is probably the cheapest direct carrier from many European countries. Iran Air also flies many internal routes that might be essential for your trip.

On arrival, or on the aeroplane, you will be asked to fill out a customs declaration. This is written in Farsi and English, and you can answer in English. It will ask about your intentions, and if you possess any of a long list of items that are prohibited or controlled. This includes items such as make-up, and it is safer to say no, as they are really looking for commercial quantities. The customs form should be retained until departure, but in fact no one ever seems to ask for it. If you have items like a camcorder or notebook computer, ask the customs officer to enter these on the customs form (or in your passport) to show that you brought them with you. Ensure that these entries are cancelled upon exiting Iran if you wish to return with that passport. Audio and video tapes will be inspected, as will magazines and other reading material, for suitability. Tapes may be retained for collection on another day, after they have been thoroughly examined. Magazines will often be confiscated if they contain unsuitable pictures. Only up to 200,000 rials of Iranian currency can be taken into the country. Although you can bring in unlimited foreign currency, amounts over U.S.$10,000 must be declared on arrival.

Foreigners may not have their baggage searched, but the arrival of an international flight in Tehran is a scene of total chaos. It can be hard to believe that the amounts of baggage really belong to individual travellers, not to import businesses. You will probably be met with more kindness than the hapless Iranians who are about to be fleeced by the customs officers, but expect long delays (you won't be disappointed). If you feel you can't really cope with the chaos, or you have fairly innocent but potentially troublesome items with you (like books, magazines or many gifts), a good idea is to enlist a porter. They wear grey jackets, and, if given a foreign bank note (minimum U.S.$10 if you want more than portering), they will steer you through customs, with whom they clearly have an accommodation.

Outside any airport, avoid the official airport taxi service and take a normal private taxi for half the price. Shared taxis are another option—either you or the driver can scout around for fellow passengers.

LEAVING IRAN

Customs Regulations

You will be asked to fill in another customs declaration and possibly asked to show your original one. If you want to exchange rials back to hard currency, you must show the original official rate exchange receipts. You must also declare your foreign currency.

You may export unlimited Iranian handicrafts, as long as they are not for trade. In the past, the value limit for purchased handicrafts leaving the country was 150,000 rials, so keep your receipts in case this rule is reintroduced. Traders will provide lower priced receipts if asked. Receipts will not help you at all in the case of exporting Iranian carpets—you may take one or two, up to 12 square metres in size. Very old, rare or valuable carpets may not get through customs. Kelims and weavings are not usually counted as carpets, although this should all be checked on before departure. It may be necessary, if in doubt, to take your planned exports to the airport or a local customs office (*edareh-ye gomrek*) up to a week before departure, so they can be approved for export. Carpet dealers can often advise on the procedure.

Up to 150 grams of gold (not coins or antiques) and 3 kilograms of silverwork can be exported. Gemstones need prior approval by a customs office. Anything vaguely antique may need special permission. Musical instruments have been banned from export at various times, as have chess and backgammon sets (gambling devices!), so always seek advice about these. It is usually a good idea to claim that they are purely decorative. Books and tapes generally need prior approval from the Ministry of Culture and Islamic Guidance, which has offices (*edareh-ye ershad*) in most towns. The officials there will check the items and give them back to you sealed and stamped for post or export. This can take several days, and it is probably a good idea to ask an Iranian to accompany you. Some texts and tapes are exempt from this, and you can ask the seller for advice, but, ultimately, only the Ministry can decide.

Most people find that a little cash or even pleading can resolve many problems at the airport. Again, porters are legendary in their ability to fix things, so it is worth being generous if you think you may have a problem with customs restrictions or excess luggage. In Tehran Airport, there is a stretch of the terminal which forces you to either drag your baggage alone to the check-in (with no trolley provided) or to hire a porter anyway.

Queues and More Queues

In addition to queuing for security checks, customs, and then the check-in counter, you will be asked to visit the police station in the airport where they will endorse your passport for departure. This is the case for both Iranians and foreigners, all of whom will be checked against a list of wanted criminals or those forbidden to leave. The police will check that you have not overstayed your visa, and they also may subject you to several searches (of both you and your baggage) before boarding, although things are increasingly relaxed. It is best to arrive as early as possible to allow for all the queuing.

Once you have passed customs, checked in and deposited your bags, you can leave the airport or go back to the public area to see your friends in the expensive and indifferent coffee shop until your flight is called.

Departure by bus may be very slow, as there is often a queue of buses to be checked, and the passengers can have phenomenal amounts of luggage. The security checks can also take time, depending on the current political and social climate.

MONEY MATTERS

The monetary unit is the Iranian rial, abbreviated to RI or RIs. There are actually 100 dinars to the rial, but everyone has forgotten this, as the rial is so hopelessly devalued. Coins of 2, 5, 10, 20, 50, 100 and 250 rials are in circulation, as well as notes of 100, 200, 500, 1000, 2000, 5000 and 10,000 rials. The bank notes have Latin numerals as well as Arabic and Farsi numerals, but the coins have only Arabic numerals.

In their daily dealings, all Iranians use an old currency unit, the Touman, which is equal to ten rials. This can be confusing, as the price will almost always be written in rials, but expressed as one tenth of that. Some low prices, such as taxi or bus fares, are expressed in rials, and this will become clear to you as you develop a feel for prices. Money is quite bulky, and the lower denomination bank notes are often dirty, torn and creased. They are useful for taxis and snacks, as are the larger denomination coins. Film canisters are useful for carrying coins, and the lower denominations can be given to beggars, although five or ten rial coins are useful for public telephones.

The Dollar Reigns Supreme

Despite Iran's official distaste for everything American, the U.S. dollar commands universal respect. It is the currency of choice for official and unofficial purposes. Dual pricing for foreigners means that you will be pressed to pay in dollars, although this should generally be avoided, due to the spoiling effect of the official exchange rate on prices. (You're much better off paying in rials bought at the black market exchange rate rather than paying for something in U.S. dollars). Other hard currencies are exchangeable, but even banks prefer the familiarity of the American dollar. Travellers cheques are only exchanged in Tehran—at a hefty commission and at a slow pace. Visa or Mastercard are accepted at major hotels and in some souvenir or carpet shops, and central banks will advance cash on them. If the card is issued in the United States, however, it may be unusable due to the trade embargo. American Express cards are not accepted. Hard currency bank accounts are offered by the major Iranian banks, but these are of limited use to foreigners. Foreigners working in Iran are often paid all or most of their salary in hard currency to a bank account at home; they can then buy Iranian currency for their needs in Iran. Whilst in Iran, you will have to acclimatise yourself to a solely cash system.

The Exchange Problem

Do not believe any official literature, which assures you that banks offer the best exchange rates. They offer the 'official' exchange rate, which is about half the free market rate. (Summer 1998 rates were approximately U.S.$1 = 5,000 RI.) You will need to exchange some hard currency at the airport bank on arrival, but apart from that, you will probably deal with the free market exchangers, who are currently legal and generally tolerated (although not encouraged). Be aware that this can change, and, in the past, free market exchange carried the death penalty, so ask people in Iran what the current situation is.

Apart from the airport bank, banks are usually open from 8 a.m. to 4 p.m., and closed on Thursday afternoons and Fridays and all public holidays, of which there are many. Banks on the Gulf coast have their own hours, reflecting the hot weather, and hotels may offer exchange to guests.

The money exchange offices exist outside Tehran, and they look like small shops, with lists of their currency prices posted outside. Usually 'currency' or 'exchange' is written in English, and anyone will point out a *sarafee* to you. Check that you are getting the unofficial rate on your transaction. If you can't find an office, a hotel employee or carpet dealer or trusted acquaintance will often arrange exchange for you. Many Iranians know of someone who wants to amass hard currency (often in anticipation of a trip) and can put you in touch with that person, who is happy to 'buy' your cash. These deals happen because Iranians are strictly limited on how much of their own money they can export.

Changing money in exchange offices is currently legal, but changing on the streets is not and should thus be avoided.

Money Transfers

It is possible, within a few working days, to transfer money into Iran through Iranian banks. This will be converted at the official rate. However, the most common method of getting money into, as well as out of, Iran is via private money-changers. These semi-legal outfits co-operate with money-changers in Europe and elsewhere to transfer money between countries, at the unofficial exchange rate, by selling the hard currency to Iranian buyers who want to export their cash. The fee for such a service is met by a fractionally lower exchange rate. This Is technically illegal, but extremely common. Such money-changers (*sarafee*) can be found throughout Iran, and anywhere there is an Iranian community. The transfer may seem shady, and there may be no paperwork involved, but in Europe they operate on a 'my word is my bond' system. Money in Iran can be transferred to any numbered bank account or collected from a network of contacts. If you want to spend any time in Iran, it is worth visiting a money-changer in your home country to inquire about possible transfer deals.

THE BUSINESS ENVIRONMENT

Foreign Investment and Privatisation

The Iranian government has an ambivalent relationship with foreign investors. All foreign concerns and many indigenous private industries and services were nationalised in 1979 (from hotels to foreign shares in Iranian oil companies), and the firm adherence to the principles of economic independence meant that foreign investors were actively denied any further involvement. However, the Iranian government also realises (reluctantly) the need for foreign capital to help heal the country's struggling economy.

The Iranian constitution specifically forbids the granting of concessions to foreigners, a reflection of Iran's unhappy past experiences with foreign concession holders, who generally abused their positions. Today, the general principle is interpreted as meaning that non-Iranians may not own more than 49% of shares in Iranian companies. In 1992, this restriction was effectively lifted, but only two cases of 51% foreign ownership have occurred: a Daewoo car assembly plant and a Nestle baby-milk factory.

In a complete reversal of earlier policy, the Iranian government has recently made increasing efforts to woo foreign investors, including a programme of privatisation commenced in 1988. But the government has bypassed the laws on privatisation, nationalisation and foreign investment rather than actually confronting them, and legislation remains a significant legal and psychological barrier to major privatisation and, especially, foreign investment.

Free Trade Zones

As a tool for liberalisation and economic growth, the Iranian government has developed Free Trade Zones (FTZ). These are mainly on the Persian Gulf islands of Kish and Qeshm, as well as the port city of Chabahar, although there are also 'Special Economic Zones' on the mainland, which function much like the FTZ. These zones allow unlimited foreign participation, a free market exchange rate, the operation of foreign banks, a twenty-year exemption from taxes, and no restriction on imports and exports (within Islamic guidelines, of course). Foreigners who travel straight in and out of the FTZ are exempted from customs duties on purchases.

Taxes

For an oil economy, Iran has a striking variety of taxes, paid by individuals and companies. All companies are subject to a tax equal to 10% of their profits (Company Tax), but this is not applied to foreign companies. Corporate Income Tax is applied to the remaining profits of all companies, and ranges from 12 to 54%. For Iranian companies, this is levied as a tax on personal income. Chamber of Commerce Tax is 0.3% of taxable income. Value Added Tax is about to be implemented. Personal Income Tax—varying on a sliding scale from 12 to 54%—is deducted by the employer on annual incomes exceeding U.S.$1,200. Social Security Charges are deducted from payrolls at 30% up to a ceiling, of which 7% is met by the employee, the rest by the employer. Ministry of Labour Charges mean that Iranian companies must pay a charge of 23% of a foreign employee's salary to the Ministry of Labour.

There are also Real Estate Taxes (2–8%) on property sales; tax payments for transfer of shares through the stock exchange by public companies (0.5%); Tax on Transfer of Real Estate (10–12%); and Stamp Duty on share capital (0.2% of the capital).

The Government is getting stricter at enforcing taxation and has allocated company codes to all businesses to aid this. Tax benefits and exemptions apply to: 20% of the profits from mining, manufacturing or assembly industries; new factories in 'underdeveloped areas' for four to eight years; profits set aside for new development projects; technical assistance contracts between foreign companies and public companies (as long as some work is performed in Iran); interest income, dividends and royalty agreements with French and German companies; and companies whose share capital is quoted on the Tehran Stock Exchange.

Customs Duties

Customs duties range from 5 to 25% depending on three main issues: if the good is produced locally or could be; if it is a priority in government programmes; and if it is considered a luxury good. The definition of luxury goods varies greatly, and explains many of the inflated prices in Iran. Export tax is negligible, and re-export is fully legal.

Wages and Employment Conditions

Salaries vary a great deal in Iran, but, generally, wages are low, even for skilled workers. Many employees survive on perks or by corruption, and an apparently low paying job may be highly desirable in terms of these opportunities. The majority of white collar employees are employed by the government in the public services on set scales of pay. This partly explains why Iranians all seem so familiar with each other's income. A semiskilled labourer earns approximately U.S.$80 a month, and a civil servant with a degree earns around U.S.$100 a month plus benefits. All employees receive an annual bonus of one and a half months' salary at the Zoroastrian New Year (Now Ruz). Retirement is at age fifty-five or after twenty-five years of work. Trade unions are legal but effectively powerless, as strikes are illegal. Minimum wage for the public sector is fixed by the Ministry of Labour. Redundancy is not permitted. There are no guaranteed state pensions, other than for civil servants. Some private companies and trades unions arrange pensions.

Working Hours

Working hours are set at a legal maximum of forty-four hours per week, and annual leave is thirty days per year. Most government offices are open from 8 a.m. to around 2 p.m., Saturday through Thursday. All offices are closed on Friday, and most either close early on Thursday or for the entire day, especially government ministries in Tehran. There are many public holidays. (See Chapter Eight.) Office hours in the south of Iran are shorter, and an afternoon siesta is the norm in the provinces during the summer.

Business Etiquette

Business transactions may appear casual in Iran, but this is largely superficial. Business dress is generally more relaxed than in other countries, and office organisation may seem chaotic, but business etiquette operates along similar lines to the social behaviour described in previous chapters. Social correctness is important, and anyone aiming to do business in Iran should be prepared for a lengthy courtship ritual with their prospective clients or partners. Ultimately a good relationship is probably more important than price or the actual details of the proposed business deal.

Private businesses tend to keep flexible hours, and generally are open for longer hours than their state counterparts. As many Iranians have two jobs, the private sector may operate in the afternoon only, when the state offices are closed. Iranians like to establish a personal relationship with business contacts, and a firm distinction is not drawn between business and social relationships. Small gifts from abroad are typical, as are gifts to mark a successful deal or the opening of a new venture. Foreign business contacts may be asked for goods from abroad or small favours such as invitation letters for relatives. This should not be confused with bribery, which is rampant but quite different, in that this type of gift giving is merely an extension of social behaviour.

Although you should never be late for an appointment, expect your Iranian opposite to be late, to cancel or change the arrangements, and you won't be disappointed. Tea and other refreshments are always be offered in offices and precede any serious transactions. Many offices have a room in which to sit comfortably and discuss business. Business lunches are common and generally informal, while evening dinners are more likely to be formal. Invitations may be to the home, rather than a restaurant, and, in this case, avoid talk of business unless initiated by the host. Except in the most conservative bazaar environment, asking after one's family and exchanging personal details is normal and all social niceties that apply to social engagements should be observed. A business contact who also becomes a friend is a double success for any Iranian.

Business cards are widely used, and often printed in English as well as Farsi. It is a nice touch to arrange bilingual cards for yourself, but generally not essential. Iranians almost always list all professional and academic qualifications on their cards.

The Mighty Bazaar

The bazaar is so much more than a labyrinth shopping centre—it is a formidable economic power in Iran. The small stalls in the bazaar are the front of major businesses and storage facilities all over Iran. The Tehran bazaar controls a third of Iran's trading and retail sector, including up to 70% of domestic wholesale trade and 30% of imported goods. It is like a city in itself, with its own mosques, schools, restaurants, banks and public baths. It has an important political role, much as Wall Street or the London Stock Exchange, in that the government needs the support of the bazaar merchants. In fact, the bazaar represents a giant commodities market, a stock exchange and a banking system all wrapped into one institution.

Through their exported goods, such as carpets and dried fruits, the bazaaris have access to foreign exchange, which remains outside government channels. The bazaar has its own banking system, and loans are arranged on the basis of reputation; no collateral is required. The bazaar merchants have strong family, social and business links with the clergy, and were instrumental in the success of the 1979 revolution by closing the bazaar and paralysing the economy. One of the problems with the bazaar system is that it emphasises short term profits from trading over long term investment and manufacturing, and this has been blamed for much of Iran's economic malaise. However, it would be a brave government that dared to challenge the supremacy of the bazaar.

COMMUNICATIONS

Telephone and Fax

Public telephone offices are easily discerned by the ranks of telephones outside, and they are often combined with the post office in smaller towns. Telephone services largely depend on the area of Iran, and ringing intercity can be tiresome, as the lines are often busy. International calls are cheaper from the public telephone office than from private lines, but not domestic calls. International calls in general are not cheap.

Public telephones use small coins, which can be hard to obtain, especially the five- or ten-rial coins used in the old telephone booths. You also will need many coins to make a call of any length, although in Tehran, many public phones allow unlimited time for a local call with one coin. Airports and bus stations often have a booth for free local calls. Many shops and hotels have private pay phones, and public card-phones have recently come to Tehran. There are none, however, that use credit cards.

Fax services are offered in main post offices and telephone offices, as well as many hotels and some shops. Hotels are generally the most expensive. Fax costs reflect the high cost of international calls from Iran. Some provincial cities, especially in border regions monitor faxed documents carefully. Main telephone offices and, of course, telegraph offices offer telegram services which are quite slow, but cheaper than a short fax, taking a couple of days to arrive overseas.

Postal Services

The postal service from Tehran to overseas and vice versa is quite reliable (and can be very fast), but this is sadly not true of the internal mail system. Both international and internal postage is cheap for letters and papers. Postboxes are unknown in the provinces and rare in Tehran, so you must visit the post office to get your mail delivered.

All mail needs a return address, and Iranians rarely repeat the address at a letter's head, so hold onto the envelope. Post cards are always put in envelopes (*paaket*), and are sold with an envelope, which, in the way of most Iranian envelopes, will need some assistance to stick shut. Letters to be sent abroad really need the country written out in Farsi at the top; addresses in English will result in late delivery of internal mail, except for straightforward addresses in Tehran and major cities.

Addresses are written in descending order, with the recipient's name at the bottom. It is generally considered necessary to name the householder, even if this is not the recipient. This is usually written as, 'the house of Mr. X, please give this to Ms. Y'. Many addresses are very complicated, with additional directions, such as 'opposite the Ministry of Justice' or 'just past the Shahpour School, on the right'.

Many Iranians live in alleys (*couchehs*), and this always requires the name of the main road.

Personal mail delivery is rare, and it is customary for the recipients to tip the postman when he visits. It is also customary to tip him for bringing good news or a parcel.

Sending a parcel is complex in that one needs to take the unwrapped items to the post office to have them checked. If for overseas, a customs official will decide on their suitability and the customs duties incurred. A minion will then usually wrap the goods and box them, and you will be asked to fill in several forms. It might be a good idea to supply any padding necessary for fragile items, although the service is usually satisfactory.

Electronic Communications

Although electronic communications are a medium quite alien to the majority of Iranians, Iran leads the Middle East in its Internet usage, and expatriate Iranians (especially those in the United States) are particularly keen 'net-surfers'. An estimated 60,000 Iranians in Iran are now using the Internet. All Iranian universities have Internet access provided by the Institute for Studies in Theoretical Physics and Mathematics, or I.P.M. (gopher://physics.ipm.ac.ir:aria.nic.ir/); AT&T mail; or SprintNET. Many websites have sprung up for lively debate between all Iranian groups, and the Iranian government and its organs have not been slow to make use of cyberspace.

Commercial Internet access is provided by four companies, of which the two largest are Neda Rayaneh Corporation (support@neda.net) and Irnet (support@Irnet.ir). Charges vary from annual accounts around U.S.$100, to one-time registration fees of U.S.$48 with a U.S.$0.50 charge for each transaction. Service is generally slow at 96,000 baud, or 12 kilobytes per second. Some commercial and private users maintain accounts with Internet providers abroad, using compressor software, and calling the provider overseas for transactions. They do this for reasons of security and reliability, although the government makes no serious attempts to control Internet use. A list of useful Internet sites can be found in the bibliography at the end of this book.

ACCOMMODATION

Settling Down: Tehran or Elsewhere?

Like most of this chapter, and, in fact, much of this book, it is generally assumed that foreigners will spend most of their time in the major tourist cities of Iran, and that foreigners living in Iran will be based in Tehran. This is a simple reflection of reality. Iran is very unevenly developed and is clearly centralised around Tehran, which has the greatest concentration of amenities and services in the country. Thus, most foreigners find themselves living in the capital. The cost of living is actually very high in Tehran, and inflation is driving prices up weekly. Where appropriate and where space allows, I refer to the situation in other parts of Iran, although most foreigners would find that life in the provinces is generally much less convenient and more restrictive than in Tehran, even if it is considerably cheaper.

Villa or Apartment?

Most Tehranis live in apartments. Even people who build their own houses (which is quite routine in Iran), often rent out the ground floor and live upstairs. Few people have big gardens, as land is expensive. The large houses in the expensive parts of cities are called *villas*, and are considered very desirable, although they are often far from amenities like shops. In Tehran, the most desirable areas are in the north of the city, although some people like to live more centrally. One advantage of living in a house is having a private swimming pool—as long as it's not overlooked by the neighbours, or if the neighbours find that acceptable. Foreigners tend to congregate in certain areas. Apartments have the possibility of making friends,

A typical walled compound in north Tehran. The rich live very well.

neighbours to advise you, and a janitor to take care of things. In 1998, rentals for foreigners in Tehran varied from U.S.$400 per month for a small apartment to U.S.$5,000 per month for a large *villa*, suitable for several people. There is usually no official deposit charged, although references will be taken up with your company, who are generally responsible for the contract anyway. However, it is usual for the landlord to take a hefty advance of up to six months' rent. The *Tehran Times* has a page of adverts every day with details of apartments, *villas* and agencies which specialise in foreigners. Two of these agencies are Bijan Housing Agency (021-8770908) and Sharokh Housing Agency (021-2055408-9).

Furnishings

Most short-let apartments and houses come with furnishings which are pretty similar. The most popular style of 'European' furnishings is the one commonly referred to by Arabs as 'Louis Farrokh'—all spindly legs, bowed backs, scrolled woodwork and gilt trim. Standard furniture is a sofa and chair set in this style, with a matching, large dining table with chairs included. Several small tables, usually onyx and gilt, will be in evidence. Most dwellings have fitted wardrobes and hall cupboards, and a family room or den to watch television. European sanitary fittings are normal in bathrooms in Tehran and for lets, although there may also be an additional Iranian-style toilet. Kitchens are usually fitted and may be open to the living area in apartments.

If you need furniture, almost all kinds are available in Iran, although the 'British country house' look is rare and such items would need to be specially ordered. Large furniture stores sell the styles popular in Iran, whilst you may find an artisan willing to make furniture to your specifications, if not your high standards.

There is a shortage of accommodation in Tehran, meaning constant building work and ever taller buildings.

Services

As rented accommodation comes with all services, you are unlikely to have to deal with the Byzantine complexities of establishing such amenities. Always ensure that an accommodation has a telephone line, as demand is such that you can literally wait years for a line. Apartment complexes may include services such as heating, hot water and gas; your bills will come monthly, and must be paid at the offices concerned.

There are occasional power cuts in most cities, and some homes have gas lamps for such emergencies. If not, and you have no backup generator, ensure a convenient supply of candles or oil lamps. Although gas has now been piped to most cities in Iran, some areas and individual dwellings are still without a supply. Also, some houses have no supply in the kitchen, and gas cookers are often run from bottled gas, which will be replaced by a gas seller when empty. Ask the neighbours for details.

Help at Home

It is possible to hire Iranian servants to help at home, although they are generally more used for heavy cleaning than for the type of light domestic duties undertaken by Western 'dailies'. They are often men, and many such workers are Afghanis. For a country with high unemployment, Iranians are very reluctant to undertake domestic tasks. Cleaners are not treated with the respect they are in the West, and they are generally not trusted with delicate tasks or alone in the house. Servants or housecleaners are found by word of mouth, or possibly through agencies advertising in the *Tehran Times*. It is also possible to find cooks, nannies and gardeners this way. Many people find that the dust and general filth of city life in Iran means that they need at least occasional help to wash the windows, scrub the woodwork and so on.

EDUCATION

Iran has quite a high rate of basic literacy—around 75%—although this is lower in rural areas and for women. School is free and compulsory for children from six to ten years, and around 90% of children do attend for at least a couple of years. Iranian schooling is very rigid in structure, focusing on discipline and rote learning of set texts. They follow the French system whereby the failure to pass exams in all subjects each summer means retaking the entire year. Islamic studies, Arabic and English are compulsory. Education after eleven years of age is similar to the French Baccalaureate, and focuses on a group of subjects, such as natural sciences, or literature. More than one million Iranians are attending university, although half of these are at the newer private universities.

Schools for Foreigners

Very few foreign children attend school in Iran, and outside Tehran, this is very unlikely. There are some schools in Tehran for foreigners, including German, Italian and French schools. The Indian community in Tehran runs an English-speaking preschool facility as well as a school. The Iranian Ministry of Education runs the fee-charging International School, which teaches in English. This is for the children of foreigners resident in Iran or for children who have a foreign parent. The system is very intensive and as rigid as in the rest of Iranian schools. Schooling in Iran is likely to be a serious problem for parents, who might consider home tuition.

SHOPPING

Luxury Products

Local Iranian produce is generally cheaper than it would be in the West (although still sometimes surprisingly expensive), but imported products have very confusing price structures. They can be wildly expensive due to customs taxes, or occasionally they are cheap because they are imported by a government-registered charitable foundation (*bonyad*). These foundations, such as *The Foundation for the Martyrs of the War* are profit-making charities which are entitled to a special rate of foreign exchange to import goods—often luxury goods. As they buy them at a cheap rate, they can then be sold off cheaply. As time passes you will learn which goods are surprisingly cheap and which ones are fakes, such as certain brands of cosmetics. Any brands of drugs, cosmetics and clothing to which you are particularly attached should be brought from home, as availability changes frequently in Iran, and there are no regular franchise outlets for foreign goods. Some goods, like disposable nappies (even the brand made in Iran) and decent sanitary protection, are ridiculously expensive.

Daily Shopping Needs

Iran is a country of small shops, and most towns have no supermarkets. *Super* means something like a corner shop, which will be smaller than a local convenience store in America or Britain, and will sell a similar range of goods, although not as varied. Most shops are contained in small shopping centres on the main roads, consisting of ten to thirty small units, collectively called a *passage*; food shops tend to be directly on the road. Prices and style of goods are generally dictated by the location of the *passage*. Prices are rarely fixed, and some small negotiation is usually possible, often depending on the size of your purchase and whether you are a regular customer. For expensive items, it is best to shop around; ask Iranian friends for recommendations, and take an Iranian with you.

Certain areas are known for certain types of shopping or services, and most locals will advise you as to where to start in your search for certain items. Shops are generally open from 8 a.m. to 1 p.m. and 3 p.m. to 7 p.m., or much later in certain areas. Some shops stay open all day, especially in the more expensive shopping areas.

Men do much of the shopping in Iran, especially in the provinces, and very traditional women my never go shopping. Peddlers sell certain products, such as fresh vegetables and dried fruits around more traditional neighbourhoods; women will then send out for these goods. In such neighbourhoods, bread is purchased once or twice a day, but some people, especially in Tehran housing estates, have to freeze bread, as there are no local bakeries. Milk is often brought by tanker in the morning to shops in certain areas, and is sold out by midday. You may need your own container to carry this milk. In expensive areas, your local *super* will deliver your order to the house.

The Tehran Bazaar.

The Bazaar Experience

The bazaar sells almost everything, but in Tehran you are only likely to go there to buy carpets or jewellery. In touristy cities, such as Isfahan, it is usually the place to look for local handicrafts and souvenirs, where you can watch them being made. In the case of a carpet purchase, it is best to go with an Iranian friend, and ideally to see the wares of a recommended merchant—otherwise, you will be pestered. Women rarely visit any part of the bazaar alone (except for maybe the gold section), as it is a very conservative place, and care should be taken to dress appropriately. The bazaar in Tehran opens at about 8 a.m. and is effectively closed by lunchtime. On Fridays it is deserted. In other cities, the bazaar is closed for a long lunch break, but it reopens in the evening, except on Thursday afternoon and Fridays.

Supermarkets

There is now a very good chain of co-operative supermarkets in Tehran known as Rifah, which offers self-service and facilities similar to Western supermarkets. It usually has a ground floor selling prepared foods (including the closest to convenience foods you will find in Iran), dry and canned goods, fruit and vegetables, frozen foods, meat and baked goods. There is usually a top floor which sells furniture, clothes, cosmetics, household items, material, toys and handicrafts. Prices are clearly marked and reasonable. There are no interfering assistants except at the individual counters for some goods like cosmetics. You take your goods to the check-out in the trolley provided. Rifah is open for long hours, and the food section may be open for twenty-four hours a day. As most of the foodstuffs sold are clean and packaged, the vegetables washed, and the meat already packaged, this is by far the easiest shopping option in Iran. They also have free car parking.

A branch of Rifah co-operative supermarket.

223

Clothes

You can buy almost any style of clothing in Iran, although the prices and quality vary dramatically. Iran's clothing industry is not very advanced, and most clothes and fabrics are imported. Very few shops will exchange shoddy goods, so check clothing carefully for likely durability. Cotton T-shirts are quite good value, although it is imported goods that have the greatest social cachet. Underwear is generally of poor quality, and Iranians often request underwear from abroad.

Tailoring is cheap and often excellent, and you should ask for a recommended tailor (most of them are men), who will copy your clothes or fashion them to your designs. Remember to discuss every detail, especially trimmings, as cheap trimmings can often ruin an otherwise satisfactory outfit. You may have to provide even the zipper on a pair of trousers, if you distrust the standard of the zipper provided. Most Iranians have a 'pet' tailor, and consider this the best way of dressing. For women who are very concerned with the fit of garments, it is worth seeking out a woman tailor, as she can take more accurate measurements than a man. Fabrics are surprisingly expensive, as they are mostly imported, and knowing which fabrics will work well for which outfits is a matter of experience.

Jewellery

Jewellery in Iran is quite addictive, and surprisingly cheap, gold being sold by weight at fixed prices. All gold is 18-carat unless specified otherwise, and although the hallmarking system is not well developed as in Europe, jewellers are inspected regularly for irregularities. Traditional designs vary with region, and the filigree work from Yazd is particularly famous. Jewellers make excellent copies of all the newest European and American designs. Gems should only be purchased from reputable shops (ideally by personal recommendation), and the combination of 18-carat gold and paste or semiprecious stones is not unusual. Gold is repurchased by jewellers at a set rate by weight, although you may get more on a 'trade up'. Watches are reasonably priced, including some decent designer copies.

Beauty Matters

For men, haircuts and shaves are very straightforward. There are numerous barbers, and they are all very cheap. A head massage is usually included.

For women, matters are more complex. Beauty parlours and hairdressers are usually combined, and they are hidden behind closed doors to avoid male eyes. Iranian women friends will recommend a salon, or maybe someone who comes to the house. Beauty salons are found in the expensive hotels and in health clubs. Do not expect the same beauty treatments available in the West, although many of these can be found in Iran, including 'slimming' and 'toning' treatments. Beauticians mostly focus on hair removal (by a 'threading' technique or waxing), eyebrow shaping, manicures and pedicures. In the provinces, they may only offer hair removal, hairdressing and bridal make-up. The facial hair removal is particularly thorough, and can leave one looking like a spotty lobster for days; experiment some time before a special occasion if you must.

You may be expected to provide your own cosmetics if you don't like what's on offer. Many Iranian women dye their hair, and it sometimes appears that the majority of Tehrani middle-class matrons are honey blonde. If you like a particular colour, you would be well advised to bring it with you.

Visiting the beauty salon is a social event for most women, who prefer to do it in groups, and who may also meet up at home to give each other beauty treatments such as homemade face-packs, hair-dyeing with henna, and painting each other's nails. The services of a beautician and hairdresser are requested in bulk before weddings or special parties, as this is all part of the festivities.

There are several indigenous beauty products, which are widely used. One of these is henna, which leaves the hair shiny and black or auburn, depending on the added ingredients. Another is *sedra*, a powder which leaves the hair fuller and shinier, without adding colour.

TRANSPORTATION: WITHIN THE CITY

Taxis

Taxis are cheap and easy to use, especially in Tehran. Taxis are usually orange Paykans, maybe blue or cream in some cities, and are either private, run on shared routes, or agency/telephone taxis. The private taxis are flagged in the street and the price is either agreed in advance (be prepared to haggle) or run on a meter. They will take you to exactly where you want to go, although they may get lost on the way or need directions.

Shared taxis run on set routes, generally along main roads between the main squares, and take up to five paying passengers, two in the front passenger seat. If you don't want to be crushed, you can pay for two spaces, although some drivers don't like this for some reason. Usually a man and woman who are not together do not share the front seat. Some shared taxis wait at specific points, but most are hailed along the way. The way to hail one is to lean into the road and shout your destination (not too specific—name a square or main road) at the driver; he will stop if your destination is on his way, he has space, and if it is far enough on his route to be useful. During busy periods, it can be hard to find a taxi with space, and you may have to walk to nearer the start of the route or to a place where a lot of passengers disembark. The other problem is positioning yourself along the correct route. Passers-by will direct you to the right route if you ask them for a taxi to your destination. You may have to take several shared taxis to get to a given place. Fares, which are set by the government, depend on the distance travelled and the city you're in; they are paid either on boarding or on arrival at the destination. Only exact change is accepted. Fares vary between 150 RI and 1500 RI (500 and 2000 RI in Tehran). Stop the taxi by saying, '*Kheilee mamnoon*' (Thank you), and be prepared to get out quickly before he pulls away again. As only the back door near the kerb usually opens, be prepared for some scrambling to get out if no one else is disembarking. Take care on entering an empty taxi to make it clear if you are not chartering the whole taxi.

Telephone or agency taxis are, as the name implies, called by telephone, or maybe outside their offices, which are often in the suburbs. Hotels usually call these taxis for their guests, and they are more expensive, but generally cleaner and more comfortable.

Buses

As taxis are so cheap and plentiful, buses are used mostly by the poor and people who have a long, fixed journey to work every day. Some areas, like the housing complexes to the west of Tehran (near the airport), are poorly served by taxis and have good bus connections to the city centre. Buses are often horribly crowded, so don't bother using them unless the route is recommended to you. Bus tickets are purchased from ticket booths at bus stations or on main streets. Tickets are 50 RI each, and journeys can cost more than one ticket. The commuter-type bus routes accept payment on the bus. Bus stops are clearly marked, usually with a red or blue circle. Do not take any timetable seriously.

Officially, men and women are segregated on buses: women at the back, men at the front, and some buses have separate doors. Again this depends on the part of the city, and you will judge from situation inside the bus what is appropriate. In any case, avoid sitting next to a person of the opposite sex, unless it is your companion. I have, however, been on buses where this is ignored by Iranians themselves. If women have to enter through the back door, then they pass their ticket to the driver through the front door—or, they don't bother at all, as rumour has it.

Avoid minibuses, as they are even more horribly crowded than the buses and often filthy.

The Trolleybus and the Metro

The one electric trolleybus route in Tehran runs from the Eastern bus terminal to Imam Husayn Square. The long-planned metro has only two stops in the south of Tehran, only of use to travel to the resting place of Ayatollah Khomeini.

TRANSPORTATION: INTERCITY

Planes

Air travel is very good value in Iran, and also has a good safety record. A trip from Tehran to Bandar Abbas will cost around U.S.$25—at the free market exchange rate—and best of all, foreigners can pay in rials. Iran Air or Iran Asseman fly to almost all large cities in Iran, and there are some other small airlines that serve specific cities or regions.

Actually booking a ticket can be rather troublesome. You need your passport to book, and the ticket is nontransferable. Some flights are heavily subscribed, and claim to be full, often days or weeks in advance. Pleading may help, as many of the seats are in fact kept for possible V.I.P.s, and you are after all foreign. Alternatively, your Iranian friends—in the time-honoured Iranian way of personal inter-vention—may have a contact who knows someone who works for the airline and can help you. Calling daily may also help, as the situation often appears to change from day to day. Allow an hour to check in, as security can be strict. Strange security rules apply on different flights. For example, from Isfahan, wrapped *gaz*, the local delicacy, must be checked in, not carried on board, and in the south and southeast, batteries must be held by the captain.

The standard of service on board is very good; light snacks and drinks are generally provided. Airports in Iran are usually clean and quite well organised.

Trains

The train service in Iran covers only a small area of the country, and although surprisingly comfortable and cheap, the timetabling is infrequent and inconvenient, with all services beginning or ending in Tehran. However, certain train journeys are recommended for the scenery or the overnight sleeper facility, as well as safety. In particular, the Tehran-Tabriz and Tehran-Mashhad routes have efficient services through lovely parts of the country. First class train travel costs around twice as much as by bus (which is still cheap), and second class travel is not recommended. Tickets can only be bought from stations and only up to two weeks in advance. Beware, as the buying process generally involves a special journey, queuing and a lot of hair-pulling.

Buses

Buses are the most common method of intercity travel in Iran, with over twenty co-operative companies offering services all over Iran. These are generally known by number—for example, 'Taavoni No 1'—and vary hardly at all as to the service offered. Except in more remote areas, buses are quite comfortable, and all passengers are seated in numbered seats.

There are two classes of bus travel on most destinations: *lux* and *super*, approximating to regular second class and first class. The difference is quite small, and mostly concerns the number of seats, but as the price difference is small also, its worth booking *super* if possible. Single seats are generally assigned by gender, and you may be asked to change places to allow same sex seating between strangers. The seats at the back are the least popular, and are where the less sophisticated types tend to be seated.

229

Although smoking on board is permitted, it is rare to be on a very smoky bus, and generally people will be sympathetic if you request to change places, or even if you ask the smoker to not smoke because you have an allergy (*hessasiat*). The driver has an assistant who should take care of your needs, but this is usually confined to water from a communal bottle and glass. Stops for refreshments or toilets are usually every five to six hours, depending on the driver, and it is safest to bring along some food. Most Iranians eat their own snacks like *ajeel* on the bus, and it is polite to offer your snacks to your immediate neighbours, as they will to you. It is also common to introduce yourself at the start of the journey, and most Iranians like to pass the time in conversation. The buckets along the aisle are for rubbish.

Tickets are available up to a week in advance from the bus terminal or sometimes inside the city from the bus company's office. Some routes have such frequent service (e.g., four buses an hour) that booking is only necessary around holiday periods. Ring the terminal to check, or ask experienced Iranians. Bus terminals are in the suburbs of cities, or some distance outside the city. Large cities like Tehran have more than one terminal, each one corresponding to certain directions of departure; for example, the Western terminal handles buses to Western cities. Terminals have eating facilities inside.

Minibus

Shorter and more remote routes are often served by minibuses, and travelling from Tehran to anywhere in the Caspian region relies on minibus transport. Minibuses are faster than buses, but depart when full rather than on schedule. There is no service on board and they can be very crowded.

Taxis

For towns less than three hours away, shared taxi (*savari*) is a common way of travelling. With two passengers squeezed into the front and three in the back, they are not as comfortable as buses, but are much faster (and therefore potentially dangerous). The price is around three times a *lux* bus, and you can buy empty seats if you want more comfort or you need to leave in a hurry. Shared taxis usually leave from bus terminals and take you to the terminal at your destination. They are unlikely to take you to a particular address.

Private taxis are available for intercity trips, and will cost roughly five times the fare of a shared taxi, although all prices are open to negotiation. Of course, this taxi will take you exactly where you want to go, including possible stops along the way.

TRAVELLING BY CAR

Hiring a Car

There are no car-rental companies as such in Iran; rather, one hires a car with driver or guide, often at very reasonable rates. Some taxi firms rent cars for short periods in urban areas, and travel agencies will have details about these. In any case, I would advise against driving in Iran unless you are actually living there and you find it absolutely essential.

Drivers Beware!

Driving conditions, especially intercity ones, are often dangerous. Some routes are littered with wrecks, and many fatalities occur. Iran has definitely one of the highest car-accident rates in the world. Most intercity routes are very busy with lorries and trucks, the distances are huge and drivers are often tired and lacking concentration. Vehicles are poorly maintained, seat belts are rarely worn and it is not unusual to see eight people crammed into a family saloon car or a family of four on a moped. Child safety restraints are very rare. In urban areas, children often run into the road, and there is a general tendency to ignore both pedestrian and traffic regulations.

Actually being involved in accident requires that you call the police, which often means the parties are imprisoned until the matter is resolved. A fatality will always involve at least the temporary imprisonment of any surviving party. Even if a fatality is not your fault, 'blood money' must be paid to the victim's family, and they can insist that you are imprisoned until this is paid (hopefully by your insurance company). This can be up to U.S.$50,000. If the accident is deemed your fault, the victim's family can insist on a term in prison as well. A similar system applies to injuries sustained in accidents. Do not try to leave the scene of an accident without informing the police, as this may come back to haunt you when the other party decides that they were injured after all.

Driving Regulations

In theory, Iranians drive on the right and yield to all traffic on the right. Speed limits are legally 110 kilometres per hour on motorways and 80 kilometres per hour in the daytime (70 kilometres per hour at night) in urban areas. Technically similar rules apply to red lights, pedestrian crossings, no entry signs, one way roads, bus lanes and roundabouts as anywhere in the world, but Iranians see ignoring traffic regulations as a personal challenge, and one to which they rise magnificently. If you must drive in Iran, be aware that you may be the only person observing the rules, so don't take anything for granted and remain vigilant at all times. Part of Tehran is a 'limited traffic zone', where only authorised commercial traffic and public transport can enter between 6:30 a.m. and 5 p.m. Such regulations apply in some other cities, for example Isfahan and Mashhad, where the main tourist centres are closed to private traffic.

In the event of a breakdown, place a warning triangle 50 metres behind your car, turn on your flashing warning lights, and either call the road police or ask a passing motorist to do so for you in the next town. The police will usually arrange for a mechanic to tow you away or repair the problem there and then.

Owning a Car

If you bring your own car into Iran you need: a current International Driving Permit; a *carnet de passage*; the care registration documents; third party insurance which is valid for Iran; a nationality plate; a warning triangle and spare bulbs. Losing your car in Iran, in an accident or to theft, is a major hassle, as the customs authorities will be reluctant to accept that you have not sold it.

Cars in Iran are phenomenally expensive. Only a few people, such as returning overseas students, can import a foreign car without paying massive duties, and there is a waiting list for new cars made or assembled in Iran. This waiting list explains why a car increases in value: the owner of a new car can sell it on to someone who is impatient with the waiting time. Cars which are twenty years old cost more than a new economy model would in Europe. There is a chronic shortage of car spare parts in Iran, and intact body work is extremely rare—owners make do with whatever parts are available, in any colour. Iranian mechanics are very skilled at adapting parts to suit.

The most common car in Iran is the Peykan, modelled on the old British Talbot saloon. American 'gas guzzlers', such as Cadillacs, were popular in the 1970s, and are still limping along, but the German Mercedes-Benz and BMW are the cars favoured by the wealthiest Iranians. Japanese cars are admired for their longevity, and Daewoo, Renault and Peugeot cars are now assembled in Iran. A car purchased in Iran will not depreciate, so it represents a good investment.

Parking

Outside Tehran and a few other major cities, parking is free and a matter of where you can find a space. In Tehran, the acute congestion means that the situation is quite complex. There are multistorey car parks throughout the city, metered bays and private parking for businesses and services. Parking violations are harshly dealt with— heavy fines, wheel clamping and the possibility of being towed away.

In rural areas, peddlers travel by any means. This travelling supermarket even has a glass display case.

FINDING YOUR WAY AROUND

Iran, unlike many other Middle Eastern countries, does not really limit the possession of maps. They have very good cartographers, and in fact Iranian maps are the only detailed maps available of eastern Iraq and eastern Turkey, as the respective governments of these countries only allow such maps for official use. The Gita Shenasi Institute has a salesroom at their office in Tehran, and many of its maps are on sale throughout Iran. The provinces all have a 'tourist' provincial map with a detailed map of its capital city on the other side; the quality depends on the ranking of the province.

In addition to the usual national, regional, topographical and city maps, there is also a range of special interes t maps, such as 'Carpets of Iran', 'Animals of Iran' and 'Peoples of Iran'. Only very major cities have street maps which are at all useful. Tehran even has several

English maps, but don't expect to find every alleyway—you will have to depend on the rest of the address to find some small roads. These maps are available at the Gita Shenasi office in Tehran, as well as in museums, expensive hotel bookshops and some book shops and newspaper stalls. I recommend the cumbersome *New Map of Tehran* with an index, or the small *Tourist Map of Iran and Tehran*, both by Gita Shenasi

A Pedestrian Warning

It is a mystery why pedestrians are not an endangered species in parts of Iran, especially Tehran. Iranian pedestrians, despite the maniacal tendencies of Iranian drivers, tend to wander across multilane highways and roundabouts at random, often facing down a vehicle at the last minute with an alarming squeal of breaks.

There are some official crossing places, including bridges and tunnels—please use them, even if you are the only one. When at a crossing, do not assume that drivers will stop for a red light; look carefully before stepping into the road. Do not read your map or guidebook whilst walking near main roads, and be observant all the time. Women pedestrians should be aware that the passing motorists who flash their lights or sound their horns are not indicating that the women should cross but rather are being nuisances.

HEALTH CARE

Health Insurance

If you work for a company in Iran, they will take care of your health insurance. Otherwise, you will need to make sure that your policy covers you for Iran, as well as any activities you might undertake there. For most major illnesses, you would be probably best advised to get home (with the aid of your insurers), although Iran has good health care in certain areas, such as Tehran.

Main Health Anxieties

Iran has few outbreaks of major infectious diseases, and the water and food are generally fairly safe. Traveller's diarrhoea is probably the most likely problem to trouble you. However, advice on preventative health care depends on your destination within Iran, as well as your likely living or travelling conditions. Malaria prophylaxis is only necessary in the south of Iran in the summer, although advice should be sought depending on your itinerary and living conditions. Most adults and children living in Iran would be advised to be vaccinated against tuberculosis, and all travellers to Iran should ensure that their diptheria, tetanus and polio vaccinations are up to date. Vaccination against Hepatitis A and B is recommended for anyone spending any time in Iran.

Preventative Health Care

Your risk of getting sick in Iran is probably in direct relationship to your place and mode of living. It is wise to follow basic hygiene precautions, especially in the summer, and remember that there are many places in which most middle-class Iranians would refuse to eat on health grounds. Very frequent hand-washing is an excellent way of reducing one's exposure to dangerous pathogens, as is eating only freshly cooked food in salubrious outlets. Carry a small box of soap with you at all times, and remember that toilet doors and so on, are a major source of infection, so wash your hands as late in the bathroom proceedings as possible. All foreigners can expect some degree of traveller's diarrhoea, which needs no treatment other than plenty of fluids, unless its accompanied by bloodstained or mucous stools, or high fever.

Insect repellents are useful in the evenings and essential in malarial areas. Rigorous use of insect repellent and adjuncts like mosquito nets or plug-in insect repellent burners, may negate the need for malaria prophylaxis, even in the south of Iran. Always seek local advice on such matters. In non-malarial areas, lavender or citronella oil make excellent, safe insect repellents, even for babies. Neither of these is available in Iran.

It can get very hot indeed in parts of Iran, and the clothing restrictions can make this intolerable (especially for women), so always plan outings in the summer carefully, pace your activities and drink plenty, especially if you have stomach problems.

Some parts of Iran pose a snake or scorpion risk; again, always seek local advice about these hazards, how to avoid them and what to do if bitten. Keep away from animals, unless they are known house pets, and, even then, be careful, as they may not be kept in very hygienic conditions.

Medications

Iranians are great hypochondriacs, and pharmacies are to be found everywhere. They are usually clean and well-run. Iranian pharmacies generally sell most medications over the counter, without a prescription. Pharmacists are doctors, and can usually advise you on minor ailments, or suggest alternative medications, if yours is unavailable. Iran manufactures most common medications, and these are very cheap. However, most Iranians are discerning consumers of medications, and they are often willing to pay high prices for imported brands or new treatments. Anyone travelling to and from Iran regularly will be accustomed to the many requests for foreign medications, and it can be tricky to oblige, as they may require a prescription. Most Iranian doctors can write prescriptions in English, and this may be accepted overseas, if it is clearly written on headed notepaper. Common medications such as painkillers or cold treatments are popular gifts from overseas!

There are occasional shortages of certain drugs, and also, Iranian drugs may differ in their prescribed dosage, so if you need a particular regular medication, bring plenty with you. Contraceptives are available in Iran, but again this is something you would probably want to bring with you from abroad.

Finding a Doctor

The Iranian public health system is very rudimentary, and most doctors spend only the morning in the hospital. The afternoons or evenings are used for private practice, and most streets advertise the services of several specialists. In Tehran, the best doctors practice along Vali-ye Asr, Keshavarz and Teleghani, or close to the main hospitals. Most doctors have rudimentary English, and maybe other foreign languages as well. Iranians usually self-refer directly to a specialist, and the nature of a doctor's speciality will be listed on his ·or her sign. For popular doctors, a waiting list may exist. Although women may consult male doctors and vice versa, all new gynaecologists and obstetricians are women, by law, and only a few men still practice in this field.

Your embassy will recommend an appropriate doctor, as will a good hotel or almost any Iranian friend. The abilities of doctors is a favourite topic of conversation for Iranians, and most are delighted to share the benefit of their usually wide experience with you.

Hospitals

In an emergency you can ring the enquiries number (115) or the emergency number (198) and ask for an ambulance, or you can call a private ambulance service, such as Iran Emdad (6436662). Hospitals with English-speaking staff in Tehran include Mehrdad Day Hospital and the Tehran Clinic. Private hospitals in Tehran are generally clean and well run, although the standard of care may still not be ideal. Much of the high-tech equipment available in the West is available in Iran (and used extensively, but often quite inappropriately), but there is a general lack of coherence about health care that makes it inadequate.

There is a considerable difference of attitude on the part of the nurses towards the patients to that in the West. Nurses in Iran consider themselves to be the deputies of doctors, and rarely become involved in the intimate care of patients, rather concerning themselves with technical tasks. Untrained auxiliary nurses do the bulk of patient care, although, you can hire a private nurse, and hope that she is willing to undertake such tasks.

Alternative Health Care

Many Iranians use herbal treatments, especially in the provinces, and certain herbal or folk treatments are used by everyone. These include an extract of mint (*arak-e na'ana*), which is used in hot water for stomach upsets, and crystalised sugar which is also soothing when dissolved in hot water.

Supernatural powers are called upon by mostly uneducated Iranians, but one should be aware that many educated Iranians have a keen interest in soothsaying and the practises of quasi-religious healers, the *do'ah-nevis*, who provide written charms to be worn as amulets. There are some faith healers and fortune tellers who are patronised mostly by the upper echelons of Iranian society. Acupuncturists are also to be found in Tehran and some other major cities. Particularly in the provinces, there are a variety of alternative medical practitioners, including bonesetters, who offer physical manipulation. Manipulative osteopathy has recently just come to Tehran from Europe. I am unaware of any homeopaths practising in Iran; any homeopathic preparations you might need should be brought to Iran, although you will not easily be able to explain their purpose to your Iranians friends.

Iranians and Hypochondria

All Iranians have a love-hate relationship with doctors. They are at the pinnacle of social respectability but are also seen as greedy and inadequate. Discussion of ailments is frequent, especially digestive troubles, kidney problems and blood pressure. Most Iranians take medications like sweets, especially antibiotics, which they buy from pharmacies. Very few drugs are prescription only, and when they disagree with the doctor, Iranians prescribe for themselves. Very few people believe that an illness can be self-limiting or requires no treatment. Medical notes are carried around in a bag with the X-rays and shown to many doctors before an agreement is reached. You are most likely to be asked to take notes abroad for medical assessment, as well as to obtain expensive and probably experimental drugs from home that, mysteriously, all Iranians know about. Few Iranians are interested in long-term preventative measures, and medication is always the preferred option. The merits of various doctors, procedures and hospitals are endlessly debated at social gatherings. If you become unwell, expect friends to become very involved, as visiting a sick person is an essential kindness (as is calling regularly for progress reports). Ill Iranians rarely like to be left alone and enjoy being pampered and having special tempting dishes prepared for them.

In Iranian lore, the liver is the seat of emotion, so if someone's liver hurts or burns, this signifies mental anguish. Being thin is not something to comment on, since this is a sign of ill-health, as is being 'yellow' rather than pale. Loss of appetite or avoiding company are signs of illness or unhappiness.

As mental illness is considered a serious social embarrassment, Iranians tend to channel their disturbances into physical ailments. An unexplained ailment is rarely attributed to depression or somatic reasons, but rather is undiagnosed due to medical inadequacy

SOME IRRITATIONS OF LIVING IN IRAN

Bureaucracy

The bureaucracy in Iran is large, slow and often beyond comprehension. There is an employee for every task in most areas of employment, especially public sectors, and flexibility of task-sharing is not common. Expect simple procedures to take several days to allow for extended lunch hours, tea breaks and unexplained absences of key officials. Although officials may be charming and hospitable, they may also wield their powers in very obstructive ways. Demonstrating base humility is one of the normal approaches to such apparatchiks; the other is bribery, which is not considered as such if handled appropriately. Bribery can be monetary, in the form of a gift, or as a suggestion of a favour, perhaps to be traded later. Relying on one's foreignness can also be a good ploy, as it allows officials to display Iranian generosity and magnanimity. Iranians in a queue will usually encourage officials to help foreigners, and will often all become closely involved in your problems.

Environmental Pollution

Tehran has a smog problem similar to Los Angeles. The traffic congestion, industrial pollution and domestic air pollution creates smog, which is trapped by the Elburz Mountains. The quality of air is a major topic of conversation in Tehran, and people with allergies or respiratory problems may find themselves suffering greatly, especially when the weather conditions can create a particular build-up. A

241

day out in Tehran can leave one desperately in need of a shower and change of clothes.

Other Iranian cities are generally not known for their smog, and, in fact, the cities in the mountains often have particularly lovely, clean air. All Iranian cities suffer from a high level of general street litter, and Iranians who are very fussy about their houses usually see nothing wrong with throwing rubbish in the street. Rubbish collection occurs daily, but disposal bags are often ripped open by feral cats and their contents scattered around.

CULTURAL QUIZ

You may feel thoroughly disheartened after reading this book. Perhaps you feel that you will never be able to grasp the complexities of Iranian social behaviour, but, remember, you are only a foreigner after all. Even Iranians don't get it right all the time, and you will be on an upward learning curve, learning from every faux pas you commit.

This lighthearted quiz is an attempt to test your knowledge of Iranian customs and everyday life. All of the examples are based on real events, experienced by myself or others, and, in many cases, there is no absolutely right answer—the correct response could only be gauged in situ, and maybe the best course of action only became apparent in retrospect.

SITUATION ONE

You are a guest at someone's house for dinner. You have eaten all that you can, having had choice morsels pressed upon you all evening. Now you are in the sitting room, and your hostess is peeling and cutting up items of fruit, which she insists you eat. You feel that you will explode if you eat any more. What do you do?

- A Force down whatever they put on your plate anyway.

- B Insist that you are full, but as the peaches look so delicious cut up like that, you will force yourself to have just one.

- C Insist that you are full, and leave the fruit, despite your host's entreaties.

- D Make your excuses and leave early.

Comments

Option D would be a shame, and your host would be very distressed. The evening hasn't finished until you have had fruit, tea, and possibly nuts and sweets. Your hosts would be delighted if you pursue option A, which many Iranians will do. Option C may be necessary, but will disappoint the host, who will feel that the fruit was not tempting enough. Option B at least satisfies the host's desire to be hospitable, and flatters their choice of fruit. B and C also offer you the choice of eating some or all of the fruit a little later on, when you feel less full.

SITUATION TWO

You have been invited twice to an acquaintance's house, but have been (genuinely) otherwise engaged each time. They have invited you again for tomorrow night, but unfortunately you have a date with another friend. Do you:

- A Explain that you are otherwise engaged, although you would love to have come.

B Accept and then hope that your other friend doesn't mind you cancelling.

C Invite the person to your friend's house with you.

D Ask if you can bring your friend with you.

E Suggest another date.

Comments

This is a tricky one. To a European, it may seem clear that A is correct, but as this is the third time, the refusal will be open to interpretation as a veiled way of declining further social closeness. Your action depends on three things: your closeness to the other friend, your desire to get closer to this acquaintance, and whether families are involved. If you want to get closer, and are already close to your other friend, you can try option B, as Iranians are used to last minute changes of plan, and he or she may not be too offended. This also depends on whether or not this friend is single, and if the date was an invitation to eat at home or not. Explaining to your acquaintance that you have a prior date with a friend may result in an invitation to that friend also, especially if he or she is single, so you might try asking if you can bring your friend (option D). Iranians are usually delighted to get to know your friends, since this is part of building a relationship with you. C is possible if the acquaintance is single, and is also socially acceptable. E is not really ideal, but may be your only choice if you really can't break your previous date. You could try issuing an alternative invitation yourself, but this may be declined. If a definite alternative date is not immediately established, you can assume that a later invitation will probably not be forthcoming. It is acceptable to delay for a few hours, explaining that you want to try to break a date, and then call your friend or just decide how important the nascent relationship is to you. Remember to appear truly unhappy if you can't accept.

SITUATION THREE

An Iranian guest arrives for dinner, depositing a wrapped package on your hall telephone table. The guest does not refer to it again throughout the evening and departs without making any move to take it with her. Do you:

A Ask if it's a present for you, and if affirmative, open it in front of them.

B Ignore it until they leave then investigate it.

C Ask if they've forgotten their package as they are leaving.

D Take it into another room and open it, thanking your guest before they leave.

Comments

Many Iranians give gifts rather diffidently, so you can probably assume that it is a gift for you. Option A would probably embarrass the guest, who clearly feels shy about the gift. Also, there is always the possibility that they are on their way to another function with that gift, having had no time to get you a gift, so D could be very awkward. Of course, the good guest would never correct your assumption. Although you can try C, it is unnecessary—moreover, in the unlikely event that they forgot the gift by accident, they would never admit this, as you would have drawn attention to the matter. Option B is the politest choice, as it shows that you were interested in the guest, not the gift. If the gift turns out to be something personal, you can call the donor and thank them, otherwise either no comment or a brief word is called for on the next meeting. Gifts are often quite impersonal, and many donors do not expect to be thanked, it was part of a guest's social obligation.

SITUATION FOUR

You are a guest at someone's house, and have neglected to tell the host that you are a vegetarian. The dishes almost all contain meat, and repulse you. What do you do?

A Explain that you are a vegetarian, and you will just eat the rice.

B Force yourself to eat some of everything.

C Claim illness and excuse yourself from eating at all.

D Explain that you have been ill and that a doctor told you today that you should avoid certain foods, including meat.

E Pick parts of the dishes with vegetables, pushing any stray meat around your plate, and hope they don't notice.

Comments

Being a vegetarian in Iran is hard. It was very rude of you not to tell your host of your culinary perversions, which may not have been fully understood in any case. As a great deal of trouble has been taken for you, the politest and most Iranian choice would be B. Failing that, E is a good choice, as you will have to accustom yourself to traces of meat anyway if you want to socialise in Iran. If your fussiness is noted, you can try D as a fallback—all Iranians are very interested in illness and many doctors prescribe dietary restrictions. However, be prepared to provide details of the illness. Option A will hurt your host, as they will feel inhospitable and feel obliged to try to whip up alternative dishes, however awkward for them. C will alarm and distress your host, who may insist on taking you to see a doctor.

SITUATION FIVE

You have become quite friendly with an Iranian of the same sex. You notice that this friend invades your personal body space constantly—holding your hand, sitting almost on top of you when seated, and patting and caressing you frequently. This person makes personal comments about your appearance (complimenting you profusely about your lovely hair, eyes, etc.), buys you small gifts, and has even sent you a card with hearts and flowers on it, praising your friendship. You are invited to dinner, and your friend strongly suggests that you stay over the night, appearing distressed when you want to go home.

Does this mean that:

    A You are about to be the subject of a homosexual pass.

    B You are lucky to have found a close friend.

    C The person is unstable and you should terminate your relationship.

Comments

Scenario A is rather unlikely, although it is of course possible. C may be possible, but in the absence of more specific behaviour, it is unlikely. Whether B is the case depends on your personality and your Western hang-ups about private space and emotional restraint. Iranians tend to have very close same-sex friendships, and Iranians also generally have less need for privacy and barriers to intimacy. It is quite normal to develop what amounts to a crush on a friend—this is quite noble and there's nothing shameful about it. There is no overt sexual connotation, although the gender segregation in Iran may mean that there is some degree of sublimation involved here. Staying over at a friend's house is all part of establishing greater intimacy, which is not likely to be aimed at sexual intimacy. If you are really uncomfortable, you can try to explain that you are used to a more distant form of friendship, although this is complicated to explain— and clearly not in the Iranian scheme of things, nor desirable. Ultimately, you may have to avoid close friendships with Iranians if you can't learn to relax and go with the flow.

SITUATION SIX

You lent a perfume or aftershave to an Iranian friend who saw it in your bathroom and then asked to use it for a social occasion the next day. That was a month ago. It was an expensive perfume, not available in Iran, and you want it back. Do you:

A Ask directly for the return of the item.

B Mention it casually, hoping that the friend will take the hint and return it.

C Buy an alternative perfume and suggest that you exchange it for the one originally borrowed.

Comments

Sorry, but the concepts of 'lending' and 'giving' show some considerable degree of overlap in Iran. When you lend something in Iran, you must accept that you may never see it again. The exchange of personal items is part of cementing friendship in Iran, and you can feel flattered that your friend felt close enough to ask to borrow something. As this is clearly not an item you need, you certainly cannot ask for its return, so A is out. C will cause offence, although you could offer a similar perfume, as you know how much your friend liked yours, and hope that they will return yours (unlikely). Option B could also cause offence. Ultimately you have to decide which is more important, a perfume or a friendship. Certainly your Iranian friend would not likely lose sleep over the loss of such an item to you, and, in fact, would probably be gracious enough to be pleased that you liked it.

SITUATION SEVEN

You are asked by an Iranian acquaintance what religious faith you follow. How do you reply?

A You are a Christian, Hindu, Muslim, Jew, etc.

B You are a rationalist atheist and humanist who despises organized religion.

C Your parents are Christian, Hindu, Muslim, Jewish, etc.

D You are an agnostic with no firm convictions.

Comments

Option A is probably the safest answer, although admitting to being Jewish can be rather awkward in Iran, depending on your companions. Answer C is irrelevant in Iran, as one's religion is inherited from the father anyway, although it may make you feel happier if you have objections to declaring a religious conviction. Answers B and D, even if true, should be saved for your closest friends, and only then if they are known to be open-minded about such ideas. Remember that the question is really meant to place you in a cultural context, not to gauge your individual depth of faith. Claiming allegiance to a major faith simply indicates something about your cultural background. Discussions about actual convictions are a different ball game all together.

SITUATION EIGHT

You are trying to cross a busy road in the city and an approaching driver flashes his lights at you. Do you:

- A Assume that the driver intends to stop for you (or at least slow down), and dash across the road.
- B Stay put until there is a definite break in the traffic or until a car actually stops.
- C Wave at the driver and hope that he stops.

Comments

The answer to this depends a little on whether you are a woman or not. Flashing headlights is a common communication signal in Iran that can mean anything, including, 'I am an Iranian man who feels free to leer at women in the street, especially foreign ones.' Any response may encourage this, and he may even stop, but possibly not to let you cross the road. Option B may never come in a city like Tehran, where the traffic is frenetic. Option A is positively suicidal. Consider that even if there is a gap in the traffic, you may fall and it is possible that no one is going to stop for you. The safest option is to use the designated crossing places, including bridges and tunnels. This may add some hundreds of meters to your journey, but it could add years to your life.

SITUATION NINE

You want to go to the toilet desperately while you are shopping. Do you:

    A Look for a public toilet.

    B Go to the toilet at the nearest mosque.

    C Ask a shopkeeper if you can use his toilet.

    D Go to a restaurant or tea house and ask to use the toilet.

    E Force yourself to buy something to eat or drink at a restaurant or cafe and then use the toilet.

Comments

Don't bother about A, since you probably won't find one, unless in a park, and it may well be filthy. B is an option for men in particular, and also a last resort for really desperate women, who may have to ask a sympathetic man around the mosque to clear the cubicles of men for her. This is not a good idea in very conservative areas or around prayer times. C is a possibility, but most shops in Iran are small and share facilities. A really helpful shopkeeper will show you to the communal facilities. E is probably not necessary—simply asking is probably adequate. Women should try to seek out a restaurant or somewhere a little salubrious, although Iranians are usually quite kind about the lack of public facilities.

SITUATION TEN

An Iranian friend asks to borrow money for a business venture. You do just about have that much money to spare for a loan, but you don't feel that you can actually afford to give it away. The best answer would be:

- A   Explain your situation and ensure that there would be a fixed repayment plan.

- B   Explain that your money is in a fixed term account and you can't get at it for a few months.

- C   Explain that you don't have the money, but you can borrow it from a friend.

- D   Ask for further details about the venture and a possible partnership.

- E   Lend the money.

Comments

Option E is fine, as long as you accept that you may not see the money for a long time, if ever. Option A is considered rather unfriendly, as it implies that you do not trust your friend to return the money. C is the sort of thing that Iranians do quite often, although you risk losing two friends if things go wrong. D is tantamount to putting up the money and accepting that you will not see it again. B is the safest option, as you can still pursue D, while having an excuse not to lend the money. Remember that many Iranian friendships founder over money, so always consider how close you are to the person and judge how much you value continuing that closeness. Or just how much you would care if you lost the money, which many Iranians accept as a necessary part of friendship.

FURTHER READING

General

Abrahamian, Ervand. *Iran Between Two Revolutions*. Princeton: Princeton University Press, 1982.

Cooper, Roger. *Death Plus Ten Years*. London: Harper Collins, 1993. A look at Iran's dark side.

Faramarzi, M.T. *A Travel Guide to Iran*. Tehran: Hamso Publishing Consultants, 1995. Available through the British Consulate, or from the publishers: Tel: 021-882-7433 or 021-882-6176.

Fisher, W.B., ed. *The Cambridge History of Iran*. 6 vols. Cambridge: Cambridge University Press, 1968. Six volumes, subsections written by specialists on almost everything you need to know about Iran's history, economy, flora, fauna, etc.

Greenway, Paul and David St. Vincent. *Iran*. London: Lonely Planet Publications, 1998. This is an updated version of the only mainstream guidebook on Iran since 1979. Although aimed at budget travellers, it contains a wealth of information on tourist attractions and travel inside the country, and is packed with practical information, including addresses and telephone numbers for many organisations and facilities.

Simpson, John and Tira Shubart. *Lifting the Veil*. London: Hodder and Stoughton, 1995. A newer, revised edition of *Behind Iranian Lines* (Robson Books: London, 1988). A 'political' travel book. Mr. Simpson and Ms. Shubart are sympathetic, well-informed and manage to cram a great deal of anecdotes and information into their accounts. They met with many senior figures in the regime, and they also enjoyed the hospitality of more ordinary folk. John Simpson has been an Iran watcher for over twenty years.

Ethnic and Religious Minorities

Cooper, Roger. *The Baha'is of Iran*. London: Minority Rights Group, 1991.

MacDowall, David. *The Kurds*. London: Minority Rights Group, 1996.

Wirsing, Robert. *The Baluchi's and Pathans*. London: Minority Rights Group, 1987.

Autobiographies

Azadi, Sousan. *Out of Iran. One Woman's Escape from the Ayatollahs*. London: Macdonald, 1987. For some reason, a hugely popular book about a spoilt rich girl and her inevitable adventures after the 1979 revolution. Best avoided unless interested in the nauseating details of the elite lifestyle in the 1970s.

Guppy, Shusha. *The Blindfold Horse: Memories of a Persian Childhood*. Penguin, 1989. A fascinating and naive account of a privileged upbringing in Tehran.

Kordi, Gohar. *An Iranian Odyssey*. London: Serpent's Tail, 1991. This is the true story of Iran's first blind female graduate, who endured a tormented childhood due to poverty, her handicap and her sex.

Tabrizi, Gholam-Reza Sabri. *Iran: A Child's Story, a Man's Experience*. Edinburgh: Mainstream Publishing, 1989.

Culture and Society

Beeman, William. *Language, Status and Power in Iran*. University of Indiana Press, 1988. Beeman expands the concept of *ta'arouf* into an Iranian cosmology, suggesting the historical and social reasons for such ritualised communications.

Beeman, William. 'Status, Style and Strategy in Iranian Interaction.' *Anthropological Linguistics* 18 (1976): 305-322.

Betteridge, Anne. 'Gift Exchange in Iran: the Locus of Self-identity in Social Interaction.' *Anthropological Quarterly* 58 (1985):190-202. An anthropologist's account of the way in which gift-giving in Iran can be viewed as a presentation of self. The formal gift is a stereotyped, generalised currency in social exchange. Personal gifts reflect the inner person, which can only be exposed to the intimate circle.

Chaqeri, Cosroe. *Beginning Politics. The Reproductive Cycle of Children's Tales and Games in Iran.* Florence: Mazdak, 1996. An examination of Iranian socialisation and its influences on values and political action

Curtis, Vesta. *Persian Myths.* London: British Museum Press, 1993. A useful, slim guide to ancient Persian texts and the origins of the mythology that still survives in popular currency.

Donaldson, Bess Allen. *The Wild Rue: A Study of Muhummaden Magic and Folklore in Iran.* London: Luzac, 1938. This is of more than academic interest, as so much about superstition still holds true.

Fisher, Michael. *Iran—From Religious Dispute to Revolution.* London: Harvard University Press, 1980. A wonderful account of the role of religion in everyday life as well as politics.

Khorsandi, Hadi. *The Ayatollah and I.* London: Readers International, 1992. This is a collection of satirical columns from this outspoken writer. His wit is biting and he is popular with most expatriate Iranians. The columns are well translated and give a valuable insight to Iranian black humour and parody. Certain of the characters he invented have entered popular culture. The atmosphere of the post revolutionary and war years is vividly drawn. The targets of Iranian humour are made very clear: mullahs, religion, middle class morality, intellectuals, human greed and aspects of the 'Iranian character'. Although many of the targets no longer dominate society, they still exist as popular targets of jets. Highly recommended and highly illegal in Iran, of course.

The Koran (Qur'an). Any English translation, but the Penguin one is well presented. A larger one with an index is useful for quick reference. Unlike other Islamic countries, Iranians rarely refer to the Hadith, or traditions of the Prophet Mohammed. Many Iranians will be appreciative of a foreigner having read the Qur'an, although as many Iranians have read it only in Arabic, their understanding of it may be very sketchy. Interpretation is often left to mullahs. Some familiarity with the lives and attributes of the Shi'ite saints, especially Imam Ali and his family will also aid communication.

Mottahedeh, Roy. *The Mantle of the Prophet: Religion and Politics in Iran.* London: Penguin, 1987. The life story of a fictional mullah from Qom—written by a Harvard professor of history— this book provides a unique insight into the politics, history and religious life of Iran. Although presenting a wealth of scholarly learning, the book is written in an approachable manner, using human interest as its means of examining various themes. It also answers key questions, such as what Islamic religious leaders actually study and teach in the theological colleges, and how religious conservatives conduct their domestic lives.

Plisken, Karen L. *Silent Boundaries: Cultural Constraints on Sickness and Diagnosis of Iranians in Israel.* New Haven: Yale University Press, 1987. Although obviously not suitable to take to Iran, this book has thoughtful sections on Iranian communications, cultural stereotypes and social hierarchy. In particular Chapters Three and Six are very useful. The book explores the cultural misunderstandings that arise between Iranian immigrants and the Israeli medical services, and examines Iranian constructions of illness and expressions of unhappiness. Much of the book holds true for Iranian society in general, and initial research was conducted in Iran.

Food

Najmieh Batmangli. *Food of Life*. Washington, D.C.: Mage, 1984.

Ramazani, Nesta. *Persian Cooking*.

Shaida, Magaret. *The Legendary Cuisine of Persia*. Henley: Lieuse Publications, 1992. Iranian cookery books available in Iran are often poorly translated and illustrated and do not explain cooking techniques. Books such as this offer a wealth of cultural information as well as a guide to the cuisine of Iran. They also use poetry to illustrate the importance of food in Iranian life.

Literature

Ahmad, Jalal Al-e. *Occidentosis: A Plague From the West*. Several editions and publishers; often known by the Persian title, *Gharbzardaghee*. Written in the early 1960s but banned in Iran until 1979), Al-e Ahmad explores the Iranian obsession with Western culture and values and proposes a return to Iranian roots, including Shi'ism. This aspect of his writing endears him to Revolutionary ideologues, but his many short stories, novels and anthropological monographs display his socialist leanings. He is one of the greatest figures of modern Iranian literature, and it is worth reading any translations of his works. Translated novels include, *The Pen* and *The School Principal*.

Browne, E.G. *A History of Persian Literature in Modern Times (1500-1924)*. Cambridge: Cambridge University Press, 1924. A very thorough grounding for the period concerned. Worth a look at the contents to familiarise oneself with the names.

Daneshvar, Simin. *Shaveshun*. Washington D.C.: Mage, 1990. Al-e Ahmad's wife and still living in Iran, Daneshvar was the first important female prose writer in Iran. This novel, the best-selling ever in Iran, follows the fate of a family in the interwar period in Iran through the feelings of the female characters. Also recommended: *Daneshvar's Playhouse* (Washington D.C.: Mage, 1989), a collection of her short stories.

Ferdowsi. *Shahnameh* ('Book of Kings'). Many editions of sections of this poem. This epic poem, possibly the longest poem ever written, details the mythic lives of heroes and Iranian Kings and has been officially rehabilitated recently, but has always been a popular poem for public recitation. Several of the mythic characters are common to everyday expressions; for example, Rostam the giant hero is frequently mentioned. The poem has only once been published in its entirety in English—that is, in nine volumes. *The Legend of Seyavash* is published by Penguin (1992). Also, *The Tragedy of Sohrab and Rustam* (J.W. Clinton, trans., Seattle: University of Washington Press, 1987).

Ghanoonparvar, M.R. *In a Persian Mirror. Images of the West and Westerners in Iranian Fiction.* Austin: University of Texas Press, 1993. It may be interesting to know how you have been portrayed!

Harvey, Andrew. *The Way of the Passion—A Celebration of Rumi.* London: Souvenir, 1995. Written by a sufi mystic, this draws on the poems of Jalal-e Din Rumi to explain the Sufi way. This is approachable for anyone interested in Sufism.

Hedayat, Sadeq. *The Blind Owl.* Various editions and publishers. Hedayat, who killed himself in 1951, was possibly the most influential Iranian writer of the twentieth century. He wrote many short stories in a critical realist manner, portraying the lives of the underprivileged in a dispassionate style. *The Blind Owl* is the best known Persian novel in the West, and could be described as the most unique, especially in its impact outside Iran. An anthology of his short stories makes very good reading, but works of his are bound to be included in any collection available of Iranian short stories.

Hedayat, Sadeq. *The Life and Legend of an Iranian Writer, Homa Katouzian.* London: I.B. Tauris, 1991.

Omar Khayyam. *The Rubaiyat.* Many editions, including Penguin. Although these tend to be very imperfectly translated, even familiarity with the themes and key quatrains will be much appreciated by Iranian acquaintances. Ditto for Saadi's *Gulistan* and Hafiz's *Diwan.* Familiarity with this triumvirate of Iranian poets will aid conversation with Iranians who are very proud of their poetic literature. Even illiterate Iranians are familiar with large tracts of poetry. Conversations are often littered with verse and verses are used to illustrate points.

Southgate, Minou, trans. *Modern Persian Short Stories.* Washington, D.C.: Three Continents Press, 1980. The short story, along with poetry, are genres more familiar than the novel in Iran, and some familiarity with the well-known short stories (and the respective authors) is much appreciated. Iranian writers have usually dwelt on social themes and common angst, so exploring their works is a good way of understanding Iranian society. This book includes a very enlightening introduction. All the well-known pre-1980 writers are represented, and all the stories are very readable.

The Tales of Mullah Nasreddin. Many editions. There are countless tales of both the wit and the foolishness of this mythical figure. He is both cunning and vulnerable, displaying the two extremes of necessary social behaviour. Anecdotes are used both to entertain and to illustrate.

Thackston, Wheeler. *A Millenium of Classical Persian Poetry.* Bethesda, Maryland: Iran Books, 1994. This book is aimed at students of Persian and provides translation of key passages.

Travellers' Tales

Bird, Isabella. *Journeys in Persia and Kurdistan (vols. I and II).* London: Virago, 1988. Ms. Bird's travels took place in 1890, and she gives an extremely vivid account.

Browne, Edward G. *A Year Amongst the Persians*. London: Adam and Charles Black, 1893. A large volume of some impressive travels in Iran.

Curzon, George Nathanial. *Curzon's Persia*. London: Sidgewick and Jackson, 1986. This is an edited version of Curzon's *Persia and the Persian Question,* published in 1892, and lavishly illustrated.

Dodwell, Christina. *A Traveller on Horseback*. London: Sceptre, 1992. Ms. Dodwell travelled to Iran in the mid-1980s, and travelled back by horse.

Novels Using an Iranian Setting

Barkhordar Nahai, Gina. *Cry of the Peacock*. London: Simon & Schuster, 1991. An epic novel, covering two centuries in the lives of an Isfahani Jewish family. Not appropriate to read in Iran.

Clavell, James. *Whirlwind*. London: Coronet, 1987. A preposterous 'action' novel based on the evacuation of Bell Helicoptors from Iran, with a cast of Iranian nobles and assorted foreigners, including a Finn.

Cronin, Vincent. *The Last Migration*. London: Hart Davis, 1957. Still widely available second hand, this is a touching account of the effects of forced settlement in the 1930s and 40s on the nomads of southern Iran. It vividly portrays the nomadic life, which is still culturally, if not economically, relevant to Iran.

Books to Deny Ever Having Seen or Read

Satanic Verses, or anything by Salman Rushdie. I usually find it is best to plead ignorance and explain that he is not a very popular writer and that no one you know has read the book in question, so you can't really comment.

Not Without My Daughter by Betty Mahmoudy. If you do see this book you will know that however unfortunate her personal circumstances, this book is very insulting about many aspects of Iranian life. The whole story has been thrown into doubt and Iranians will be reassured to know that you don't believe a word of what you have heard of it anyway. Also deny having seen the film, which was made in Israel, thus confirming it as a Zionist plot to humiliate Iran.

Health

Lessell, Colin. *The World Traveller's Manual of Homeopathy.* Saffron Walden, England: C.W. Daniel Co., 1993. A monumental work with chapters on all ailments likely to be encountered by travellers, with suggestions for homeopathic treatment.

INTERNET BIBLIOGRAPHY

Iranians are avid users of the Internet, and there are sites on just about every aspect of Iran and Iranian society. Due to the politicised nature of Iranian expatriate society, many of these sites are tiresomely political, and can be wearing. All Iranian opposition groups have web sites, but I have not provided these for obvious reasons. The Iranian government has not been slow to keep up with technology, and provides numerous, worthy web sites, often to inform expatriate Iranians of what they are missing. A cornucopia of sites follows, but you will probably benefit best from your own net-surfing.

- **The Iranian Cultural and Information Center**
  http://tehran.stanford.edu/
  The 'mother of all websites for Iranian topics'.

- **PersiaNet**
  http://userwww.service.emory.edu/~sebrahl/PersiaNet.html
  A listing of various web sites.

- **Export Promotion Centre of Iran**
  http://www.iranexport.com
  Advice on business matters.

- **The Iranian government**
  http://www.netiran.com
  Embassy details, customs rules

- **Neda Reyaneh**
  http://www.neda.net
  Commercial provider with good information about Iran. Offers an Iranian Yellow Pages

- **Iran Culture and Information Centre (Canada)**
  http://www.IranVision.com
  History and culture of Iran.
  http://www.payvand.com
  Travel advice and links.

- **Iranian Embassy (Ottawa, Canada)**
  http://www.salamiran.org
  Useful information, much lifted from travel guides. Children's section.

- **University of Texas**
  http://www.lib.utexas.edu.Libs/PCL/Map_collection/ Atlas_middle_east
  Maps and geography.

- **The Iranian**
  http://www.iranian.com
  A magazine site, 80% of articles in English.

- **Soroush**
  http://www.soroush.com
  An interactive network for Iranians.

- **IranNet**
  http://irannet.com
  Topics of interest to Iranians businesses .

- **Iran Net**
  http://aria.nic.ir
  Iranian national academic network.

- **Zan**
  http://www.zan.org
  An apolitical women's site.

- **Iran Business Digest**
  http://www.neda.net/ibd
  From Tehran in English.

- **Islamic Republic News Agency (IRNA)**
  http://netiran.com/news/irnafile.html

- **CIA's unclassified report on Iran**
  http://www.odci.gov/cia/publications/97fact/ir.html

- **Amnesty International's Report on Iran**
  http://www.amnesty.org/ailib/aireport/ar97/MDE13.htm

- **Ferdowsi's Shahnameh in English**
  http://www.cit.ics.saitama-u.ac.jp/hobbies/iran/shahnameh.html

- **Omar Khayyam's Rubaiyat in English**
  http://cit.ics.saitama-u.ac.jp/hoobbies/iran/khayyam.html

- **Iranian music site**
  http://www.iraian.com/mar96/web/music.html

THE AUTHOR

Dr. Maria O'Shea is a writer, researcher and independent consultant on Middle Eastern affairs, particularly those of Kurdistan and Iran. She teaches political geography and Middle Eastern geography in the School of Oriental and African Studies at the University of London, one of the world's foremost centres for research on the Middle East.

She has spent considerable time in Iran, both for family reasons and to undertake doctoral research. In addition to *Culture Shock! Iran*, she is the author of several titles for children on the countries of the Middle East, and of many articles on the political, cultural and historical geography of the Middle East, Iran and Kurdistan.

INDEX